Teaching English at Japanese Universities

Written by leading English-language educators in Japan, this *Handbook* provides an in-depth guide for the new generation of teachers at Japanese universities. In clear, accessible prose, it offers practical and detailed advice on effective classroom pedagogy, student motivation, learning styles, classroom culture, national language policy, career opportunities, departmental politics, administrative mindset, and institutional identity. Its four parts—The setting, The courses, The classroom, and The workplace—examine issues faced by university language teachers as well as challenges confronted by the increasing number of scholars teaching English as a medium of instruction (EMI) and Content and Language Integrated Learning (CLIL) courses. Firmly grounded in contemporary teaching method and theory, the *Handbook*'s 23 chapters also acknowledge the influence of diverse movements such as world Englishes, global issues, gender, and positive psychology. Its three appendices contain information on organizations, books, journals, and websites particularly useful for Japanese university educators; explanation of types and rankings of schools; ways to learn more about individual institutions for job-hunting; and detailed information on the structure (and Japanese titles) of faculty and non-teaching staff at the typical university. This *Handbook* is an invaluable resource to anyone teaching, or aspiring to teach, at a Japanese university.

Paul Wadden, PhD, is a Senior Lecturer in the English for Liberal Arts Program of International Christian University, Tokyo. The editor of the original *A Handbook for Teaching English at Japanese Colleges and Universities* (1993), he is the author of articles on language teaching and academic writing appearing in *TESOL Quarterly*, *ELT Journal*, *RELC Journal*, *College Literature*, *Composition Studies* and many other journals; articles on culture, politics, and education in *The Washington Post*, *The Wall Street Journal*, *The New York Times*, and *The Japan Times*; and more than 50 textbooks. He has taught in Japanese universities for the past 30 years.

Chris Carl Hale, EdD, is Associate Professor in the Graduate School of Global Communication and Language at Akita International University, Japan and formerly the Academic Director of the Tokyo Center of the New York University (NYU) School of Professional Studies (SPS). He has taught undergraduate and graduate courses related to language acquisition and teacher training in the United States and in Japan for over 20 years at universities such as City University of New York (CUNY), Queens College, Teachers College Columbia University, and International Christian University, Tokyo. His articles have appeared in *Language Testing in Asia*, *TESOL International,* and Teachers College Columbia University *Journal of TESOL and Applied Linguistics.* He is also an avid DJ and techno music producer.

Teaching English at Japanese Universities
A New Handbook

Edited by
Paul Wadden and
Chris Carl Hale

LONDON AND NEW YORK

First published 2019
by Routledge
2 Park Square, Milton Park, Abingdon, Oxon OX14 4RN

and by Routledge
52 Vanderbilt Avenue, New York, NY 10017

Routledge is an imprint of the Taylor & Francis Group, an informa business

© 2019 selection and editorial matter, Paul Wadden and Chris Carl Hale; individual chapters, the contributors

The right of Paul Wadden and Chris Carl Hale to be identified as the authors of the editorial material, and of the authors for their individual chapters, has been asserted in accordance with sections 77 and 78 of the Copyright, Designs and Patents Act 1988.

All rights reserved. No part of this book may be reprinted or reproduced or utilised in any form or by any electronic, mechanical, or other means, now known or hereafter invented, including photocopying and recording, or in any information storage or retrieval system, without permission in writing from the publishers.

Trademark notice: Product or corporate names may be trademarks or registered trademarks, and are used only for identification and explanation without intent to infringe.

British Library Cataloguing in Publication Data
A catalogue record for this book is available from the British Library

Library of Congress Cataloging in Publication Data
Names: Wadden, Paul, editor. | Hale, Chris Carl, editor.
Title: Teaching English at Japanese universities : a new handbook / edited by Paul Wadden and Chris Carl Hale.
Description: London ; New York, NY : Routledge, 2019. | Includes bibliographical references and index.
Identifiers: LCCN 2018029318| ISBN 9781138550384 (hardback) | ISBN 9781138550391 (pbk.) | ISBN 9781315147239 (ebook)
Subjects: LCSH: English language—Study and teaching (Higher)—Japan. | English language—Study and teaching (Higher)—Japanese speakers. | English teachers—Training of—Japan.
Classification: LCC PE1068.J3 T35 2019 | DDC 428.0071/052—dc23
LC record available at https://lccn.loc.gov/2018029318

ISBN: 978-1-138-55038-4 (hbk)
ISBN: 978-1-138-55039-1 (pbk)
ISBN: 978-1-315-14723-9 (ebk)

Typeset in Galliard
by Swales & Willis Ltd, Exeter, Devon, UK

Contents

List of figures	viii
List of contributors	ix
Advice to foreign teachers at Japanese universities	xvii
Foreword by John F. Fanselow	xviii
Acknowledgements	xxiii

PART 1
The setting   1

1 The landscape of Japanese higher education: an introduction   3
CHRIS CARL HALE AND PAUL WADDEN

2 Making a career of university teaching in Japan: getting (and keeping) a full-time job   11
JENIFER LARSON-HALL AND JEFFREY STEWART

3 The *ronin* teacher: making a living as a full-time part-timer at Japanese universities   25
CHRYSTABEL BUTLER

4 The chrysanthemum maze: understanding your colleagues in the Japanese university   32
CURTIS KELLY AND NOBUHIRO ADACHI

PART 2
The courses   41

5 Tearing down the wall of silence: constructing the English conversation class at a Japanese university   43
JOHN WILTSHIER AND MARC HELGESEN

6 The blind spots of reading: switching on lights in the Japanese university classroom 54
GORDON MYSKOW, PAUL R. UNDERWOOD, AND ROB WARING

7 Mandatory 'sentencing': breaking loose in the Japanese university writing classroom 64
GORDON MYSKOW

8 Real world listening in the Japanese university classroom 75
CHRIS CARL HALE

9 Teaching and learning vocabulary in the Japanese university 84
PAUL WADDEN, CHARLES BROWNE, AND PAUL NATION

10 Teaching presentation in the Japanese university 97
CURTIS KELLY

11 Teaching subject content through English: CLIL and EMI courses in the Japanese university 103
HOWARD BROWN AND ANNETTE BRADFORD

12 Using technology in the Japanese university classroom (and beyond) 109
DAN FERREIRA AND JOACHIM CASTELLANO

13 Homework in the Japanese university classroom: getting students to do it (and then evaluating their performance) 115
THOMAS N. ROBB

PART 3
The classroom 123

14 Nails that still don't stick up: revisiting the enigma of the Japanese college classroom 125
FRED E. ANDERSON

15 Creating engagement and motivation in the Japanese university language classroom 137
BILL SNYDER

16 The Japanese student and the university English teacher 144
DONNA T. FUJIMOTO

17 English language policy in Japan and the Ministry of Education (MEXT): emphasis, trends, and changes that affect higher education 150
PAUL R. UNDERWOOD AND GREGORY PAUL GLASGOW

PART 4
The workplace — 157

18 "He said, she said": female and male dynamics in Japanese universities — 159
    DIANE HAWLEY NAGATOMO AND MELODIE COOK

19 The Japanese university teacher of English — 165
    ASAKO TAKAESU AND MIKIKO SUDO

20 Beyond the native speaker fallacy: internationalizing English-language teaching at Japanese universities — 174
    TIINA MATIKAINEN

21 Walk a mile in the shoes of the non-Japanese administrator — 180
    STEPHEN M. RYAN AND PETER McCAGG

22 Conflicts, contracts, rights, and solidarity: the Japanese university workplace from a labor perspective — 187
    GEROME ROTHMAN

23 Navigating the chrysanthemum maze: off-hand advice on how to tiptoe through the minefield of the Japanese university — 196
    A DIALOG WITH CURTIS KELLY AND CHARLES BROWNE

Appendix 1: Resources for university educators in Japan — 202
GLEN HILL

Appendix 2: Types of universities in Japan — 211
CHRIS CARL HALE AND PAUL WADDEN

Appendix 3: Academic admin hierarchy chart — 216

Index — 218

Figures

1.1	Total number of youths (1970–2013)	4
1.2	Number of colleges and universities in Japan (1955–2014)	5
2.1	Job search checklist	22
5.1	Sample pair work activity	46
5.2	Dialogue sample from a textbook	48
6.1	*Spot the Difference* focusing on lexical and grammatical differences	59
6.2	Summary of extensive reading practices	60
7.1	Sample genre analysis activity	67
7.2	Plagiarism awareness-raising activity	68
7.3	Error code handout with translations and examples	70
7.4	Rubric for an argumentative essay assignment	73
8.1	Sample authentic listening text: *Looking for Love in the Big City*	79
9.1	Sample readout showing NGSLT results	86
9.2	Screenshots of student feedback from Quizlet.com	88
9.3	Illustrations of NGSL Builder	89
9.4	Sample word-part activity	92
21.1	I was likely appointed to a leadership role based on (check all that apply):	181
21.2	"Instruction manual for non-Japanese administrator initiating change" (break glass in event of emergency)	186
A1.1	JALT SIGs	202
A1.2	JACET study groups	203
A2.1	Japanese university rankings	214
A2.2	Ranking in Asia according to the *Times Higher Education* 2018 rankings	215
A3.1	Academic administration hierarchy	216
A3.2	Names and titles of non-teaching staff and offices	217
A3.3	Teaching staff titles and ranks	217

Contributors

Nobuhiro Adachi, PhD, is Emeritus Professor in the Department of English Language, Faculty of Foreign Languages, at Kansai Gaidai University, Osaka. He taught undergraduate and graduate courses at Kansai Gaidai for more than 35 years, including three years at Gustavus Adolphus College, St. Peter, Minnesota, as an exchange professor and one year as a visiting scholar at the University of Hawaii at Manoa. His research interests lie in socio-historical analysis of linguistic assimilation of immigrant groups in the United States and teaching public speaking fundamentals to Japanese university students.

Fred E. Anderson, PhD, is a U.S. native and Professor of English Linguistics at Kansai University, Osaka. He first arrived in Japan in 1977 and has since taught English-related subjects at universities in Hokkaido, Kyushu, Kanto, and Kansai areas as well as in the United States and Sweden. He received his doctorate in linguistics from the University of Hawaii at Manoa on a fellowship from the East-West Center. His interests include language socialization, world Englishes, intercultural communication, and minority language education and revitalization. He co-edited (with Craig Alan Volker) *Education in Languages of Lesser Power: Asia-Pacific Perspectives* (John Benjamins 2015).

Annette Bradford, EdD (The George Washington University), is Associate Professor in the School of Business Administration, Meiji University, Tokyo, where she teaches in the English-medium instruction program. Previously, she held a Council on Foreign Relations International Affairs Fellowship in Japan and taught at universities in Japan, the United States, and Indonesia. She is the co-editor, with Howard Brown, of *English-Medium Instruction in Japanese Higher Education: Policy, Challenges and Outcomes* (Multilingual Matters 2017). Her research on the internationalization of higher education and English-medium instruction can be found in publications such as the *Journal of Studies in International Education* and *International Higher Education*.

Howard Brown is a Professor at the University of Niigata Prefecture, where he is the coordinator of English-medium instruction programs. He has more than 25 years' experience in language education, including work as a teacher, teacher trainer, and administrator at high schools, private language schools, and universities in Canada, Turkey, and Japan. Howard has published extensively on English-medium instruction and the links between English-medium and English-language programs in Japan. He is the co-editor, with Annette Bradford, of *English-Medium Instruction in Japanese Higher Education: Policy, Challenges and Outcomes* (Multilingual Matters 2017).

Charles Browne, EdD, is Professor of Applied Linguistics & TESOL at Meiji Gakuin University. He served as the first National Chairman of the JET Program from 1987 to 1988 and as a member of many MEXT committees including a national committee on teacher training, a national steering committee for the JET Program, and the national junior and senior high school textbook advisory committee. He is a specialist in second-language vocabulary acquisition and extensive reading, especially as they apply to online learning environments, and has created several important new corpus-based word lists for second-language learners as well as a wide range of free online apps, tools, and websites to teach, learn, research, and create texts based on these lists (all downloadable from newgeneralservicelist.org).

Chrystabel Butler came to Japan in 1990. She has experienced the full range of teaching contexts in the country, having taught at high schools, junior colleges, and universities in both private and public settings. At the university level, she has held positions, ranging from part-time adjunct teaching posts to full-time and tenured posts, at top-ranked universities as well as at small junior colleges in the remote countryside. She has published research in the areas of socialization in the Japanese classroom, patterns of hierarchy and authority in Japan, and cross-cultural studies analysing the organization of intra-psychic structures which determine relational patterns to self and other.

Joachim Castellano is a language and media educator with a specialization in technology. He earned a BS from Northwestern University and a Master of TESOL from Teachers College, Columbia University. Since 2009, Joachim has taught at the university level at Kanda University of International Studies, New York University School of Professional Studies Tokyo Center, and presently at Aichi Prefectural University. Joachim's career includes stops at the EdLab of Teachers College and the Center for the Study of Languages and Cultures at the University of Notre Dame. In 2013, Joachim's work in technology and education was recognized when he was selected for the Apple Distinguished Educator award of Japan.

Melodie Cook, PhD (Macquarie University), is Professor at the University of Niigata Prefecture and has been teaching in Japan at the tertiary level for over 20 years. She is a former Associate Editor and Editor of *JALT Journal* and a reviewer for several journals. Her research interests lie in the areas of expatriate experiences in Japan, including foreign faculty involvement in large-scale testing, mixed-roots family experiences of schooling in Japan, expatriate adoptive and foster parents, as well as gender representation in educational materials.

She writes a regular column for *Savvy Tokyo* about her experiences as an adoptive and foster parent.

John F. Fanselow's journey began as a U.S. Peace Corps Volunteer at a teacher training college in Nigeria in 1961. John has worn many hats during his long career but his main interest remains challenging teachers to think about what happens in their own classrooms. "Beyond Rashomon" and "Let's See," two of John's seminal articles in *TESOL Quarterly*, have been reprinted in many anthologies. "Beyond Rashomon" was the basis of *Breaking Rules* (Longman 1987) and "Let's See" was the basis of *Contrasting Conversations* (Longman 1992). His latest book *Small Changes in Teaching, Big Results in Learning—Videos, Activities and Essays to Stimulate Fresh Thinking about Language Learning* was published by iTDi in 2017, on the 30th anniversary of his groundbreaking *Breaking Rules*.

Dan Ferreira has been teaching in the greater Tokyo region for over 15 years. He is a Google Certified Trainer and Apple Teacher and conducts faculty development workshops. A doctoral candidate at Northcentral University, San Diego, he is currently focusing his research on professional development in e-learning in higher education in Japan, and his action research particularly explores the use of a conceptual tool that will help instructors systematically link the use of technology with their teaching context and learning objectives. His other specializations include academic writing and vocabulary development at the university level.

Donna T. Fujimoto, EdD, is a Professor at Osaka Jogakuin University and Temple University Japan. For over 40 years she has taught courses in all skill areas of English as well as courses related to intercultural education. She is the Coordinator of the Pragmatics Special Interest Group of the Japan Association of Language Teaching (JALT), the Coordinator of the Society for Intercultural Education, Training and Research (SIETAR Kansai), and one of the founders and current Coordinator of the Contrast Culture Method (CCM), an intercultural training group. Her main research methodology is conversation analysis where the focus is on classroom interaction. Her other research interests include pragmatics, intercultural communication, and narrative studies.

Gregory Paul Glasgow, PhD (University of Queensland, Australia), is an assistant professor at Rikkyo University, College of Intercultural Communication, and has taught English in Japan for nearly 20 years. Dr. Glasgow has served as an English Language Specialist for the Embassy of the United States in Tokyo, conducting teacher training seminars and skills development workshops throughout Japan. He holds a PhD in Applied Linguistics and a Master of TESOL from Teachers College, Columbia University. His research interests are language policy and planning, native-speakerism, the pedagogy of English as an International Language and a *lingua franca*, and the professional development of native and non-native English-speaking teachers.

Chris Carl Hale, EdD, is Associate Professor in the Graduate School of Global Communication and Language at Akita International University, Japan and formerly the Academic Director of the Tokyo Center of the New York University (NYU) School of Professional Studies (SPS). He has taught undergraduate and graduate courses related to language acquisition and teacher training in the United States and in Japan for over 20 years at universities such as City University of New York (CUNY), Queens College, Teachers College, Columbia University, and International Christian University, Tokyo. His articles have appeared in *Language Testing in Asia*, *TESOL International*, and Teachers College, Columbia University *Journal of TESOL and Applied Linguistics*. He is also an avid DJ and techno music producer.

Diane Hawley Nagatomo, PhD (Linguistics, Macquarie University), is Professor in the Graduate School of Humanities and Science at Ochanomizu University. She has taught graduate and undergraduate courses in Japanese universities for more than 30 years. She is the author of 21 EFL textbooks for the Japanese audience and numerous academic articles, and has presented at numerous conferences. Among her books are *Exploring Japanese University English Teachers' Professional Identity* (Mutilingual Matters 2012) and *Gender, Identity and Teaching English in Japan* (Multilingual Matters 2016). Her research interests include teachers' and students' beliefs, professional identity, gender issues, and materials development.

Marc Helgesen is Professor in the Departments of Intercultural Studies and *Gendai* Business at Miyagi Gakuin Women's University, Sendai, where he teaches a variety of English speaking, reading, and teacher development courses. He also teaches a course on Positive Psychology in ELT in the Master of TESOL program at Nagoya University of Foreign Studies. He is the author of over 180 articles, books, and textbooks related to ELT and has been a featured or invited speaker at conferences on five continents. The former chair of the Extensive Reading Foundation, he is particularly interested in extensive reading, positive psychology in ELT, and mind, brain, and education issues.

Glen Hill is an American who has been teaching English in Japan since 1998. His teaching experience includes university, private high school, conversation school, and private clients. At Obihiro University of Agriculture and Veterinary Medicine, he is an Associate Professor teaching reading and technical writing to science majors, and manages the English Resource Center. In addition, he has been the Publications Chair for the JALT CUE SIG, where he serves as the Editor of *OnCUE Journal*. His research interests include extensive reading, ESP curriculum development, and English for science careers.

Curtis Kelly, EdD (Nova Southeastern University, USA), is Professor of English at Kansai University in Japan. He has worked for 40 years in Japanese universities and written over 30 books, including *Significant Scribbles* (Longman 2005), *Active Skills for Communication* (Cengage 2008), and *Writing from Within* (Cambridge 2011) and has made over 400 conference presentations. Since his life mission is to "relieve the suffering of the classroom," his main research interest is the neuroscience of motivation and learning. He is the founder and Coordinator of the Japanese Association of Language Teachers' Mind, Brain, and Education SIG, a Director of the NeuroELT FAB Research Group, and the Director of the Center for Applied Social Neuroscience (CASN).

Jenifer Larson-Hall, PhD (University of Pittsburgh, USA), is Associate Professor at Kitakyushu University in Japan. She has taught undergraduate and graduate courses in second-language acquisition and teacher training in the United States and Japan for over 15 years. Her best accomplishment is raising four bilingual children; however, she was mostly too busy to document their fascinating language acquisition! She is interested in statistics and methodology in SLA, age effects, phonological acquisition, and language attrition. She hopes everyone will stop using bar plots in their results, unless they have count data (see "Moving Beyond the Bar Plot and the Line Graph to Create Informative and Attractive Graphics" in *Modern Language Journal* 2017).

Tiina Matikainen, EdD (Temple University, Japan), is a native of Finland and currently Visiting Lecturer in the Faculty of Environment and Information Studies at Keio University Shonan Fujisawa Campus. She has been teaching EFL and second-language acquisition undergraduate and graduate courses in Japan for the past 15 years. Before coming to Japan, she taught academic English courses in the United States. Her research interests include L2 lexicon, English for academic purposes, and professional development of non-native English speaker teachers.

Peter McCagg, PhD (Georgetown University, USA), is Vice President for Academic Affairs and a Trustee at Akita International University. He has been involved in higher education administration in Japan for over 35 years. Prior to his current position, he served as a Professor and Director of the college-wide academic English program, Chair of the Division of Languages and Dean of International Affairs at International Christian University, and Director of the American Language Institute at New York University. Peter's academic interests lie in cognitive linguistics and conceptual metaphor studies.

Gordon Myskow, PhD, is Visiting Assistant Professor at Keio University, Department of Law and Politics, where he teaches CLIL-based academic literacy courses. He has taught in Japan for 18 years, including pre-service teacher education and in-service Master of TESOL courses at Teachers College, Columbia University (Japan). His research interests include the language of school subject matter and the implementation of CLIL in the Japanese EFL context. His work has appeared in the *Journal of English for Academic Purposes, Linguistics and Education, ELT Journal,* and *Functional Linguistics.* He is an advisor to the United Nations Association's Test of English in Japan.

Paul Nation is Emeritus Professor in Applied Linguistics at the School of Linguistics and Applied Language Studies (LALS) at Victoria University of Wellington, New Zealand. He is the author of more than 250 books and articles, including *Learning Vocabulary in Another Language* (Cambridge

University Press 2001, 2013), *Teaching Vocabulary: Strategies and Techniques* (Heinle 2008), *Teaching and Learning Vocabulary* (Newbury House 1990), and *New Ways in Teaching Vocabulary* (Ed.) (1994) and is one of the foremost scholars in second-language vocabulary.

Thomas N. Robb, PhD (University of Hawaii at Manoa, USA), is Professor Emeritus at Kyoto Sangyo University where he taught linguistics, CALL, computer literacy, and communicative English for over 35 years. He is Chair of the Extensive Reading Foundation and is a past President of JALT and PacCALL. He is also Editor of *TESL-EJ*, the first electronic journal for ESL, and an organizer of the GLoCALL conference held in a different Asian community annually. His main focus is on educational technology for language learning. For extensive reading practice, he has created the MReader software, which is used worldwide by over 100,000 students.

Gerome Rothman is Field Director and Organizer at Zenkoku Ippan Tokyo General Union (Tozen Union for short). As an organizer at Tozen he is a Case Officer for several of its locals, responsible for leading collective bargaining, drafting demands and legal documents, and representing the union to third parties such as the Labor Relations Commission. He is also Tozen's representative to the executive of Rengo Tokyo, Rengo being the national federation with which Tozen became affiliated in 2016. Prior to coming to Japan, he worked as an organizer for Service Employees International Union Local 775 in Seattle.

Stephen M. Ryan is Professor in the Department of Language and Culture, Faculty of Human Sciences at Sanyo Gakuen University, Okayama, and former President of Eichi (St. Thomas) University, Amagasaki, Japan. He has taught English and intercultural communication at the undergraduate and graduate level in Japan for over 30 years and has held an unusual number of administrative and management positions in Japanese universities. His research interests include intercultural communication, study abroad, and neuroscience.

Mikiko Sudo is a Lecturer at Soka University in Tokyo, where she teaches content-based academic writing courses and a variety of EFL courses. She has taught undergraduate courses for more than 18 years at universities such as Kwansei Gakuin University (Kobe-Sanda Campus), Konan University (Kobe), and International Christian University (Tokyo). Her research interests include identity and motivation in language learning, classroom participation structure, and classroom discourse analysis. She earned a Master of TESOL and completed her doctoral courses (ABD) in TESOL at Temple University Japan.

Bill Snyder, PhD (Northwestern University, USA), is Specially Appointed Professor and Assistant Director of the Master of TESOL Program at Kanda University of International Studies, where he teaches a foundation course in teaching practice and pedagogical grammar. In addition, he works with students in the program on their writing, encouraging them to highlight the teacher's voice in talking about teaching in Japanese classrooms. He has worked in teacher education for 20 years in Russia, Korea, Turkey, Armenia, and Japan. After a stretch of administrative work, he has returned to research, writing on flow and engagement in teachers' work.

Jeffrey Stewart, PhD (Swansea University, UK), is an Associate Professor at Kyushu Sangyo University's Language Education and Research Center in Fukuoka, Japan. He has over 10 years' experience teaching in Japan at the university level, and is a founding member of the JALT Vocabulary Special Interest Group. His research involving language assessment and vocabulary acquisition has appeared in journals such as *TESOL Quarterly* and *Language Assessment Quarterly*, and he serves as a reviewer for journals such as *Language Testing* and *Modern Language Journal*.

Asako Takaesu is a lecturer at Soka University in Japan, where she teaches academic writing focused on global issues and TOEFL preparation classes. For more than 20 years, she has taught undergraduate courses at Japanese universities, including Aoyama Gakuin University, Senshu University, Tokyo Metropolitan University, and International Christian University. Her professional interests include global issues, academic writing, reflective journal writing, and the use of news in the EFL classroom. In addition to teaching EFL, she has also worked as an interpreter, translator, and English-language journalist. Her publications include more than 120 articles on culture, politics, travel, and current issues that have appeared in English-language newspapers and magazines in Japan. Her master's degree is in American Studies from Michigan State University.

Paul R. Underwood, PhD (Lancaster University, UK), is Associate Professor of English and Teacher Education in the Department of Social Sciences, Toyo Eiwa University, where he teaches ELT methodology in the high school teacher training course. He also teaches the "Perspectives on Global Politics and Society" CLIL course in the Center for Global Interdisciplinary Courses (GIC), Keio University. He has been teaching in Japanese universities and across Japan in pre- and in-service teacher education programs since 2007, and prior to that, in Japanese junior and senior high schools.

Paul Wadden, PhD, is a Senior Lecturer in the English for Liberal Arts Program of International Christian University, Tokyo. The editor of the original *A Handbook for Teaching English at Japanese Colleges and Universities* (Oxford University Press 1993), he is the author of articles on language teaching and academic writing appearing in *TESOL Quarterly*, *ELT Journal*, *RELC Journal*, *College Literature*, *Composition Studies* and many other journals; articles on culture, politics, and education in *The Washington Post*, *The Wall Street Journal*, *The New York Times*, and *The Japan Times*, and more than 50 textbooks. He has taught in Japanese universities for the past 30 years.

Rob Waring, PhD, is Professor at Notre Dame Seishin University in Okayama, Japan. He is an acknowledged expert in extensive reading and second-language vocabulary acquisition. He has published over 60 articles and has given hundreds of lectures, plenaries, and featured speaker presentations in 28 countries, and has been Chair of several major international conferences. He is an Executive Board member of the Extensive Reading Foundation responsible for the promotion of extensive reading globally. He is also author and series editor of a six series of graded readers by various publishers, and the administrator and co-founder of the websites ER-Central.com (extensive reading) and word-learner.com (vocabulary).

John Wiltshier is a professor in the Department of English Literature at Miyagi Gakuin Women's University, Sendai, where he teaches speaking, listening, and TESOL teacher training courses. He is an author of *English Firsthand*, the communication course widely used in universities across Japan. His research is highly practical and focuses on discovering, practicing, and refining effective class-based teaching. He has presented nationally and internationally in Asia, Europe, and the United States, including twice being Featured Speaker at the International JALT conference.

Advice to foreign teachers at Japanese universities

June 4, 1894

Excerpt from a letter by Lafcadio Hearn, Foreign Instructor at the National Fifth High School (now Kumamoto University), to Basil Hall Chamberlain, newly appointed Professor of Japanese at Tokyo University.

I should say these were the general rules for a foreigner in Government service:

Never to ask any questions concerning business.

Never to ask why.

Never to criticize even when requested.

Never to speak either favourably or unfavourably of other officials, of students, or of employees.

If obliged to speak, to remember that favourable criticism may prove much more objectionable than the other.

Give no direct refusal under any circumstances, but only say 1. "It is difficult for the moment—"; or 2. "Certainly"—but take care to forget all about it. Direct refusals are not forgiven. The other devices are respected and admired.

Never imagine intimacy possible, —or imagine reserve possible. Both are entirely impossible; but one must steer carefully between the two.

Consider that all adverse criticisms upon national or official matters are thrown out as "feelers" and that any expression of sympathy with them is likely to provoke immediate hostility.

Do not imagine that the question of application, efficiency, or conduct in relation to students is of any official importance.

The points required from the foreigner are simply 2: (1) Keep the clams in good humor. (2) Pass everybody.

If told you give too high marks, pay no attention—except to give higher still when possible. The suggestion is policy.

Be very much afraid if praised, that something awful is going to happen to you.

Be perfectly sure that the result of making any complaint will be that you will be held responsible for the cause of the complaint—because that is the easiest way of settling the matter.

Foreword by John F. Fanselow

> Before starting our teaching careers, or at times when we are considering moving from one institution to another, we all ask the question, "Where, who, and how should I teach?" Later, after we have made the decision and are in the position we decided to accept, we ask the question, "What does it all mean?" Common as these questions are, they have rarely been dealt with in a concrete, useful way—that is, until the publication of this *Handbook*.

That was the opening I wrote more than 25 years ago for the volume that preceded this one, called *A Handbook for Teaching English at Japanese Colleges and Universities* (Oxford University Press, 1993). My Foreword continued, identifying the same questions and issues this new and revised *Handbook* again fully addresses, though in the present moment and current context,

> How can I best teach my students? What does my institution expect of me? What is my role in curriculum design and university policy-making? What is the meaning of my teaching in this foreign country? Why am I frustrated with how the students sometimes respond to my teaching methods? Why are some of my relationships with colleagues so bewildering? It is these kinds of questions, ones that grow out of our need to determine where, who, and how we want to teach that this *Handbook* deals with in specific, realistic ways.

Once again in this volume—drawing upon their extensive experience as language-teaching professionals—leading educators at Japanese universities share, with refreshing candor, experiences with their students, their colleagues, and their administrators. For language teachers and foreign faculty newer to the Japanese university setting, the observations the authors offer will help them understand their students, sharpen their pedagogies, and appreciate their colleagues. For more experienced university teachers, these chapters will help them compare their own teaching practices with those of other veteran teachers and more fully comprehend the complex cultural, political, and academic dimensions of the Japanese university.

For non-Japanese university instructors seeking tenured, full-time, or part-time employment—to get their foot in the door or land a coveted tenured position—the information in this book will be invaluable. For Japanese faculty and administrators, the authors' observations and reflections should also prove valuable. As I previously wrote,

> Japanese professors and administrators who want to discover the thoughts and views of their English-speaking colleagues will find a rich mine of insights and revelations in this *Handbook*. The book's observations on Japanese students, teachers, and administrative staff reflect to a large extent the values, attitudes, and beliefs commonly held by foreign teachers in Japan. It is crucial that these values, attitudes, and beliefs be more widely understood because they determine many of the differences that separate foreign and Japanese faculty on a university staff and that often create a gulf of misunderstanding. This book can help bridge that gulf.

In this current volume, in which 21 of the 23 chapters are completely new and the other two are extensively revised, some of the returning authors tackle the same issues they did in the 1993 edition but focus on the contemporary milieu—the educational background and learning styles of the students, the expectations and assumptions of institutions, the character and principles of the faculty, and the need to consider differences among them. It is important to consider how even words such as *consensus, listening, responsibility* have different meanings in Japanese and English and are interpreted differently, and how important it is to understand internal policies at universities (written and unwritten), Ministry of Education regulations, and labor laws.

In 1993, I wrote that while each author provided concrete and specific advice, the authors didn't claim that they were presenting "the" truth but rather "a" truth. I observed,

> They have bared their feelings in as genuine and sincere a way as they can with faith that others will consider their suggestions and present view of reality as the basis for attempts to understand themselves, their students, and their colleagues in a deeper, more complete way.

And their insights and observations have evolved.

As I consider my previous comment, I do not think it was strong enough to urge you, the reader, to see how broad and diverse the interpretations of the reality of teaching English in Japan are. So this time around, I suggest you consider these chapters the same way you would consider the comments and questions from participants in a round table discussion, respectfully dialoging and debating with each other. For example, those who focus on cultural explanations would question those who base their teaching philosophy on universal principles. Those who believe that we need to listen for years and gain a consensus before we suggest "change" would question, in a round table, those who advocate for more immediate pragmatic change. What this volume does is provide the diverse perspectives to get such discussion started. In short, I want to remind each reader of what most do anyway—to learn through dialogue and to question everything we read. To that end, I see these contributions as a rich source for teacher development. Selecting a chapter every few weeks to discuss at a staff meeting, or a faculty retreat, or informally over tea or lunch I think would lead to deeper and deeper insights for all of us. Of course, the more discussion leads to change in our perceptions, understandings and, most important, actions, the better.

I emphasize *change* for two reasons. First, the new authors contributing to this volume bring to bear viewpoints from contemporary educational theory including cultural studies, applied linguistics, global issues, world Englishes, and gender studies that provide insight into how the present teaching context has changed. Yet each returning author has also changed to varying degrees in the last 25 years, as have many of the pedagogical practices and cultural interpretations they discuss in their chapters. There is no need to re-read the earlier volume to confirm my claim. Taken together, these changes in our collective thinking about our relationships with colleagues and students and policies in Japanese higher education help us become more informed and mature.

The second reason I mention *change* is that our role as teachers is not only to deepen our own understanding of our cultural and educational context but also to challenge and change our ideas about what types of learning are most beneficial for our students. Here, for example, is what some claim Darwin wrote about *change*: "It is not the strongest species that survives nor the most intelligent but the one most responsive to change."[1]

Though it is obvious that learning requires change, in fact there are forces arrayed to prevent change, such as textbooks that contain a wider range of grammatical principles, sentence patterns, and technical vocabulary items than students can cope with. Cultural conventions that equate learning with test scores coupled with examinations that require memorization rather than thinking also inhibit change.

Professor Kensaku Yoshida from Sophia University has for many years surveyed Japanese adults on their feelings about the English classes they have taken. He has consistently reported that 90 percent of adults, looking back, consider their English courses to have been a complete waste of time. Could any business or government in the world survive with an approval rating of 10 percent? Of course not. In 1993, I wrote,

> The *Handbook* you are holding is not meant to be just a quick read, though the concrete and specific nature of the chapters does enable us to read them quickly, without getting bogged down. And because we can easily move through the readings, we should not forget that the suggestions and reflections cannot be really useful to us unless we re-read them slowly, compare our own reflections with those in the book, and translate some of the suggestions into practice. A quick read can reveal what is available. But without re-reading and reflection, re-reading and discussion and finally action, we will not get the full value of the book.... Reading about the misconceptions, nodding our heads, sighing, or even disagreeing, yet continuing to

teach as before, means we are not really engaging ourselves with the insights provided, but rather going through motions.... This *Handbook*, whose authors share their experiences and values so directly, is designed to move us beyond simply going through the motions. The authors encourage involvement and candor in your work and relationships in the same way that they have shared their own.

As I re-read the lines above and the chapters in this volume and reflect on traditional policies that inhibit language learning, discriminate against non-native speakers and teachers of English, and are complicit in the continuing occurrence of sexual harassment and bullying, I feel that I and many in our field have been too complacent. The proclamations and ads from universities, private language schools, government offices, and so on supporting the use of language for communication, critical thinking, and globalization are often contradicted by policies and practices, as exemplified in the mandated tests and textbooks, in hiring practices, and in lack of investment in the preparation and development of Japanese English teachers and in the importation of 60,000 mostly native speakers of English in the JET program in the last 30 years.

The myth that native speakers are superior to non-native speakers, discussed in several chapters, reminds me of the long history of discrimination against *the other*. Segregation in the United States and racial discrimination in many other countries has to varying degrees eased, but it is grounded in the same fallacy: the superiority of one type of person over another, whether men over women, or young over old, or one color skin over another. *Hierarchies of privilege have also been reinforced within the field of language teaching.*

Having said this, I still look at language teaching through rose-colored glasses. One of the reasons is that teachers such as those who have contributed to this book, as well as the two editors, boldly invite professional educators in Japan and other countries to reflect on and analyze and re-reflect on and re-analyze their experiences in their classrooms, in their faculty meetings, in their presentations at conferences, in their writings, in their reading of the wide range of articles and books in our field, and in their conversations with colleagues.

Moreover, though the authors teach in universities and focus on issues in higher education, teachers at all levels can benefit from their insights, questions, practices, and suggestions.

The most important lesson for me in my professional life is: Question everything! The Nobel Committee commissioned a book to explore common values and practices of those who have received the Nobel Prize in all fields since the inception of the award. The conclusion was that all the recipients questioned accepted practice. When Japanese Nobel recipients were interviewed a couple of years ago each said, "I had to forget and ignore everything I had learned and look with fresh eyes on reality."

Science historian Jacob Bronowski equates such questioning with the habit of truth. He writes, "In science and in art and in self-knowledge we explore . . . by turning . . . to ask, 'Is this so?' This is the habit of truth, always minute yet always urgent."[2]

The invitations to renewed inquiry from Paul Wadden and Chris Carl Hale to the authors of this *Handbook* relate to every aspect of English-language teaching in Japanese higher education and are important because they led to these new chapters, each asking, "Is this so? Is this still so?" The original *Handbook for Teaching English at Japanese Colleges and Universities* had a major impact on language teaching in Japanese higher education. I expect this volume that you are holding in your hand will have an even greater one.

John F. Fanselow
Professor Emeritus, Teachers College, Columbia University
Faculty Member, International Teacher Development Institute

Notes

1 The source of his quote on change is unclear; some think that it is a streamlined version of a similar idea that Darwin wrote in *The Origin of Species* in 1859.
2 Bronowski, Jacob. *Science and Human Values* (Harper and Row 1956), p. 43.

Acknowledgements

The editors thank the inspiring students and wonderful colleagues—Japanese and non-Japanese—who over the years have made our careers at the Japanese university worth having and this *Handbook* worth writing. Curtis Kelly and Tom Robb, notable contributors to the earlier *A Handbook for Teaching English at Japanese Colleges and Universities* in 1993, deserve special mention for encouraging us to take on a new one and giving insightful feedback along the way. So does distinguished professor John Fanselow of Columbia University Teachers College who graciously wrote the Foreword to both editions. John has worked tirelessly to raise the quality of English education in Japan for more than 30 years, and almost any book on that topic, directly or indirectly, bears his influence.

I, Paul, thank Stanford University—particularly Associate Vice Provost Marvin Diogenes and colleague and collaborator John Peterson in the Program in Writing and Rhetoric—for support as a visiting scholar while editing this volume, Earl Skidmore for his personal generosity during my stay, and International Christian University, Tokyo, my home institution, for a sabbatical that made it possible; two daughters Elena and Kari, both university students, for never letting me take myself (or my writing and research) too seriously; and last but never least, partner Mee Hey Chang, who has put up with and borne up these kinds of projects since the day we were married.

I, Chris Carl, wish to thank the amazing authors of this volume for contributing their insights and expertise. Many of them I have known for years, and others I have only known from reading (and learning from) their work. It was a true honor to put this volume together with such an amazing roster. Paul Wadden, for finally (finally!) taking me up on my offer to help him update his classic. I'm sure there were times he was second-guessing that fateful decision. Thanks for sticking it out and for in fact handily taking the lead once Soma Roger was born halfway through the project. From that moment on, you never once complained about my emails sent all in lowercase because I only had one free hand to type with.

We both would like to express our thanks to Routledge for enthusiastically taking on this project, and offering fast and expert guidance, and a lot of patience, whenever we asked. Samantha Phua and Katie Peace from the Singapore office, in particular, deserve special note. Also to AIU graduate assistant Stephen Tucker for helping us get over the finish line. Finally, however unconventional, an acknowledgement is owed to the spirit of adventure in language teaching and language learning that leads us, in far lands or in our home country, to expand our minds and broaden our hearts to other cultures and peoples (teacher and student alike), while remembering, as intrepid Melville reminds us of our destination, despite *Handbooks* like this, "It is not drawn down on any map. True places never are."

Part 1
The setting

1 The landscape of Japanese higher education

An introduction

Chris Carl Hale and Paul Wadden

Changing demographics, paradoxical realities

Over the last 25 years, since the original *A Handbook for Teaching English at Japanese Colleges and Universities* was published, there has been anxiety over Japan's low birth rate, declining population, and dwindling number of college-age students. In such an environment, many readers of this new *Handbook* might wonder, "Why pursue a teaching career in Japan at all?" Looking at the trend line in Figure 1.1, one would certainly be forgiven, demographically, for climbing aboard the panic bandwagon.

Since the early 1990s when the sharp decline of Japanese youth began, predictions of mass firings of faculty and mass shutterings of universities have abounded. Yet like many trends in Japan, there has been a paradoxical shift from what was expected to what has *actually* happened. According to MEXT, while the overall college-age population *has* significantly declined—from 2 million in 1990 to 1.2 million in 2017—the percentage of that population now attending college has sharply risen from 30% in 1990 to 50% today. And counter to widespread expectation (and even current belief), the overall number of four-year colleges and universities has steadily *increased* rather than decreased over this same period, as shown in Figure 1.2. This suggests there are more positions for foreign teachers at Japanese universities, and more diverse positions, than ever before.

In addition to the four-year colleges and universities shown in Figure 1.2, there are 352 two-year colleges in Japan; these junior colleges have, admittedly, seen a modest thinning out over the same period. Yet overall there are currently 1,133 institutions of higher learning in Japan, with an astonishing 274 *more* four-year colleges and universities than in 1993 when the original *Handbook* was published.

The contrasting shifts illustrated by these two figures suggest that Japanese higher education has skillfully surfed a demographic tidal wave—in part by enrolling more domestic students and in part (in a story untold by the chart) by attracting more international students, particularly from East Asia. As a result, Japanese college and university campuses are more diverse and dynamic than at any time in post-war history. Moreover, in order to attract international students, many universities are expanding their course offerings and

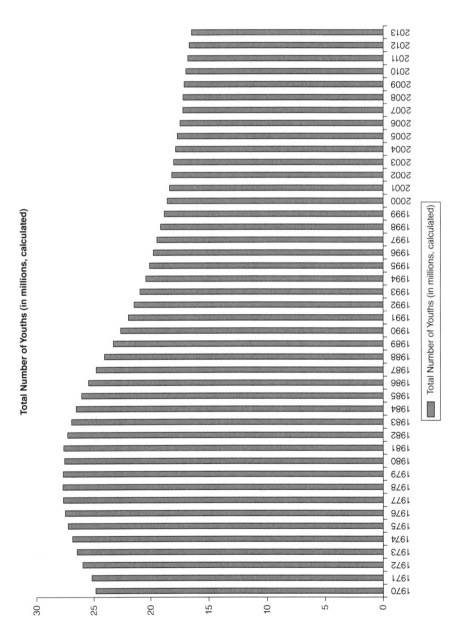

Figure 1.1 Total number of youths (1970–2013)

Note

a This graph was derived from OECD data. The percentage of youths in Japan (%) was multiplied by the population of Japan (#) to derive these figures. All data is originally sourced from OECD online resources.

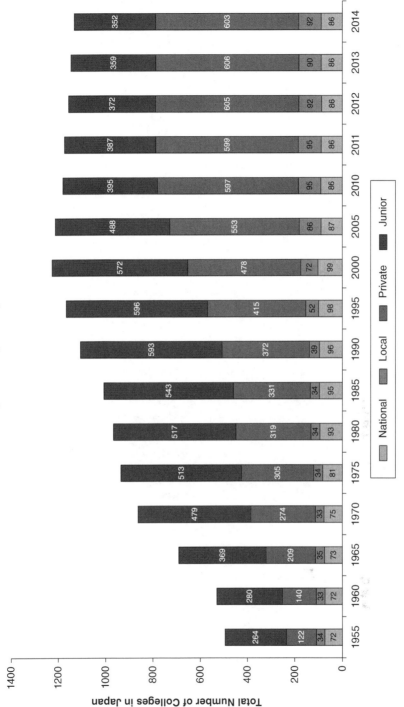

Figure 1.2 Number of colleges and universities in Japan (1955–2014)

Notes

a Data from Ministry of Education, Culture, Sports, Science and Technology (MEXT).

b The data for junior colleges is also divided into national, local, and private colleges, and the value here represents the combined total of those three groups of data. They are presented as a sum here primarily because the ratio of private junior colleges to national and local junior colleges starts and ends very high (77.3% in 1955 and 94.9% in 2014).

even establishing full degree programs in English. As imperceptibly slow as it may appear to the long-time casual observer on the ground, the country is starting to re-envision itself as an educational hub for the region. At my university (Chris's), for example, nearly 30% of the undergraduate students are non-Japanese, and foreign faculty—both language teachers and subject-specific professors—are being hired to teach them. In other words, despite popular belief and raw data suggesting an impending higher-ed apocalypse, the reality is that there has never been a better time to find work teaching English—and teaching in other academic fields in English—at Japanese colleges and universities.[1]

Perhaps what *has* changed in the past 25 years is that while the number of universities has risen, so too have the academic standards for their faculty. As will be evident in Chapters 2 and 3, which discuss in detail many aspects of university hiring and employment, the days of foreigners being offered full-time positions by showing up as native speakers with college degrees in hand have long since passed. And this is a good thing. In fact, the professional qualifications of the foreign professoriate in Japan are the best they have ever been.

Leaving generalizations at the door

A common refrain about higher education in Japan is that it isn't very rigorous (some have even gone so far as to call it a "myth").[2] Among Japanese it is often said that universities are hard to get into (brutal entrance exams), but easy to get out of (a glide to graduation), which is generally the opposite of higher education systems in other developed countries. This generalization is bolstered by comparing the percentage of the population that enrolls in higher education of some kind (80% in Japan, compared with 69% in the U.K and only 52% in the U.S.) and university completion rates (72% in Japan, compared with 55% in the U.S. and only 44% in the U.K.). One interpretation of these OECD figures[3] is that a lot more students in Japan attend a college or university of some kind, and they have a far easier time completing their study. In other words, the U.S. and the U.K. are more rigorous: fewer attempt to enter at all, and of those who do, fewer can "cut it" and graduate.

As we have spent a combined half-century working in Japanese universities, we can attest that there is *some* truth to this generalization. There are more than 1,100 colleges and universities, including junior colleges, and some are indeed less rigorous. If students can get to the first step at the bottom of the "escalator," as another Japanese metaphor for college study depicts it, they can rise without much effort from freshman year to senior year and step off the top of the escalator with a diploma in hand. But we also both work at two universities that decidedly *do not* fit this characterization. Many of the authors of this volume can attest to schools that do not fit this stereotype either. Interestingly, one of the benefits of having more international students on Japanese campuses is that they are voting positively with their feet and expect quality teaching for their tuition payments. Thus, faculty are under pressure to "up their game" and abandon—or at least limit—old-fashioned pedagogies such as droning on in weekly lectures for an entire course with one multiple-choice exam at the end. New predominantly English-language universities are being founded, such as Akita International University and Ritsumeikan Asia Pacific University, as well as free-standing new colleges within traditional universities, such as Waseda University's "School for International Liberal Studies" (SILS).[4] Other trends putting positive pressure on courses and curricula are the Ministry of Education's successful efforts to get universities to lengthen terms, regularize credit hours, and implement student evaluations, as well as the newfound emphasis companies are placing on continual and lifelong learning skills needed for success—for employees and employers—in the twenty-first century. A series of well-funded Ministry of Education initiatives to globalize Japanese higher education through massive multi-year grants—in particular, the Super Global University projects—has spurred innovative curricula at leading universities and raised the demand for qualified foreign teachers, scholars, and researchers.

One strategic generalization that we and other contributing authors have made in this book concerns the term "the Japanese university." For us, this phrase functions in the same way that the term "species" does in biology: it names an overlying category of educational institutions within which there are many different types (subspecies such as "national," "prefectural," "private," "elite," "technology," "liberal arts," "foreign studies," etc.) as well as significant differences in each individual institution as a phenotype. We urge you, the reader, to approach your particular school the way an anthropologist investigates a foreign culture: put aside your personal assumptions and cultural predilections and observe as clearly as possible the actual environment in which you work; it will be completely different from your university back home in Sydney, Liverpool, Hamilton, Dublin, Singapore, or San Francisco. It will also be significantly different from any previous school at which you worked in Sapporo, Osaka, Tokushima, or Fukuoka. Learn about its history (how and why it was founded), its faculties (which are largest and most influential), its organizational structure (and how power flows within it), and its student demographic. Observe without judgment the behavior of the faculty, students, and staff around you and try to discern the web of relationships and values in which they are embedded. Continually interview and casually question members of each group to better understand this unique island culture and ecosystem on which you have landed. Just as each community and each family is distinct, each university is one of a kind. The maps provided in the following pages won't be the actual territory, but they may prevent you from getting disoriented in that territory as often, and when lost, may help you more quickly find your bearings.

Navigating this *Handbook*

This first section, Part 1, contains two important chapters dealing with how to get (and keep) both full-time and part-time university work in Japan. They describe positions, qualifications, hiring processes, typical responsibilities, and the general dos and don'ts of finding employment. For those seeking full-time positions, Chapter 2 identifies a fundamental yet common error of focusing one's educational qualifications only on TESOL and applied linguistics, while Chapter 3 explores the potential to earn a decent living—and live a freer life—as a permanent part-timer. Chapter 4, "The chrysanthemum maze: understanding your colleagues in the Japanese university," is essential reading for anyone trying to grasp the political, psychological, interpersonal, and administrative infrastructure of the Japanese university; it is a quasi-user's guide for making sense of the functioning of your faculty and administration.

Part 2, "The courses," begins with four chapters written by leading teacher–educators on principles and pedagogy to optimally teach the primary English skills courses—speaking, reading, writing, and listening—at Japanese universities. These are followed by chapters on the teaching of subject-specific courses (such as CLIL and EMI) and the art of presentation (both are expanding throughout college curricula), and by chapters on skills and pedagogy underlying nearly all university coursework—acquisition of vocabulary, use of technology, assignment of homework, and standards of evaluation.

Part 3, "The classroom," focuses mainly on Japanese students. Who are they? What are their attitudes and expectations? Why are they often "silent"? What accounts for their interaction patterns? What is their educational experience to date? How can a teacher create engagement and heighten motivation? What particular dynamics exist between students and their "foreign teachers"? Why? How does national language policy from elementary school through university impact their language skills and learning styles? These topics—and many more besides—are explored in this section.

Part 4, "The workplace," engages an even wider range of issues including those encountered by Japanese teachers of English, "non-native non-Japanese" teachers of English, and non-Japanese administrators. These chapters examine the challenges and contributions of non-native English teachers (belying the "native speaker fallacy" and the newly posited "native speaker learner fallacy") and share the perspectives of two non-Japanese faculty who have served as senior administrators (a former university president and a current vice president for academic affairs). Other chapters appraise female–male dynamics in the university based upon a nation-wide survey ("'He Said, She Said': Female and Male Dynamics in Japanese Universities") and the laws and labor conditions of the workplace, including possible recourse when conflict occurs ("Conflicts, Contracts, Rights, and Solidarity: The Japanese University Workplace from a Labor Perspective"). The final chapter, "Navigating the Chrysanthemum Maze: Off-hand Advice on How to Tiptoe through the Minefield of the Japanese University," is a casual conversation between two contributing authors—and wizened language-teaching faculty—in which they ponder general rules of thumb for working in a university and elaborate on insights offered in this *Handbook* by recalling their own experiences.

Appendices are often regarded as superfluous, but we urge you to browse through the ones in this book. We include them because we wish someone else had compiled them previously so we could have used them. Appendix 1 features resources available to English teachers and foreign faculty, from professional associations to academic journals, and from useful websites to research groups (including some little-known but intriguing scholarly study groups). Appendix 2 offers a brief explanation of types of universities and how to find out more about them; some of this information is much more accessible these days as a complete list of Japanese universities is now available, by region, on Wikipedia, and many universities have their own English webpages. Appendix 3 presents (A) a hierarchical table of administrative offices at the typical university (it may need to be slightly reconfigured for your own); (B) the offices and titles, in Japanese and English, of non-teaching university staff; and (C) the Japanese and the English translations for the titles and ranks of teaching staff, from professor emeritus to part-time lecturer.

The chapters in this book are intended to be accessible and interesting. To that end, we have attempted to avoid academese and opted for reader-friendly endnotes instead of reader-interrupting in-text citations. We have also embraced a rich variety of voices, perspectives, and even genre, including chapters rhetorically framed as question-and-answer, survey response, scenario sequences, and even, with a nod to Plato and the origins of western educational philosophy, a dialogue. Topically and thematically, the chapters are meant to present a diversity of viewpoints. For instance, Curtis Kelly and Nobuhiro Adachi favor understanding the soft power of human relations at the university, while Gerome Rothman focuses on the hard reality of labor relations. We hope this multitude of voices and multiplicity of perspectives inspire readers to consider all of them through a critical lens and to thoughtfully "question everything." We also hope the shared insights, knowledge, and experience help readers to both better succeed and greater enjoy life at a Japanese university.

150 years of friendly advice

The original *Handbook* published in 1993 was not the first attempt to explicate and explain the Japanese university for the foreign teacher. We can reach back as far as 1894 when Lafcadio Hearn, one of the first westerners to teach university-level classes and become a regular faculty member in Japan, wrote to Basil Hall Chamberlain to give him advice upon commencing his new position at Tokyo University. He instructed him:

> Never to ask why. Never to criticize even when requested. Never to speak either favourably or unfavourably of other officials, of students, or of employees. . . . Do not imagine that the question of application, efficiency, or conduct in relation to students is of any official importance. The points required from the foreigner are simply 2: (1) Keep the clams in good humor. (2) Pass everybody.[5]

We should respond to this advice in the same way that John Fanselow suggests in the "Foreword," that readers consider the *Handbook* authors' observations, reflections, and claims, by asking, "Is this so? Is this still so?" Some foreign university teachers might conclude that the more things change the more they stay the same. We feel that the more they seem to stay the same, the more they may have actually changed. We and the authors offer you this new letter of advice, in 23 chapters and three appendices, with a deeper, more detailed, and somewhat different message.

Notes

1 While the overall employment trend is positive, especially among higher profile public and private universities, about 40% of less prestigious private schools were unable to meet their enrollment quotas in 2017. These lower and mid-tier institutions remain under stress.
2 See Brian McVeigh's powerful and provocative *Japanese Higher Education as Myth* (Routledge 2002), for instance.
3 See enrollment rates and graduation rates on OECD website: stats.oecd.org
4 Several years ago *The Nikkei Shimbun* asked human resources departments at major Japanese corporations which universities' graduates they were "paying more attention to" in recruiting talent. The three most often named were The University of Tokyo (the nation's oldest), and Akita International University and Asia Pacific University. The latter two didn't even exist 20 years ago.
5 See the frontispiece for text from this letter.

2 Making a career of university teaching in Japan

Getting (and keeping) a full-time job

Jenifer Larson-Hall and Jeffrey Stewart

I, Jenifer, was spending the day at a small Japanese seaside town watching the local festival with my family when the phone call came. It was a professor from Kitakyushu University inviting me to a job interview, that much I could tell, but I needed to be alone to focus all my attention on understanding what she said. So I separated from my family and walked around the gravel courtyard, crunching small pebbles under my feet, while she told me that I would be asked to teach a *mogi* lesson on *oningaku*. Panic! What is a *mogi* lesson? What is *oningaku*? I kept making noises like I understood ("*Hai,*" "*Hai,*" "Mmm," "Mmm") while my brain feverishly tried to decode what I was agreeing to do. After all, I didn't want to show my ignorance at the very start of the hiring process! I scribbled down the interview date and finally worked out I would be doing a *demonstration* lesson on *phonetics*.

So began the saga of what eventually became my current job as a foreign tenured faculty member. You may think such positions are rare, and there are certainly fewer of them than part-time adjunct or full-time contract positions. But there is reason to be optimistic about a career in a Japanese university if you stay in Japan over the long haul. We imagine our typical readers are in their 20s or 30s, perhaps coming to Japan initially as an ALT (assistant language teacher) in the JET (Japan Exchange and Teaching) program and now hoping to pursue a career here, or someone with a TESOL/TEFL master's degree currently teaching part time but who can't see a tenured position in the cards. You may also be one of the growing number of people coming to Japan to teach a content area in English. You have some proficiency in Japanese or are serious about putting in the work to get there. You're academically inclined and willing to eventually get a PhD in a field you're interested in, or at least would be provided you were convinced it wouldn't be a waste of time and money. Most importantly, you're someone who thinks about the long term and stays the course toward a goal. The truth is, although tenure is numerically rare for foreigners, and jobs are increasingly competitive, *genuinely* qualified candidates for these positions (i.e., credentials in the relevant field and proficiency in Japanese) are even rarer still. So rare, in fact, that they may never fully outpace the number of available positions, even with shrinking enrollments. Our knowledge of jobs at Japanese universities largely relates to *bungakubu* faculties (generally translated as humanities but including history, literature, geography, and other departments), language centers which provide English as a foreign language (EFL) classes, and, to a lesser degree, the social sciences. Yet from what our colleagues in the natural sciences report on the number of applicants per position available, positions may be equally obtainable in their fields.

Getting your foot in the door

There are two paths toward teaching at a Japanese university. Since most four-year university degrees in Japan require at least two years of language credits regardless of students' majors, for part-time and fixed-term full-time contract positions, the majority of opportunities are in the fields of English-language education or EFL. Most foreigners teaching at Japanese universities in humanities and social science faculties teach EFL classes. These types of jobs are typically advertised on the JREC-IN (jrecin.jst.go.jp), Linguist List job site (linguistlist.org), or the JALT Jobs List.[1] For JREC-IN, the jobs that show up in an English keyword search are often different from the ones that are displayed in a Japanese keyword search, so if you have a Japanese accomplice to help you or the Japanese ability to do it yourself, check both.

Contract full-time is usually 8–10 classes a week, although 10 classes is becoming more the norm. Usually you teach 3 or 4 weekdays and have the remaining days free of class with the expectation you will devote this time to your research. Many teachers use these days when they have no classes scheduled to teach extra part-time classes at another university, but some universities do not permit their staff to teach elsewhere and may even require faculty to be present in their offices for non-teaching days during the term (see Jenifer's experience with a contract job, pp. 15–16), or they may limit outside teaching to a single day a week. Typically, there are two (or three) terms in the academic year totaling 30 weeks of instruction, plus several test days or an exam week at the end of each term. As a full-time contract teacher, you'll collect your salary throughout the year, but typically, you don't have to be on campus during the five months you're not teaching.[2] These kinds of positions now usually start in the 5–6 million yen range, although the salary varies widely by university, region, and the qualifications and experience of the teacher. On the low end, some pay as little as 4 million for 8 classes. You can get 7 million in Tokyo, and as much as 8–9 million a year is possible at elite private universities, but obviously those jobs are a lot more competitive. You also receive an annual research/travel budget between about 120,000 to 400,000 yen, depending on your institution and its research and publishing expectations. While we hope these rough estimates help you adjust your expectations, it may be safest to assume a salary on the low end before you accept a job; in Japan, applicants typically do not know what their salary will be with any certainty until after an offer is made. Negotiation has never been a possibility as far as we can tell!

To determine starting salary, universities use formulas based on a new hire's age (or the number of years since receiving a bachelor's degree) and years of university-related experience. Generally, the older the teacher and the more teaching and academic-related experience, the higher the starting salary. However, any time *not* spent teaching since getting your bachelor's degree will be a deduction in the points used to determine your starting salary. Also, time spent teaching part time is usually given a lower point value than full-time teaching, but it is still given something. Therefore, when filling in the work-experience forms for a personnel department after getting hired, it is important to maximize the time spent engaged in teaching and minimize the "gaps" between teaching posts. Under this system, teachers who get their degrees later in life can find themselves seriously penalized when it comes to salary calculations. In such cases, it (literally) pays to list on these forms any kind of teaching you have done, even that student-teaching work you did in college or the part-time job you had in the library while a graduate student, and to be generous to yourself in the periods covered.

Contract terms are typically limited to a maximum of three years and may be shorter. Renewals of terms are possible, but due to a 2012 change in contract labor law and a 2013 revision regarding university faculty, it is rare for universities to renew such contracts for more than 5 years, and nearly all will limit renewals to an absolute maximum of 10, because if university educational staff continue in the same position for longer than this, the law unambiguously states that permanent contracts must then be offered upon request.[3] However, if you manage to string together several such positions, you could potentially get to old age doing these jobs, preferably moving to better ones as you go. That option is a distant second to tenure, but even if this is as far as you get, it's still a lot better than most EFL teachers in Japan achieve.

Here's how you can eventually move from work as a JET or ALT (or a similar entry gig) to that kind of EFL work. First, start becoming proficient in Japanese. People that hire you will want to know you can participate in faculty meetings, read simple memos, communicate with students in basic Japanese, and handle the assorted duties that come with the position. Prospective staff with Japanese ability have a huge leg up on otherwise highly qualified competition. Second, get a master's degree in TESOL or Applied Linguistics. (Just being enrolled in a program makes you eligible for most part-time jobs.) If you already have a master's degree in another field, a TESOL certificate is a helpful credential. If you're living in Japan, master's programs held at physical locations are often best because you can make contacts with people already in the system. Some distance programs are acceptable, but be sure to check the reputation of your program to avoid the perception that you got your degree from a "diploma mill."

Third, join your local JALT (Japan Association for Language Teachers) chapter (see Appendix 1 for more professional organizations in Japan). This is the de facto organization for university-level foreign English teachers in Japan. When members need someone to do some classes part time at their university, they often just ask around at the JALT meetings. It's the simplest way to get your foot in the door and acquire the university-level teaching experience you'll need to get better jobs down the road. Don't go once or twice just to "make contacts"—attend regularly, and better yet assume some responsibility in the local chapter or in a SIG (special interest group). If you're not pushy and people feel comfortable around you, sooner or later someone will give you a chance and ask for a resume.

For more interaction with your Japanese counterparts—and more connection with Japanese professors and language-teaching faculty who administer and staff many university departments—consider joining JACET (Japan Association of College English Teachers) which has nearly 3,000 members, an annual conference, SIGs, regional chapters, and regular seminars. In addition to JACET, there are scores of more specialized academic associations (the American Literature Society, the Japan Association of Higher Education Research, the Japanese Association for American Studies, the Japanese Association for Social Research, etc.) that are worthwhile joining in order to meet your Japanese colleagues in these fields. It is through genuinely sharing like-minded interests that friendships and professional connections are made, which then often open doors to professional opportunities and teaching posts.

Fourth, try to publish something even at this early stage. This is because, increasingly, universities ask for three publications even for part-time EFL positions. It doesn't need to be anything flashy at this early stage of your career; our suggestion is to simply publish your teaching ideas locally. Even short 500-word lesson plans will show that you are professionally active. JALT has all kinds of SIGs with publications in which you can share activities and games. As soon as you land a part-time university position, begin contributing to your department's in-house journal. Every publication, no matter how short, counts.

Fifth, cast your net wide. Your chances of getting a job go up dramatically if you consider lesser-known universities in rural areas as well as reputable universities in major cities. Ask everyone you know, especially your Japanese friends and acquaintances, for help and advice in the process. A friend of a friend may provide a crucial contact.

Last, learn how to handle interviews. In Japan, if you've made it as far as the interview stage you can take it as a given that you're considered qualified and your credentials are no longer an issue. Here, the interview is often more of a jerk test than anything else: sure you look good on paper, but are you the kind of person who is pleasant (or at least not unpleasant) to deal with every day? Are you arrogant or humble? Are you culturally chauvinistic or interculturally aware? Be positive and friendly. When you're asked if you're willing to teach various classes at various times or to handle responsibilities beyond teaching, respond with unqualified enthusiasm. When the topic turns to pedagogy or your research, don't be too forceful in your answers. If you are just finishing a PhD, committee members may worry that you will soon jump ship for a better position, requiring them to do a new search all over again a year or two later. Ease their concerns. In general, try to "read the air" and allow space for your interviewers' own opinions (many will be willing to share them if given the chance).

If you minimally follow the above steps in the current climate (online master's degree, three activity-oriented publications in small venues, basic Japanese, plus some part-time experience you got via the people you met at JALT), you should be able to get a contract full-time job *somewhere*. The challenge at that point lies in getting a job that allows you to stay in your current city, rather than having to move to a remote area. If you're willing to live in Tohoku, Hokkaido, or Shikoku, the steps above can sometimes be enough to get you a tenured full-time job after a round or two on the EFL contract circuit, at least for the time being. There is one catch though: check online for the finances and *hensachi* (偏差値) ranking of rural colleges you're applying to, particularly the private ones. You could wind up getting "permanent" employment at a place that won't exist in 5 years.

Experiences with contract jobs

Your authors—and most of the contributors to this volume—have experience with part-time and full-time contract EFL teaching in Japan, as well as most things in between. The two of us are both lucky enough to have tenured positions now. I (Jenifer) would like to talk about some of my experiences to illustrate the variation in EFL jobs depending on the size of the institution and whether it's public or private.

My first trip to Japan was with my husband, who had a government scholarship to study Japanese history in Japanese. I, on hiatus from my master's study in Russian linguistics, had nothing to do but learn to speak Japanese and acclimate to life in Japan. To make extra money, I worked three long days a week in a windowless room teaching English to Japanese of all ages, from 2-year-olds who cried at the sight of me to grandmas who wanted to travel and learn a little English before they went (traveling, that is). I remember when the English school owner, a practical Japanese businesswoman, created a little scheme where students could attend *manabihodai* (my own made-up word for an "all-you-can-learn" buffet!) for just 10,000 yen a month. She got a nice influx of students, and I asked for a raise from my 170,000 yen per month salary. After all, she was making more money, and even if I wasn't working any more hours, why shouldn't I share in the profits, as I was doing all the teaching? She said no and I quit, taking my talent to the streets, or rather, to the students of a nearby university where I advertised my own *manabihodai* and was soon making the same amount of money doing a lot less work.

While moving back and forth between Japan and the US, I held full-time contract jobs at two different private universities. The first one was a private university that specialized in language learning and had a very large English program. I was interviewed by the Australian head of the program while still in the States. I thought the atmosphere there rather sophomoric, with a large contingent of young but qualified teachers (everyone had a Master of TESOL degree) but unspoken jockeying for being the most "popular" teacher with the students. However, the students were in general quite interested in learning English and I taught about 8 classes per week, with few administrative responsibilities (I think looking photogenic might have been the main one).

One thing that rankled, though, was that I was forbidden by the head of the program to stay home on the days I was not teaching. When I told him it was quite normal at an American university for teachers to not be present at the school on days they were not required to teach, he accused me of cultural imperialism. I didn't know then that many Japanese professors routinely do the same thing with no repercussions. I thought, "I can't stay home with my child? I'll take my child with me then!" I thought it would be fun for him and the students to interact in the English lounge, a place where students could come and just shoot the breeze for extra English practice. However, the head of the program heard about it and soon squashed that idea as well. In my future jobs, I always made sure to check what was required for days when I was not teaching. After this, I had no other jobs which required me to be present at the school when I was not scheduled to teach or attend meetings.

Later, in the early 2010s, I worked at a private women's college for about the same pay as my previous job (prices and pay in Japan have really not moved much in 20 years) but was required to teach 10 *koma* (classes) per semester. The two semesters, 15 weeks each, meant I had teaching assignments for 30 weeks of the year, which still left a good 4 months where no one was bothering me with any administrative duties. However, the grandfathered-in foreign faculty taught only in the first-year English program, which was compressed into an intensive 10 weeks, meaning they had literally the other 32 weeks of the year free. As evidenced by my situation, it seems the sweetest deals are a thing of the past, but I felt that my own position was still a very comfortable one: I had one "research day" off per week with no classes, a research budget of about 200,000 yen, a secretary to run to when I got notifications in Japanese from the school that I didn't understand, and a very nice office of my own. The school did ask me to submit one article per year for its in-house journal (called a *kiyou*). If what you want is a job teaching only EFL classes, then this type of situation is quite nice, in my opinion. The basic problem is the typical limit on how long you can work there.

I also twice had the experience of having a full-time contract position at a national university. This was a special *gaikokujin kyoshi* (foreign teacher) position, which required a PhD and was understood as being limited to one stint of 2 or three years only. These positions are funded by the national government, as I understand, and pay quite handsomely along with a subsidy for housing (in other words, no need to pay any deposits or "key money," and rent is quite cheap). Such positions and benefits are used to attract foreign faculty to Japan, and this type of position may even provide funds for moving to Japan and moving back to your home country when it is finished. The teaching load was fairly light, too (about 6 *koma* per semester), and one position involved teaching content courses as well as EFL courses. Administrative work was not required. However, it is difficult to land these kinds of positions successively if one wants to stay in Japan. For short-term stays, though, they are attractive.

Some minor caveats

One difficulty of being a foreigner working in Japan is that you are handicapped in comprehending the unspoken realities and expectations of your Japanese colleagues (see Part 4 of this book, The workplace, for insights into this area). In my first such position, I had a large office that I invited my husband, who was still finishing his dissertation, to share with me. I went about my teaching as seemed normal to me, holding office hours and even advertising a weekly English lunch hour when students could eat together with me and practice speaking. I conducted research and worked on publishing my own dissertation in journal articles. When a female foreign colleague unexpectedly died, I agreed to take over two of her classes the next semester just to show that I was a team player for the university. So it came as a shock when I was told in December of my second year that I would not be kept on for a third year, as every other *gaikokujin kyoshi* before me had been in that department. The reasons? (1) I had allowed my husband to share my spacious office and (2) too few students visited me in my office. Whether these seemed like legitimate reasons or not, I'll leave to you, the reader, to decide, the point being that I was given no warning or opportunity at all to remedy the situation. I do not claim this is unique to Japan, of course (I have heard of people losing tenure-track positions in the US with sudden claims of "uncollegiality" and no warning given as to problems with behavior either), but it serves to underscore that it is good to note and learn more about cultural workplace norms, whereupon you can decide whether you are comfortable flouting them or not.

Pivoting to tenure

If you're reading this book, odds are you're already on your way to finding part-time or contract full-time work. Now we'll cover an even harder part: getting tenure. This is by no means exclusively a difficulty faced by foreign academics who wish to work in Japan, as tenure is becoming harder to obtain all over the world. But with an ever-declining number of college-bound 18-year-olds, many of the less prestigious tertiary institutions in Japan are struggling just to keep their doors open, making the holy grail of tenure all the more elusive. To improve your odds of getting tenure in Japan, it's important to consider what you're qualified to teach and what types of teachers universities need to hire.

The basic qualifications for tenure-track or permanent positions are easy enough to explain and understand. Applicants should have a PhD, experience teaching the types of classes that the position involves, and preferably a history of publishing in respected journals and obtaining research grants. It is also advantageous to be active in academic societies and on the conference circuit, not only to burnish one's CV but also because hiring committees typically prefer to hire trusted acquaintances (or at least those recommended by trusted acquaintances) over unknown entities.

However, even with all of the above, landing tenure at a good university in a major city can be difficult for EFL teachers. While the credentials listed above will certainly make a candidate competitive, the grim reality is that by taking the EFL race all the way to the PhD level, English teachers here are qualifying themselves to become tenured professors in what is largely a non-specialized "general education" field with few such positions, and one that in the future will likely employ even more contract teachers and fewer tenured professors than it does now.

To appreciate why it's so difficult for foreigners with EFL credentials to get tenure, it's important to understand what tenure is in Japan. Regular full-time (正社員 *seishain*) employment is protected by strong labor laws which make it very difficult for even truly incompetent employees to be fired. As a consequence, at Japanese universities "tenure" is in practice, if not in name, really just a matter of securing regular, non-contract, full-time employment in the first place. However, such employment has become increasingly harder to obtain, and not just for foreign staff at universities.

Japan's generous system of lifetime employment with age-based raises worked well during the country's boom years, but by the late 1990s, it was becoming a burden on major corporations trying to compete with more flexible foreign counterparts. Japanese politicians were understandably reluctant to relax labor laws that protected the electorate, but they allowed a loophole: instead of having to give every new employee a lifelong deal, companies could contract or subcontract new limited-term workers in a manner that liberated firms from the responsibility of paying for the legally required benefits due to regular employees, and freed them up to hire and shed new workers as needed. Unfortunately, what started as a stopgap measure for employers to temporarily staff less important positions has increasingly become the norm. Today, large numbers of Japanese workers under 35 are stuck in various forms of irregular employment as companies take on fewer full-time employees and instead use contract workers to manage routine tasks.

Universities have by no means bucked this trend. With the domestic student population shrinking, they want to avoid increasing payrolls with more permanent staff. That isn't to say that *all* new jobs are limited-term contracts, just that many institutions try to make as many new jobs contractual positions as they can. There is one principal question university administrators ask before approving a new tenured position: will the classes this particular faculty member teach be necessary for any students to graduate? If the answer is no, the position may become contract, if it is created at all.

This brings us to the role of EFL teachers: although nearly all tertiary institutions in Japan offer some English courses, unless the university specifically offers a degree in English as a foreign language or a certificate in English-language teaching, these credits often aren't critical concerns for major requirements or even for graduation. Since universities have a great deal of latitude in determining the content of their general English language credits, it is relatively easy to find part-timers who can cover these courses.

In light of these circumstances, the fact that any non-Japanese English teachers have been able to rise from the ranks of EFL up to tenure at all has often been the result of a mismatch between what humanities faculties want from foreign staff and what they've actually been able to obtain given the state of the existing academic labor force.

Universities in Japan face a dilemma: they may be open to hiring competent foreigners who can teach their research specialties and have impressive publication records, but it is difficult to entice these people to live in Japan. Even if they manage to do that, most non-Japanese face a real difficulty in their lack of Japanese ability. An impressive CV is less impressive a year or two later if students complain they can't understand the foreign professor's classes. It's less impressive still if the candidate's lack of language skills prevents them from having a meaningful role in meetings or departmental decisions, or if other faculty have to shoulder what should have been a foreign professor's share of administrative responsibilities. A relevant PhD may qualify them as experts in their field, but they may not have the fundamental language skills to be fully functional members of a department, to communicate one-to-one with students, or even to teach effectively.

As a result, some faculties essentially opt to tackle the language/culture barrier problem rather than the qualification problem, which is to say some prefer "known-entity" foreign staff that their colleagues can vouch for, who actually speak Japanese and have experience dealing with Japanese students. Foreigners who speak Japanese and are known entities, of course, tend to already live in Japan. And foreigners that live in Japan and lobby for jobs in subjects like English literature tend to currently teach EFL. EFL teachers' willingness to pursue advanced degrees makes the practice of hiring them feasible, but the problem is by getting master's degrees and PhDs in various branches of applied linguistics, they're getting advanced degrees in the wrong subject; only so many EFL teachers can get wedged into positions in humanities faculties.

The result of this race among EFL teachers to professionalize by upping their existing skill set and professional credentials, then, is a mismatch between labor supply and employer demand. Even in a relatively out-of-the-way area, a tenured position for a person with advanced degrees in TEFL can easily attract 50 applicants. An equivalent position for a foreigner in a literature department may only get 15, and in the majority of cases, those 15 people include some of the same TEFL teachers desperately trying their luck.

So here's the important point: as impossible as it may initially appear to you, if you're acculturated to Japan, have experience teaching Japanese learners with limited English, speak Japanese at a business level, *and* have a non-TEFL PhD in a relevant field such as literature, cultural studies, or history, your odds of getting tenure in humanities are actually reasonably good relative to your odds of getting such a position back home. Options for prospective foreign staff may even go beyond humanities faculties; the Ministry of Education's increasing promotion of English-medium instruction (EMI) programs and curricula has led to an expansion of the number of high quality contract and tenured positions across departments at many universities, including departments in the social sciences and natural sciences.[4] This isn't to say that a TEFL master's degree and EFL experience aren't useful; there is often a tacit understanding that foreign staff will handle English courses that the other staff can't, and any class you conduct in English will be a de facto English class to an extent. But the problem is that's all many non-Japanese trying to find work in universities ever try to qualify for. Very few English teachers in Japan have genuine credentials to teach university-level courses in subjects such as English literature, American cultural studies, or European history. But if you do a search for tenured jobs open to non-Japanese in the humanities and social sciences, that's where the majority of permanent work is available. All the larger universities seem to have more non-Japanese tenured in fields such as literature and cultural studies than they do in language education. So great is this imbalance in qualifications and types of openings that even in a climate where ESL teachers struggle to obtain tenure, Jenifer knows *Americans* who were able to obtain positions teaching Japanese history *in Japan*!

We do not say this to denigrate the field of applied linguistics. It is a noble branch of the social sciences, and if you have a passion for the subject, you should by all means pursue it. But while we are both applied linguists ourselves, the tragedy of the current university job climate in Japan is that many people who initially click with teaching English in Japan tend to be liberal arts majors in the first place and would have gone on to advanced degrees in other fields in the humanities all along if they had known there was some hope of landing a job afterward. We would like you to know that there is.

Once you've made it to a tenured position

Basically, once you've been hired with tenure, you can kick back and relax—you are set for life! Well, not exactly. Positions with tenure vary in many ways, just as with the full-time contract jobs described on pp. 12–13. The number of classes that you are asked to teach may vary quite a lot, from 3–10 per semester, and there are research and publication expectations, faculty and committee meetings, and other administrative responsibilities. But if you are looking for a career in academia, Japan is not a bad place to end up. Based on our experiences with tenured positions in Japan as well as outside it, we believe that Japanese positions compare quite favorably in many ways. Since I (Jenifer) held a tenure-track position in the US, I can say a bit about this.

First, the base pay is at least on par if not slightly better than the North American pay scales, at least for humanities-oriented PhDs. U.S. universities, for instance, do not add allowances for transportation, dependents, or housing as many Japanese universities do. Second, in Japan your salary will automatically increase every year, even if not by much, while in North America and Europe pay increases might be tied to your "productivity." In both Japan and the US there is a substantial bump in pay with promotions, particularly to full professor in Japan, and to both associate and full professor in the US.

Another pleasant feature of Japanese universities is having a guaranteed research budget, basically yours to do with as you see fit. Some universities may demand that you present a paper in order to use your budget to go to a conference (as we would recommend in any case), but others do not. On the other

Step 1: Qualifications for University Positions	
Full-Time Contract EFL Positions (and part-time, too, in many cases)	
✓	A minimum of 2–3 years experience teaching EFL courses preferably to Japanese students at or near college age.
✓	At least 3 publications (short reports and teaching ideas published locally are acceptable), and preferably 3 or more presentations (conference, symposium, workshop, etc.)
✓	Japanese ability of preferably N4 or higher on the Japanese Language Proficiency Test
Tenured Positions	
✓	Completed PhD (or its equivalent as a company executive for a business position or as a veteran reporter for a journalism position)
✓	At least 3 publications in journals respected in your field (international, impact-factor rated journals preferable) and 3 or more conference presentations
✓	Prior experience teaching courses specific to your field (part-time classes and distance instruction for foreign universities also beneficial).
✓	Japanese ability of N2 or higher on the Japanese Language Proficiency Test.
✓	A track record of handling the types of responsibilities regularly expected of tenured staff (e.g., supervising theses, editing in-house journals, writing entrance exams, chaperoning students on trips abroad, etc.)

Step 2: Looking for openings (posted or unannounced)	
✓	Search JREC-IN, JALT and linguist lists
✓	Consult with full-time professors in any departments currently teaching in or previously taught in
✓	Contact personal friends, professional acquaintances, and members of professional organization you belong to

Figure 2.1 Job search checklist *(continued overleaf)*

Figure 2.1 (continued)

Step 3: Preparing the CV and application	
✓	Carefully categorize previous study and previous teaching and any other education-related experience to avoid gaps (try to minimize unaccounted for years and periods unrelated to education)
✓	For universities that require their own standardized CV template (written in Japanese), seek translation help from a Japanese colleague familiar with your academic field—avoid asking Japanese friends or spouses to do this unless they are academics
✓	Double check you've submitted every item requested in the position announcement (overlooking even one will usually result in your application being set aside and you being disqualified)
Step 4: Getting ready for Interviews	
✓	Prepare a 30–50 minute "sample lesson" in the cases where asked to perform one
✓	Be familiar with the university, its mission, the faculty in the department, and what they are looking for from candidates
✓	Be friendly, gracious and humble. Be self-deprecating when asked to describe your "strong points." (They are trying to determine if you are a good "fit" with the department, and how much trouble you are likely to cause others.)
Step 5: After being offered a position	
✓	Talk with as many sources as possible on the hiring committee and, if possible, other faculty at the university, about workloads and working conditions (tap your personal and professional contacts to see if they know anyone teaching there)
✓	"Off the record" (and in addition to the official information) check on the number of classes per term, number of teaching days, typical administrative duties, treatment of faculty, and turnover rate
✓	Try to discreetly get some idea of typical salaries, bonuses, and research allowances BEFORE accepting position[6]

hand, at most western universities, seeking funds for going to conferences often involves begging your department for funds or writing a successful grant proposal, and funds may be limited according to whether the conference is domestic or international, and even then there will probably not be enough money to go to more than one of each kind per year.

I thought a big difference between a Japanese university and an American university would be the amount of publishing required. Of course, to gain tenure in the US, one must have published a certain number of articles or books in peer-reviewed, international venues, which are ranked in importance (the committee may also appraise your importance by running search engine checks to see how many times, and where, your published work has been cited). From what I had learned of Japanese universities, it seemed there was little pressure to publish at all, although of course, to get hired in the first place one would need publications. I was wrong about this and pleased to see that my current university does seem to care about publication even if the pressure to publish is not as strong as in the US. For example, my university will award an extra 200,000 yen to our yearly research budget if we receive an outstanding yearly evaluation, of which publication can play a major role.

Conclusion

Many of us first came to Japan in our early 20s as part of a goal to travel and see the world. However, as fun as that is, many eventually feel the call to return home, get a "real" job and settle down, under the assumption that for all the short-term advantages of working in Japan, permanent employment and the stability it brings aren't possible for those who enter the workforce outside of the traditional *shushoku* system, where college students either find a lifelong job immediately upon graduation, or never. While the odds of finding such a job may seem slim at first, with a mixture of language skills, cultural sensitivity, academic qualifications, and hard work, a university career in Japan is one way a dedicated educator can still beat the odds and find employment that is personally, professionally, and financially fulfilling.[5]

Notes

1 This list is actually not the easiest thing to find on the JALT website; it is under "JALT Publications"->The Language Teacher->Career Development Corner->Jobs Available: jalt-publications.org/tlt/departments/career-development-corner/jobs
2 Signing a full-time contract carries with it the assumption that you are a "full-time" member of that university who receives a salary 12 months a year and who can be expected to be on duty for 12 months a year. You may be asked to attend meetings during months when classes are not in session or to attend functions (such as entrance exam proctoring) on weekends during the school term.
3 Another interpretation, yet to be established in court, is that permanent contracts must be offered upon written request after more than five years of employment in the same university teaching position. See Chapter 22 in this *Handbook*, "Conflicts, contracts, rights, and solidarity: the Japanese university workplace from a labor perspective" for

a detailed discussion of labor law and university positions. In addition, see Nick Wood's "The Renewal of Fixed-term Contracts: The Law" (2015), available from nugw.org/utu/downloads/FixedTermContractRenewal.pdf. The underlying theme here is that the legal interpretation of the 2013 revision to the law is still ambiguous.

4 In this *Handbook*, see Chapter 11, "Teaching subject content through English: CLIL and EMI courses in the Japanese university" and Chapter 17, "English language policy in Japan and the Ministry of Education (MEXT): emphasis, trends, and changes that affect higher education."

5 Initial drafts of portions of this chapter were previously accessible at sites.google.com/site/japanesehumanities/japanese-universities

3 The *ronin* teacher

Making a living as a full-time part-timer at Japanese universities

Chrystabel Butler

> *For centuries, samurai who had lost their lords—or who didn't want to serve a lord—wandered Japan freely with their swords for hire. Some of these free agent warriors did quite well for themselves. In the twentieth century, university lecturers followed in their path. Welcome to the* ronin *teacher.*

The *ronin* teacher

There are many reasons to choose to teach university courses part time, such as when concentrating on doctoral study, caring for young children, or staying active as a retired professor. Full-time faculty themselves often teach part time at other universities to make some extra income or teach specialized courses. Perhaps the two most common reasons to teach part time are to eventually land a full-time position (nearly everyone who teaches full time initially started part time), or to make a living as a full-time part-timer.

Making a living as a part-timer is a distinguished tradition in Japanese higher education. During the post-war period, most universities were two-thirds staffed by part-time lecturers; they wrote books, participated in academic associations, and supported their families much like their full-time counterparts. Because foreign nationals were seldom employed as regular professors until the 1990s, English teachers in particular were more likely to pursue their profession at multiple universities as part-timers.

However, the landscape for teaching English in Japan at the university level has changed dramatically in the past 30 years. Most of these changes are simply due to supply and demand; others have evolved in the "lost decades" following the economic crash of 1991—the effects of which still linger to this day. So while it may be more difficult to secure long-term, part-time work than it used to be, it is still very much worth the effort.

The main difference between part-time and full-time teaching is freedom from the extensive administrative duties of full-time teachers that range from creating curricula to coordinating teachers to writing entrance exams. Many universities regard their faculty as de facto company employees, and some now even require full-time teachers to punch in and punch out on a time clock to prove they have been on site for a set number of hours every week. Part-time teachers escape these duties and indignities. However, while part-time teaching certainly affords more freedom, it typically comes with less job security, fewer benefits, and lower pay. This chapter will give a "lay of the land" for the would-be part-timer, describe how part-time teachers piece together classes to earn a living wage, and make the case for why some teachers go *ronin* and forgo the demands of full-time positions altogether, instead teaching only part time or, more precisely, teaching part time *full time*.

The job hunt: supply and demand

The fundamental force driving working conditions for part-time university teachers is the oversupply of qualified teachers. The number of foreigners coming to Japan to teach English first started to accelerate in the 1980s due to the high yen and the relative ease of landing a teaching job (if you could speak you could teach), then continued to increase through the 1990s due to government programs placing new college graduates from English-speaking countries in assistant language teaching (ALT) positions in public schools throughout the country. Many of these teachers decided to stay on in Japan, and subsequently procured qualifications necessary for university work (a nominal master's degree in almost anything). However, as Japan is at present the fastest aging society in the world, the number of university students, which rose until 1992, then steadily fell, dropping from its 1992 peak by 50% in 2014. The number of university students remained steady through 2018, but is predicted by experts to decline precipitously. Many smaller universities are now closing their doors due to falling enrollment, a trend that will continue. In contrast, the number of foreign teachers has steadily risen over 30 years with no increase in the Japanese student population; the future will likely lead to reductions in the number of teaching positions available, for foreigners and Japanese alike.

In this environment, job hunting has become intensely competitive for both full-time and part-time positions. The salary, bonuses, and benefits of a full-time position used to make it the obvious financial choice. However, during the early 2000s, the government imposed severe cuts in funding for private and public universities. Nowadays, many full-time contract positions for smaller or lower status schools have reduced salaries and increased course loads. University departments at present rely on small armies of part-time instructors to teach the majority of their courses. Whereas in the recent past, part-time teaching often served as a temporary alternative for a teacher who hadn't yet landed a good full-time position, it is now a default mode for many teachers who will continue their entire careers as part-timers. The silver lining in this state of affairs is that even if one can't land a full-time contract position at a choice university, skillfully piecing together a sufficient number of part-time teaching gigs can often allow one to make a higher monthly salary than many of the low-paying, heavy teaching-load, full-time positions available, while enjoying considerably more freedom.

It's who you know

The transparency of the job application process has improved considerably in the past decade, as job announcements are now posted in English on internet portals. Although these public postings on JREC-IN, JALT, JACET, and the universities' own websites are the primary means for finding full-time positions, word of mouth is an effective and sometimes essential way to procure part-time work. This is because departments may first send out announcements to part-timers already teaching at the institution and ask them to teach available part-time classes. If they can't, they are often asked to "recommend" someone who can. Many departments are loath to spend the time and energy to formally announce part-time job openings, review a large number of resumes, and interview potential candidates. If they can fast-track the process by hiring a "trusted" part-timer recommended by someone they know, they will. Moreover, even if some universities go through a formal review process for hiring part-timers, many others prefer to employ a "reliable" applicant rather than someone whose CV may be superior but whose character and commitment may be unknown.

Being "minimally" qualified

Requirements for part-time teaching candidates have been strongly affected by the glut of teachers in a shrinking educational economy. Previously, for a part-time teaching position, a master's degree in anything was sufficient (with a TESOL certificate or applied linguistics degree preferred), along with at least some teaching experience. However, standards have become increasingly stringent as universities can comfortably increase their minimum requirements due to the huge number of applications they will receive for any single job posting. Now, the master's degree you have matters and should be in a field related to what you are being hired to teach. Even lower status universities are increasing application requirements without concern for response rates. In fact, many part-time teaching positions now ask for a minimum of three publications and three years of university teaching experience on an applicant's resume, which are often also the requirements for a full-time post.[1] Though typically unstated in the job postings, applicants should remember this "three-and-three" rule. Luckily, these requirements are frequently seen as "boxes to check off" for those reviewing the applications and receive little scrutiny (nearly any publication will do). For the vast majority of university part-time positions, one doesn't need to be concerned with the impact rating of the journals one is published in or if they are refereed. The goal is just to get those three publications so the reviewers can sort the resumes quickly, with yours in the "acceptable" pile. And while it may seem like a "catch-22" that applicants need university teaching experience to get their first university teaching job, depending on your other teaching experience, professional activity (such as presenting at academic conferences), and the strength of the people who can vouch for you (hopefully in the same department), universities will often be flexible in hiring someone without the full three years of experience.

Job security

As counterintuitive as it may seem, part-time positions can now be more secure than contract, full-time positions, as many universities allow part-time contracts to be renewed indefinitely whereas most full-time contracts are strictly limited to three or five years and non-renewable. After several years of building a good schedule with enough classes, one traditionally could expect to continue permanently with this stable employment as a part-timer. However, while it is still common to "keep" a part-time position in perpetuity, with the declining student enrollments, long-term employment is becoming less common for everyone. A department may change the classes on your schedule to a different day or offer you different classes you would prefer not to teach. Unfortunately, rejecting a class usually means that you will have that *koma* (generally a weekly 90-minute class for one semester) cut from your schedule, resulting in a reduction of your monthly salary. While university departments are typically respectful of the work schedules and the assigned classes of part-timers, teachers have little recourse if such changes occur. A further disheartening development is the growing trend of universities to "outsource" the teaching of their language classes to dispatch companies that contract foreign teachers on three-month contracts (the length of one academic term at a typical university). These teachers, often with little or no teaching experience, are keen to spend a few months in Japan and make a little money at the same time. In essence, it is a several-month JET program for college teaching, just without all the job security a JET receives. For the experienced career teachers in Japan, these low-cost, low-commitment temporary teachers have become our competition for *koma* at an increasing number of universities.

There is one brief moment when the power balance reverses in the part-time teacher's favor, though. As hiring decisions are finalized at the beginning of the year (in January), teachers resign from current jobs to accept new ones at universities that pay more or are higher in status. Then departments have to advertise quickly to fill recently vacated positions. This begins a mad two-month scramble as a domino effect ripples through the entire system, ending with the last unfortunate departments advertising openings in March for classes starting in April (the traditional start of the school year). Or departments may ask their own faculty to telephone or email potential part-time teachers they know who might be interested. Depending on how desperate the university is, there is actually a bit of bargaining power at this time in terms of class days and times and even, in some rare situations, wages.

Residence and commute

When first hiring a part-timer, universities are hesitant to offer more than a few *koma* (they first want to try out a teacher), and so your initial task will be to cobble together enough work for a visa and financial survival (the first year or two is often rough). This means that unless you are already well established in a particular area, you will need to live fairly near a large population center in order to find enough work to meet the criteria for the work visa and to make enough money to live. A working visa based on part-time work at present requires about 10 *koma* per week. Over the past 15 years, it has become more common and therefore more bureaucratically straightforward for a part-time teacher to combine enough part-time contracts to fulfill the minimum salary per month (around 200,000 yen) to get a work visa.

It sometimes takes several years to piece together a "good schedule"—meaning, a sufficient number of classes, courses you prefer to teach, and tolerable commutes. You may, for example, have to criss-cross a metropolitan area in one day. One common sight in part-time teacher rooms is lecturers slumped in the comfiest chair they can find, trying to recover from multiple commutes each day; many work at one university for the two morning classes and rush to the next university for afternoon classes via public transport. They may then teach evening classes. Some teachers find the rush-hour trains unbearable so they get up at 5:00 am to beat the packed trains. While commuting is part of life for the part-timer, it is at least still customary for the university to pay all transportation costs from one's home to the university, and back. This arrangement can work in the busy part-timer's favor when multiple universities (which are not aware of where the teacher was previously working on the same day) all pay the commuting costs between the part-timer's home and the university. If one is able to get teaching positions at two universities a short distance apart from each other, the teacher's travel expenses are essentially paid twice to come to the same area. I know of several teachers who are able to bank an extra 20,000 to 50,000 yen a month this way.

One seldom discussed but potentially crucial aspect of part-time teaching is paying taxes! Most universities withhold a standard 10 percent of a part-time teacher's salary under the assumption that part-time teachers have such modest salaries that they are only in the 10 percent tax bracket. Yet part-timers who teach a large number of classes—part time full time—may have far higher incomes than this minimal tax withholding assumes. As a matter of law, any worker who is employed by more than one employer in Japan or who has more than one source of income is expected to file his or her own individual tax return and to pay the legally obligated income taxes. This also holds true for full-time faculty who teach part time at other universities. The nation-wide "MyNumber" system, a personal tax ID for every person in Japan, now makes it much easier for national and municipal tax offices to catch tax cheats. Back taxes and steep penalties for unpaid taxes are the result. Yet another reason to faithfully file and pay your taxes is that if you decide to apply for a major loan, such as for a mortgage to buy a house, you will be asked to provide the paperwork that shows you have properly paid your taxes for the past three to five years.

Courses and workload

Cobbling together sufficient classes to make a decent living really requires between 11 to 15 *koma* per week, depending on the area in which one lives, with Tokyo having the highest cost of living. Because surviving financially requires taking on many *koma* per semester, the departments one teaches in become quite important as they determine course load and one's ability to balance workload.

Program structures in Japanese universities vary widely and may also differ interdepartmentally. Part-timers' courses can vary from strictly controlled syllabi to complete freedom. For example, some universities have developed extremely controlled curricula, particularly in English for academic purposes (EAP) programs where there is little flexibility for individual teachers; one must follow a common syllabus including what textbook pages to cover each class and what tests to administer. These courses may entail a heavy workload of grading mandatory assignments, quizzes, and reports according to a complicated point-allocation system, with the added responsibility of preparing students for a program-wide examination. Other departments may have some general syllabus aims and a choice of several textbooks. Most often, though, particularly at mid- and lower level universities where English is not a priority, departments provide very general guidelines, sometimes just a course title, and give free rein to the instructors on what and how they teach.

Relationship building and networking

While there tends to be heavy administrative demands on full-timers, part-timers have few responsibilities. Most departments hold only one meeting a year for part-time teachers, and attendance at that may even be only quasi-mandatory. Teachers who find departmental politics distasteful, or close relationships with people at work burdensome, or having their time wasted by long meetings repugnant, may definitely prefer part-time over full-time positions. Among part-time teachers, some like to socialize in the part-time teachers' room, while others prefer privacy and near anonymity, slipping in and out just to check their mailboxes. One useful long-term survival strategy for part-time teachers is to build relationships with full-time faculty in a department, especially the Japanese faculty, as the strength of your relationships with them will have a large influence on whether you are offered further classes and what classes you are offered. Part of cultivating that positive relationship is doing whatever you are asked to do with a positive attitude but also being culturally sensitive and "knowing your place." In general, as a part-timer, it is best to avoid advocating curricular changes (that's the job of full-time faculty) and best to be seen but not heard (except for showing a positive spirit by greeting colleagues).

Since Japan is a relationship-based culture, the relations that you can develop with your students will be pivotal to their participation, attendance, and attitude. Yet forging good relationships with your students as a part-time teacher will be particularly challenging since you may have numerous classes each week spread across multiple universities, meaning hundreds of students that you see en masse only once a week for 90 minutes. Learning students' names, if feasible, is helpful for creating good relationships. At the very least, taking a benevolent, mildly maternal/paternal attitude toward your students will go a long way in creating a positive classroom atmosphere with students willing to engage with you. This will also work to your benefit at evaluation time, as some universities place value on "student satisfaction" surveys, particularly for part-time teachers. These surveys can determine whether or not you have a job long-term.

The *ronin* perks

Despite increasing competition and a demand for higher qualifications, there are still plenty of opportunities for foreign *ronin* teachers in Japan to live a comfortable life on part-time work alone. It may require patience and endurance, as building the perfect schedule is like putting together a complicated puzzle over several years. But once all the pieces are in place, the schedule just repeats year after year. And really, who wouldn't prefer spending breaks on a beach in Greece in March or at cafes in Paris in July, than serving their lords in faculty meetings?

Note

1 See Chapter 2, "Making a career of university teaching in Japan: getting (and keeping) a full-time job" for a detailed discussion of requirements and an excellent checklist for the process of applying for teaching positions.

4 The chrysanthemum maze

Understanding your colleagues in the Japanese university

Curtis Kelly and Nobuhiro Adachi[1]

For newcomers, Japanese universities can be full of unexpected twists and turns. The preponderance of meetings and the difficulty starting new initiatives can be especially disheartening. On the other hand, the extreme positive support from your colleagues and the staff can be humbling. While it makes sense that the key to understanding the way things work is to understand your Japanese colleagues, here we'd like to change that perspective: The key to understanding your Japanese colleagues is to understand how things work. Each university and college has its own culture, but most of the values and behaviors of your colleagues come from a kind of university cultural determinism. Your colleagues might not be very different than other Japanese, but their actions and values are shaped by the institutional systems they operate in. Behavior and bureaucracy are not just linked; they are inseparable.[2]

The purpose of this chapter is to provide a better understanding of the university system and your Japanese colleagues in the faculty. Note that by "faculty" we mean tenured Japanese faculty only. Contract and part-time teachers (meaning untenured rather than having fewer classes) are generally invisible to the tenured faculty, except when they coordinate their classes or form friendships.[3] To start with, let's consider a typical university scenario.

A solution to a problem

> Ben found a way to solve a particular educational problem that had been plaguing his department. He was absolutely sure it would work. It would only require a few small changes to the curriculum and buying some relatively inexpensive equipment. Ben explained his plan to a young Japanese colleague and she agreed. They took the idea to the Department Chair, who also agreed it would solve the problem, but with a bit less enthusiasm. The Chair said he understood and would see what he could do.[4] Then, nothing happened. Someone else told Ben his proposal was "impossible," which made no sense, but actually, the idea just seemed to disappear. Ben and his young colleague were confused and disappointed.

In my early days, I was also confused by experiences like these, and disappointed that changes that could reap so many educational benefits were seldom implemented. Now I know better. Changes, even those obviously necessary, are usually hard to make for three reasons: the bureaucratic structure of the university, the complex system of decision-making, and the many tethers of responsibility pulling at faculty. To understand our Japanese colleagues, we need to look at these all-important aspects of Japanese university life.

The bureaucratic structure of the university

Universities are generally made up of four groups: the students, the faculty, the staff, and the upper administration. The same is true for Japanese universities except there typically is no real "upper administration." Aside from cases where the university is owned by a family, company, or religious group, the upper administration is *also* composed of faculty. The President, the Deans, and the Faculty and Department Chairs are professors elected to those positions by the faculty (voted on at the *kyoujukai* often after involuntary nomination and arm-twisting).[5] Becoming the Dean of Students, the Dean of a Faculty, or the Dean of the Graduate School is an honor, but one that requires a huge amount of additional work. In many, maybe even most cases, the person elected to an administrative post does not really want that position, but accepts it with a tenuous smile. In one case, I saw a newly elected Dean bury his head in distress.

Using faculty as administrators has advantages and disadvantages. The upper positions are usually filled with professors who are hardworking, politically adept, and know their institution, but few are trained in how to run a school. The President is more likely to be an academic expert in particle physics or medieval literature than have expertise in business, education, or management. Most of the day-to-day, and sometimes major, operations are run by a highly skilled staff.[6] Since the elected professors might only be in office until the next election, and since almost all of their decisions must go to the General Faculty Meeting (*kyoujukai*)[7] for final approval, in most universities, the power of the upper administration is severely limited. Instead, although it is slowly changing, the power lies in the general faculty itself, in departments, factions, and individuals.

Therefore, rather than having a graded hierarchy of power, like a company with a president directing from the apex, most universities have power structures that resemble pyramids with the tops lopped off.[8] Power is not centralized but spread among groups throughout the university. Those groups might be faculties, departments, or even subgroups within. One type of subgroup, *gakubatsu* (school group or *gakkai* group), used to be the norm 30 years ago. They are less common today, although they still might have power in national universities.[9] A *gakubatsu* is a group of younger academics beholden to an older professor, who probably got them their jobs. More common today, as Poole informs us, are individuals with allies made from friendships, joint research, shared committee roles, and drinking sessions together (*tsukiai*). The latter is where frank opinions are shared, alliances made, and a lot of planning is performed. These individuals tend to be older and recognized in their fields, such as Department Chairs and Deans.

The exception to the topless pyramid are those universities that are privately owned by families, companies, or religious groups. The son or daughter of the founder might be both president and owner, and in most cases, they run the school in a top-down manner. Such schools can be more innovative and flexible—and are best understood as private companies—but often have relationship problems between the administration and faculty, just like companies between management and workers.

MEXT, the Ministry of Education, has taken note of how flexible these universities are. Therefore, it is encouraging other schools, especially national universities, to adopt similar systems, such as ceding more power to the president or consolidating power in a chairperson of the board (who may also serve as president). Such changes reduce the factious power of the faculty and increase the speed of decision-making.

University staff members are support teams. I have found them courteous and hardworking in every school I've taught at, the true heroes of the university, but I also know of instances where staff have withheld support and even obstructed faculty decisions, especially in schools facing financial problems. At present, declining enrollment in some schools is causing the administration to simultaneously reduce staff and increase its workload. That makes staff members less able to offer services. Keep in mind, too, that from their ten-hour workday perspective, a professor who only teaches a few hours a week barging in and ordering them to do things he could do himself—look up information, explain policy, translate documents, make copies, tasks that will just make their days longer—seems selfish and lazy. Foreign faculty in particular are often unaware of how much extra work they cause for staff just because they are not Japanese. Staff workers usually deserve more appreciation and respect than they are given; expressions of gratitude, occasional gifts such as *omiage* after a summer break or an overseas conference, and sensitivity to the limits of their authority go a long way in maintaining good relations with them.

The final component of the system, the outside bureaucracy—the *Monbukagakusho* (MEXT: Ministry of Education, Culture, Sports, Science and Technology)—is the only outside organization with a significant impact. By controlling certain funding its staff can set the terms universities are run by, such as rulings to have as many classes taught by full-time teachers as part-time, limiting the number of new students a university can accept, and determining whether or not a school can establish a new department. The *Monbukagakusho* tends to be blamed for more university problems than it should, but the restrictions it imposes to maintain educational standards often impede innovation, especially when the university wants to change its existing structure.

The complex system of decision-making

A university is largely run by committees and other administrative groups. If a proposal is made at the appropriate committee,[10] it is examined, modified and approved, rejected, or put on hold. If approved, it goes on to the next level committee, which also examines it. It eventually gets to the General Faculty Meeting (*kyoujukai*). Proposals that make it to the General Faculty Meeting have been worked out in detail and discussed extensively in advance, so most are approved without discussion. Traditionally, proposals made by upper administration affecting the entire university must also be approved by each faculty and department at their own official meeting. They are not always passed.

Approval is by consensus, so even one person in opposition can sometimes block a proposal. I once saw that very occurrence, though somewhat exceptional, at a General Faculty Meeting in a small college. It seemed everyone was in favor of a proposal made by the Entrance Examination Section except one Department Chair, who seemingly had poor relations with the Entrance Examination Section Dean. She asked difficult question after question about the proposal until the Dean announced that he would take it back for reconsideration, which meant withdraw it permanently. By all appearances, the entire college faculty, over 50 people at that meeting, were ready to accept the proposal, but the opposition of one outspoken, and generally not very well liked, professor killed it.

In fact, scores of books discuss how Japanese decide by "consensus," but since that term suggests uniformity of opinion and harmony it is misleading. Consensus might be better defined as "passive acceptance," "compliance," and "deterred opposition" to majority opinion. The vast majority of proposals, usually on mundane matters, are passed without discussion or a vote. They are accepted because the faculty trusts the group that made the proposal, there is little at stake for them personally, and because starting a public debate can be costly in time and human relations. Once in a while, however, a proposal is made that (a) does not fully square with policy, (b) is poorly thought out, or more likely, (c) will require major changes impacting the faculty or university structure. Several outspoken members of the General Faculty Meeting are likely to make comments or ask questions. The questions might be just that, questions, or they might be vehicles of opposition. The representative of the proposing group will answer (or counter) those questions, explaining why that particular proposal is necessary. More influential professors might join the discussion, a show of force that pushes opinion one way or the other until the proposal is either accepted or withdrawn.[11] The discussion might become so repetitive or emotional that the person in charge of the meeting is forced to intervene. "Consensus," then, is not always harmonious.

A proposal must fit strict rules of form and scope as worked out by the committee putting it forward. It must be complete *before* it goes on to the next group, or it will instantly be sent back. As Dean C. Barnlund once pointed out in an intercultural communication training workshop,[12] American organizations tend to decide to do something and then work out the details. By contrast, Japanese organizations tend to work out the details, including minutia, and then decide whether to do it or not. Proposals follow that rule as well. Every detail must be provided including when, where, and how the proposed action will be performed, how it will be funded, who will be in charge, possible problems that might arise, and so on. Putting a proposal together might entail months of private consultation and committee work.

In short, the decision-making system imposes a heavy restriction on what can be done or, more specifically, what can be done with a reasonable amount of work and with surety of success. Predictably, these barriers have a huge effect on faculty behavior and values. Most Japanese academics tend to be conservative by nature, but what is often seen as excessive reluctance to change or even "narrow thinking" is more likely to be just a realistic assessment of whether an idea will be approved or not.

So let's go back to Ben's proposal. Ben's idea might have provided an easy way to solve a problem, but the Department Chair might have anticipated problems with it on the administrative side. It might not have fit the jurisdiction of any particular committee, so it could not be discussed, vetted, and launched. The details might have not have been sufficiently worked out, especially funding; even proposals requiring just a few thousand yen must have a budget source. The Chair might have believed that the committee which would have considered it—knowing its members—wouldn't be able to reach a consensus. Or more likely, it just did not seem to be important enough to invest the large amount of time and energy it would require or divert from other committee tasks.

Another problem might have been risk, which as we will see in the next section, Japanese avoid. If the related committee perceived any possibility of opposition to the change from faculty, students, parents, staff, or Ministry officials, they might have dropped it for that reason. Opposition could mean as little as "that is not what the students were expecting" on the student side, "we have always done it the current way" on the faculty side, or even "who is going to look after that new equipment" on the staff side.

There is also an unusual phenomenon which could be called "proposal gestation." More than once I have made a proposal that was somewhat innovative and yet no one on the committee reacted. I assumed the proposal was dead, but then, to my surprise, one or two years later it would appear again, and proceed to be passed. The silence I assumed was a lack of interest was really just the inability of my colleagues to react at that moment, since they had to ponder many more aspects of the innovation than I did.

The tethers of responsibility on full-time faculty

As discussed above, the university is run by committees and General Faculty Meetings. Committees are made up of full-time faculty and often administrative staff. Faculty members are typically assigned to three to six committees, but Deans will have many more. Administrative work and the committee meetings often consume more of their time than their classes.

In addition, promotion in a university and success in academia in general requires faculty to publish research papers, with minimal expectations being more than one paper per year. In fact, publishing a paper is not always voluntary. At this very moment I am working with a colleague who must either submit his research paper to the university journal by the end of the week, or return the one million yen grant he received to do the research project.

Considering this time-consuming publishing expectation and administrative committee work, it is no surprise that Japanese faculty sometimes view teaching as a less important duty. This is not to say that Japanese professors are lax in their teaching, some are among the most skilled and devoted teachers I have ever met, but in general, considering all they must do and their orientation towards perfection, most faculty are overloaded. The demands on a full-time professor are often misunderstood by part-time teachers who mistakenly see course load as equivalent to workload.

Still, though most Japanese behavior and attitudes are heavily influenced by the system, there are certain salient values and behaviors that have emerged as well, most rooted in Japanese culture. As much as the school regulations (*gakusoku*) themselves, these also drive the workplace.

Japanese values especially present in university practices

Sekinin: *Sekinin* is usually translated as "responsibility," and the meaning is similar. Like responsibility, *sekinin* suggests who is in charge of what, the "who" being a group such as a committee, not an individual, for whom "Planning the Open Campus is their responsibility." It connotes attitude and behavior, as in "being responsible." However, the meaning also denotes the "obligation" an individual has as well. *Sekinin* refers to being able to do the task assigned to you completely, without error, so that it does not cause extra work for others.[13] *Musekinin*, being irresponsible, is closer to "undependable" in meaning. So, being responsible means overdoing it a bit, dotting every "i" and crossing every "t". This value is the force behind proposals being worked out exhaustively in advance.

Sekinin impacts the system in another way that I quite like. If you say that such and such should be done, be prepared to be put in charge of that task. If you feel it is important, then you should be willing to take on the extra work rather than expecting someone else to.

Nemawashi: An important proposal needs almost total support. It is not unusual for the professor making a proposal to take it privately to key people before the meeting. This is called *nemawashi*, which means literally "to bind the roots of a tree before its transplantation."[14] This practice serves many purposes. It shows respect to those consulted. It gets support for the proposal beforehand, often through shared authorship. And most importantly, it informs others in advance what the particular proposal is. As discussed on page 36, Japanese faculty and staff often need time to consider the aspects of a particular proposal before they can support it. If their first encounter with a proposal is at the meeting where it is to be decided on, that makes it harder. The system does not work well with surprises.

***Hansei* and *Kaizen*:** *Hansei* (review, self-criticism) and *kaizen* (reform, continuous bottom-up improvement) have been discussed extensively in business literature. Poole also elaborates their importance in Japanese universities. My own impression, confirmed by Japanese colleagues,[15] is that they are only occasionally practiced in Japanese universities, with the exception of MEXT-ordered self-evaluations. There might be a feedback session after a project, listing what went wrong, but usually existing systems stay in place with only minor changes.

***Private and public*:** Concern with privacy is a worldwide trend, and Japanese in particular draw firm lines at all levels between what can be made public and what must remain private. In general, committee work must stay within that committee until announced officially. University information, even student names, ID numbers, and email addresses should never be made public. CVs and grades should be password protected when sent by email, and collected and disposed of if distributed at a meeting on paper. In fact, in a nationally reported incident, a teacher was fired for losing a USB memory drive with student names and test scores on it.

***Humility and self-deprecation*:** Even mentioning your skills or accomplishments can be seen as crude. What might be acceptable in English, "I am an expert on grammar, so I have some suggestions," can seem arrogant in Japanese. The offending word here is "expert," which seems haughty. More acceptable would be "I have been doing research on grammar, so I have some suggestions." If you have certain accomplishments and skills, it is better to assume your colleagues already know about them. Public declaration is seen as conceited. A better practice is to call attention to your weaknesses. Consider these Japanese proverbs: "A talented hawk hides its talons," "Mouth is the source of trouble," "Not saying is a flower."[16]

***Conformity*:** Takeo Doi gained fame from a brilliant insight on the different way English speakers and Japanese ascertain maturity.[17] English speakers tend to think of maturity as being emergence of self: possessing self-sufficiency, having strong values, and living by them. Japanese define maturity completely differently: the ability to give up one's self for the sake of the group. This value is critical for university work. Opinions should generally not be given at meetings unless asked for. One way to express an opinion when not asked is through a question: "Why are we going to do A instead of B?"

***Tatemae* and *honne*:** Conforming to the group allows it to move forward, and sometimes so does *tatemae*—giving a somewhat dubious reason for something that is not the main one but that is more palatable. "If we give students lockers, there might be problems with theft" might be said in a meeting, when everyone knows the real problem would be the large expense incurred to install and manage the lockers. *Tatemae* is often used instead of *honne* (true personal feelings) as a social lubricant and face-saver. It has an important and highly valued function in Japanese organizations, but is often mistakenly interpreted by English speakers as deceit or two-facedness or irrationality.

***Attention to form*:** Japanese pay particular attention to form, sometimes more so than content, as a sign of personal refinement and professionalism.

Filling in forms properly and neatly (without using whiteout) shows that you care and are respectful of the receiving party. Email exchanges follow forms, too. If you grew up in the "message" age, you might write mail-like exchanges in pieces of conversation, being informal and chatty, and not bothering with a "Dear X" opening. You might also cc in a different colleague who might be interested in the topic but not part of the project. As has long been true with written letters in Japan, this is seen as sloppy, crude, and unprofessional. Correct mail forms include (a) a proper greeting and opening, (b) humility, (c) apology for making other people do things, such as reading a long email, (d) gratitude, such as appreciation for the message that prompted your reply, and (e) respect for everyone's contributions.

The map to the maze

Understanding Japanese culture alone is not enough to understand your Japanese colleagues. You also need to understand the intricacies of the university system and a few key values reinforced by that system. (In fact, Charles Browne and I discuss this further and try to apply some of these principles in the workplace in Chapter 23, "Navigating the chrysanthemum maze: off-hand advice on how to tiptoe through the minefield of the Japanese university"). Knowing the system removes barriers and reduces misunderstandings between "you" and "them," eventually making you one of them. What is often interpreted as discrimination against foreign faculty is more likely a deficit of skills they need to be productive in the system. When I composed an initial explication of *The Chrysanthemum Maze* more than 25 years ago, I knew of no foreigners in the upper administration of any Japanese university. The maze seemed intricate and impassable. That many of my American, British, Canadian, and Australian friends who have mastered the language and system have now been elected to university Deanships, and even Presidency, confirms that the maze can be learned and negotiated.

Notes

1 Curtis Kelly was the main writer and has written this from a Westerner's perspective, thus the use of "I." Nobuhiro Adachi contributed and corroborated many of the ideas. Gregory Poole and Bernard Susser offered important advice. Also, see Chapter 21 in this *Handbook*, "Walk a mile in the shoes of the non-Japanese administrator" for elaboration on many of the concepts touched upon here.
2 A disclaimer: This is a revised analysis I wrote for the chapter "The Chrysanthemum Maze: Your Japanese Colleagues" in *A Handbook for Teaching English at Japanese Colleges and Universities* (Oxford University Press 1993) more than 25 years ago. It was a lot easier for me (Kelly) then, because my colleagues were more Japanese and I was more American. Since then, I have worked as a professor in four Japanese universities and experienced a huge variance among those schools and thus, my Japanese colleagues. I face the dilemma any "fly on the wall" does. I simply cannot distill this milieu into a few stereotypical differences between "us" and "them." We overlap considerably and the differences within each group are far greater than those between them.

3 See Chapter 3, "The *ronin* teacher: making a living as a full-time part-timer at Japanese universities" for this relationship from the part-time teacher's perspective.
4 According to Masao Miyamoto in *Straitjacket Society: An Insider's Irreverent View of Bureaucratic Japan* (Kodansha International 1995), pp. 39–41, "I understand," "It is difficult," "I will examine it," etc. are polite ways to turn down a proposal.
5 In general, a university is composed of faculties, such as Faculty of Humanities, which are usually subdivided into departments. In smaller universities, all the departments might belong to just one faculty, so the faculty is just a construction on paper. In some cases, faculties are not subdivided into departments.
6 Bernard Susser, personal communication, August 18, 2017. See also Chapter 21, "Walk a mile in the shoes of the non-Japanese administrator" in this *Handbook* for more insights into the role of staff at the Japanese university.
7 Gregory Poole translates *kyoujukai* as "faculty senate," which I think is a better description, but I am using the more common term "General Faculty Meeting" from p. 2 of his book *The Japanese Professor: An Ethnography of a University Faculty* (Sense Publishers 2010). Yet this term is not completely accurate, since, according to the size and structure of the school, the main *kyoujukai* might be held at any one of these levels: *gakka kyojukai* = department faculty meeting; gakubu *kyoujukai* = division faculty meeting; and zengaku *kyoujukai* = university-wide faculty meeting. His excellent book, and his personal advice, was used extensively in writing this chapter.
8 See Karel van Wolferen's classic, *The Enigma of Japanese Power: People and Politics in a Stateless Nation* (Macmillan 1989).
9 Mikiyoshi Hirose, personal communication, July 26, 2017.
10 For simplicity's sake, I will refer to *iinkai, bukai, senta, shujikai*, etc. as committees.
11 For extremely important proposals, a vote might be taken, but such cases are rare.
12 The workshop, held in Kyoto in 1982, was hosted by SIETAR (The Society for Intercultural Education, Training and Research).
13 Robert Murphy, personal communication, June 10, 2017.
14 Gregory Poole discusses this topic and the one below in *The Japanese Professor: An Ethnography of a University Faculty* (Sense Publishers 2010).
15 Hiroshi Oikawa, personal communication, August 6, 2017.
16 能ある鷹は爪を隠す、口は災いの元、言わぬが花
17 Takeo Doi's amazing *The Anatomy of Self: The Individual Versus Society* (Kodansha International 1987) is a classic.

Part 2
The courses

5 Tearing down the wall of silence
Constructing the English conversation class at a Japanese university

John Wiltshier and Marc Helgesen

Introduction

It's mid-April and you have just walked through the door of the classroom on the first day of school. Before you lay rows of desks filled with students. Some are staring at you with wide eyes; others are talking to each other. Several appear to be struggling to stay awake, their heads resting on crossed arms. You greet the class, try to begin, but nothing happens: a wall of silence. So you throw out a few questions just to get some communication going—still, it doesn't start. "How can I get these students speaking? They've studied English for years. Why don't they . . . or won't they . . . or can't they . . . say anything? Have they nothing to show for all the time they've spent learning junior high and high school English? Didn't they learn anything?"

Actually, they learned a lot. By the end of junior high school, they had studied English for over 400 hours and were expected to know 1200 words.[1] Then, during their next three years of senior high school, studying and learning continued. Most of them mastered what they were taught. Not all, of course, but you're dealing with the ones who mostly did: college and university students.

False beginners

So what were they taught? To translate, to analyze, and to read and answer comprehension questions. What they weren't given was the opportunity to engage in speaking. They are classic *false beginners*: students who have studied and attained some language skills, but because the instruction was limited in focus, function at a beginner level.

As false beginners, they do know a lot of English, but may have difficulty giving anything more than the most basic information when expressing themselves. Yet to ignore what they have learned is to waste the previous six or more years, and besides, to start at the beginning again would bore and belittle them.

The key, then, at least initially, is to *activate* the English they already have. By *activation*, you put them in touch with what they already know and help them develop the ability to use it.

English learner to English user

Moving your false beginners from being English learners to becoming English users is the aim. This requires your students to take a step into the unknown—to move beyond their comfort zones. It also requires us—the teachers—to recognize that although the knowledge students bring to the classroom may appear passive and inert, the learning is in there, and this receptive knowledge is ready and waiting to be ignited. As teachers, we need to activate it—light the fire.

Activation and active learning through listening and speaking

Activation through listening uses receptive knowledge to slowly and surely build language skills, especially if the listening activities in your course book are task based. Tasks, simply put, are actions students must take either before, during, or after listening; for example, labeling or numbering pictures, filling in forms, or taking notes. Having a task to do provides a reason to listen; it ensures students are paying attention and actively searching for meaning as they listen or read. This searching for and thinking about meaning and then arriving at understanding is integral to the process of *active learning*.

Active learning through listening has two steps. First, the students need to identify their task—that is, they need to know what they are listening for. Second, they need to anticipate—predict, really—not only what the answers will likely be, but also the language that might come up in the audio. This "language" will be phrases and patterns related to the topic perhaps pre-taught in the unit, as well as vocabulary that might be illustrated on the page. For example, by looking at a series of photos before listening, students can predict the words relating to color, pattern, and style that they think are going to come up in an exercise or try to guess which image will be focused on and why.[2]

Since oral communication classes typically involve listening alongside speaking—and sometimes involve too much listening and too little speaking—it is worth remembering that no one can become a speaker of English without actually speaking English. The teacher must therefore provide speaking opportunities, and the students must do their best to take these opportunities. They need to make the effort required to try to speak. Effort is important. It isn't easy to try to speak in a foreign language for the first time. Stepping out of one's comfort zone is stressful, and it requires a certain amount of confidence even to start. Feeling somewhat foolish as you "um, argh" and stumble through your first efforts at speaking is natural and unavoidably uncomfortable.

So, as teachers, how can we help? First, good *rapport* among everyone in the class—teachers and students—goes a long way. This means making the classroom a non-threatening place where errors are expected and seen as chances to learn rather than mistakes to be laughed at. Second, the attitude that English is something to be *used* should be clear from the methodology, class content, and description of the course. Third, assessment should be ongoing, mirroring skills and activities practiced in the classroom and clearly explained in the class syllabus.

These three factors—plus personalizing information about the students themselves for the contents of drills and activities—will lead to high levels of student "buy-in." Students need to initially buy into a course and continue to feel buy-in throughout the duration of the course to optimally learn.[3]

Speaking activities

These false beginners in your class tend to have two language strengths: fair-sized vocabularies and at least a rudimentary understanding of grammar. In addition, they have 18 or more years of life experience. These three areas—vocabulary, grammar, and experience—can be used to provide speaking practice through drills, pair work, dialogues, and group discussions.

Drills: controlled practice

Several years ago, as the legend goes, a teacher walked into a beginners' class. He began with a drill:

Teacher: This is a table.
Students: This is a table.
Teacher: That.
Students: This is a that.
Teacher: Wait!
Students: This is a wait!

Apocryphal or not, the story points out a basic problem with drills: If a drill is poorly constructed, students don't have to know what they are talking about to do it. Equally harmful, they don't have to care. Nevertheless, some controlled practice is essential because, as stated, Japanese speakers are generally false beginners who have had few opportunities to try to speak English. Drilling in a mechanical way using a substitution drill can help students overcome the physical difficulties that often accompany saying something for the first time in a foreign language. But such drills should be done at a high tempo and for a short period of time—we suggest about five minutes. Drawing out this type of drill for long periods of class time, or doing them too slowly, that is, one question to each member of a 35-student class, will be boring and lead to demotivation. In addition, it wouldn't be the best use of class time because although such drills can help with articulation of the language, the students do not have to think about the meaning of what they are saying.

Pair work as drills

Disguising a drill as information-gap pair work provides drill-like structure and support while at the same time requiring students to think about meaning. In pair work, students work together in English to accomplish a task. That task requires

46 *John Wiltshier and Marc Helgesen*

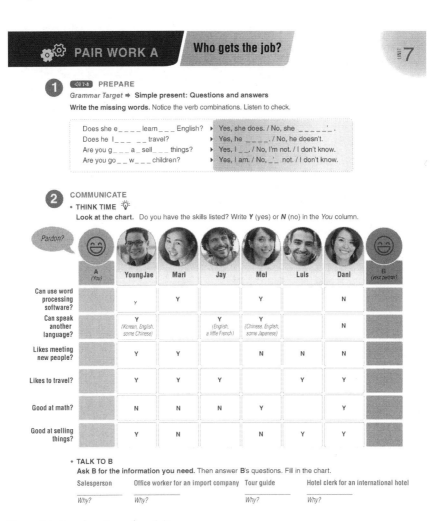

Figure 5.1 Sample pair work activity

information to be moved through communication in English. Hence, students practice speaking English by actually *using* it.

Figure 5.1[4] is student A's page of a pair work activity. Student B has a similar page with different information; what Student A knows, Student B doesn't, and vice versa, hence creating the "gap." By using English, they can get the information required to fill in the skill-set for each person in the chart. After that, they can recommend a person for each of the jobs listed under the chart. This final step gives the pair work task a clear outcome and purpose.

The activity is in fact a drill, though it is more interesting for students than a traditional "listen and repeat" drill because there is an information exchange with a focus on meaning. The language box at the top of the page makes clear the language to use; such boxes are particularly useful with false beginners as they act as a reminder to students of what they already know. This type of reminder allows them to get involved with real communication as quickly as possible. A bit of advice here: If you are using a pair work activity that doesn't provide a language box, write one on the board or project one onto a screen so students have the support they need. You may even want to put in a few "fill in the blanks" for key words. The students, alone or in pairs, try to figure out what goes in the blanks. This helps them focus on form (FonF) just before the main task. In this activity (Figure 5.1), the teacher would first lead a listen and repeat drill using the language box at the top of the page. As mentioned earlier, this helps articulation and directs students to language that can be used to complete the task in part②.

Notice that before actually doing the pair work activity in part②, a step called "think time" is included. Here, students take time to think about their own skill-set and complete the column farthest right in the chart. This achieves two things: It gets the student thinking about the topic (schema activation) and it *personalizes* the activity. Opinion-gap pair work is similar, but all the content comes from the students in the form of opinions, hence the label "opinion gap." For example, students may consider their favorite dessert or type of coffee or restaurant and then exchange the information. Such *personalization* helps students engage and become motivated to talk.

Dialogues as drills

Dialogues are one of the most common types of drill-related language exercises and use of them offers several advantages. Dialogues provide a more complete context than sentence-level work: They have a storyline to make them potentially interesting; they are more like real conversation; and they can provide models for students to use on their own. Perhaps the key reason why dialogues are useful (and popular) is that they are easy to use. The students know what they are supposed to do and exactly what to say.

To be effective, a dialogue should be short and contain high frequency vocabulary and chunks of language. Such dialogues should be practiced several times, with practice time being kept short enough for students to quickly get the practice benefit before moving on to modifying the language to include their own information, experiences, and opinions. Many teachers prefer to have students stand and face each other while practicing a dialogue; this allows for better eye contact, and ungluing the students' eyes from the book helps the dialogue enter working memory. Also, when standing, students can gesture more easily. This adds a kinetic quality to the exchanges and keeps the students more involved. Further practice can be encouraged by having the students change their voices (high/low, loud/soft, etc.), change roles (you are a busy business manager), or change physical or emotional states, for example, you are very happy, sad, tired, and so on. This keeps the conversation practice fresh and is an example of what we refer to as *repetition with change*.

Figure 5.2 Dialogue sample from a textbook

Dialogues with substitutions

One of the greatest challenges for students is moving from the dialogue on the page to a conversation based on their own information. One way to enable this shift is by using substitutions. Figure 5.2 shows a section of conversation taken from the textbook *English Firsthand Access*. The words "go to karaoke" can be substituted with either "go dancing" or "watch TV" written in blue under the dialogue. Of course, substitutions are not limited to the words given. Students can put in whatever words they choose in order to say what they want to say. Substitutions are like stepping-stones, helping students cross from set dialogues on one side to their own conversations on the other.

Using substitutions requires that students listen to each other carefully and react with appropriate responses. This, together with regular changes of partners, keeps conversations fresh and active. This is another example of the principle of *repetition with change* in action.

Activity frames

At times, it is possible to use activity frames. These are speaking templates which can be adapted to fit nearly any theme, function, or grammar point in order to create tasks for otherwise vague discussion topics. In a *Fluency Frame,* the teacher assigns the speaking topic and then students work in pairs. One member of each pair (A) speaks about the topic for exactly two minutes while the other member (B) listens. After the two minutes are over, B asks questions to clarify what (A) said. Then B speaks for two minutes, and A listens and asks clarification questions. All students then change partners by moving to the next desk. Round two begins with the A's giving the "speech" again as the new partner listens. This time, the speakers have only 90 seconds to speak, during which they try (and usually can) say the same amount they said during the first round. The cycle of B's questions, B's speech, and A's questions continues. The students change partners again and repeat the cycle, this time trying to complete their "speeches" in just 75 seconds. Although the content of what the students say will vary greatly, the time limits make the task clear and the effective use of the *repetition with change* principle ensures the "free" conversation is repeated, which leads to increases in fluency.

The range of drills, pair work, and dialogue practices outlined above will probably figure prominently in your classes, giving your students a lot of controlled practice actually using English. If you are choosing a textbook for your course, you should consider ones with all of these features. Of course, students also need freer activities in your class in the form of discussions.

Discussions: task based

Discussions[5] are more open-ended than the other practices outlined earlier, aiming to build actual fluency in the language. Types range from simple question-and-answer to guessing, role-play, group problem-solving, opinion-giving, and full debate. A discussion that works, as Ur reminds us, is one in which as many students as possible speak as much as possible in the target language. This seems obvious and is easy to state as an aim, but it is not so easy to actually achieve as discussions are commonly dominated by just a few students, or even if many students do speak, they only speak a few times during the period.

Let's consider the classic example used in December to activate the future tense and then again in January to activate the past tense: "Discuss your winter vacation." Students might begin with "I'm going to stay with my grandparents" or "I'm going to go skiing." Then what? The conversation breaks down.

The problem with this "winter vacation" discussion, as with many discussion activities, is that it lacks *a clear task*. For a discussion to work there needs to be a defined goal. For example, if you want the students to discuss vacation plans, use think time first, then have them talk in pairs to find three things both partners are planning to do and three things that only one partner is planning to do. Simply adding the "three and three" goal makes the target clear. We find the following rule of thumb useful when planning discussions: An activity has a task if you can tell when you have completed it. With instructions like "discuss" or "talk about," students don't know when they have finished; that is, when they have accomplished the goal. If the instructions are "list x things," "decide which," "find x," there is a task. Discussions + a clearly defined task can achieve both the language-learning aim of efficient fluency practice while at the same time achieving a non-language outcome, such as deciding a best course of action or completing a group questionnaire through the exchange of opinion.

A classroom discussion will work better if students prepare before the class, such as by reading an article on the topic or writing answers to questions on the topic, or both. Such preparation activates schema and primes vocabulary, grammar, and useful expressions. When they engage in discussion this language is recalled and recycled, helping it to be internalized. Rotation of group members after 10 or 15 minutes provides further practice.

Of course, a clear goal means some groups will finish before others. In such instances, a teacher's first instinct may be to cut the activity off early, believing the process more important than the product; that is, completion of the task. But both are important. One problem with cutting off the discussion is that the less proficient students who need more time to complete the task and who need more practice, don't get it. Or sometimes the opposite happens. The less proficient students do the task quickly in a quite shallow way while more engaged students take longer and go deeper. Either way, many of the students don't get the satisfaction of completing the task, which can be damaging to future buy-in. One solution is to warn students before starting that the time is set for this activity. Tell them you will announce when, for example, one minute is left, and then you will stop it. Another solution is to provide extra "mini tasks" for those who finish quickly. Ideally, your textbook will include such activities on the same page as the main activity, but if not, you could plan them before class and write them on the chalkboard ("How many of the same things will you and your partner—or group—do this weekend? Make a list."). This additional option allows students who finish the main task to go on to a further related activity and gives those who are working more slowly time to complete the first task.

If possible, use discussions in the middle part of a lesson. This allows for differences in the finishing times of pairs and groups. Also, as discussions tend to "stir up"[6] the class, having them in the middle part of lessons allows the start and end of classes to be more settled.

Avoiding the interrogation

Students tend toward interview-style conversations or discussions. Conversations like the following are commonplace:

Question.   What's your name?
You.   I'm _____
Question.   Where are you from?
You: I'm from _____
Question.   Can you use chopsticks?
You: Of course. Can you use a knife and fork?
Question.   (Ignoring the question) Do you like sushi?

You may well expect one of the next questions to be, "Where were you at the time of the crime?" What often passes for conversation is more like an interrogation—a series of ready-made questions and answers strung together. The result, not surprisingly as students spend so long with question and answer in class, isn't conversation.

To help students overcome this "question–answer, question–answer" habit, they can be taught strategies to "carry on" in conversation. One such strategy called "the A+" simply involves having the students follow up each question with an answer "plus" a fact, an opinion, or a question. Look at this example:

Q: Have you ever been to a soccer game?
A: No. Have you? (answer + questions)
OR
A: Yes. I went last January. It was a very cold day. (answer + fact)
OR
A: No. I don't find watching soccer very interesting. (answer + opinion)

Because of the way a student responds (with answer + fact, opinion, or question), more information is added and the conversation can continue. Also, the likelihood is increased that a partner is actually listening to the answer rather than getting ready with the next question.

Keeping them "in English"

Although pair work and group work are excellent ways to provide opportunities for learning English in nearly any class, some students may tend to use Japanese when speaking with each other. As the teacher, you must clearly lay down your expectations for a class. You can say when using Japanese is okay (it can be useful) and when it is not. Most students do know that to make progress they need to keep themselves in English, yet stepping out of a comfort zone sometimes causes the reversion of slipping into Japanese. There are some techniques teachers can use to encourage English as the classroom language. Early in your course, teach phrases such as "How do you say . . . in English?" and "What does that mean?" so students have the language needed to ask for help. Perhaps consider using a point system. Give points for each correct answer or for *anything* said in English. Use poker chips, toothpicks, or other small objects as counters. When a student uses Japanese, any other student can playfully say, "Give me a chip!" and take a point away. That student keeps the point. Another technique, using "contracts," may also be effective. Before an activity, students write down the percentage of English and Japanese they will use. After the activity, have the students estimate their actual percentages. This technique not only makes the student aware of when they are using Japanese, it also encourages them to take responsibility for speaking English. Yet another method is to appoint one member of each group as the "reminder" to others to stick in English.

Choosing a text

Since most university English teachers have heavy course loads, large classes, or both, it is impractical to create all learning materials for a class from scratch. Yet there are important factors to consider when choosing a textbook. Does the book look interesting? Textbooks should be attractively designed—visually appealing books immediately generate buy-in—and students want to use such books. Unit layout should be clear and regular. Too much variation between units makes books difficult for students and teachers to use. Small type and crowded pages also frustrate and confuse. A textbook must be easy to use—intuitive, in fact. For the teacher, how to teach the book should be clear from the first page.

The textbook should also contain a variety of activities. Is there a balance of controlled and freer speaking activities? Are the activities task based, and are the tasks clear? The content should reflect the students' interests and encourage personalization through adding their own opinions and experiences. This is in fact a principle that should guide your activities throughout the class as well as your choice of textbooks, since using information about the students themselves as the content of activities encourages buy-in.

The level should be appropriate. If you are teaching average first-year students, you want a book that is for false, not true, beginners; they have studied vocabulary and grammar before, and the textbook should clearly present them with an aim to *activate* their previous knowledge.

Another consideration when choosing a textbook is how easy it is to adjust the content and task difficulty to match different groups of students. Particularly when teaching large mixed-ability classes, the flexibility and ease in which a course can be leveled up or down for different groups is important. This can be done by assigning extra activities, and if such extra activities are already included within the student book (or come in a separate workbook), it makes the teacher's life easier and the class better. Check whether your course book has online components. If it does, it may allow you to use a flipped classroom, and grammar, vocabulary, and even listening practices can be done outside of class, freeing up class time for interactive speaking practice. Always try activities yourself to see whether they are easy and intuitive to use and match the textbook style and aims. Be sure to look at the teacher's manual and see if assessment materials are available before ordering a text.

As important as your text is, you will want to occasionally depart from it for a change of pace or to do extra activities in areas where your students are weak. ELT publishers offer a wide range of supplementary activity books, which are great sources of ideas. It is always good to have such resource books handy to dip into when you want to spice up a class.

Constructing the conversation classroom

By using the principles and activities in this chapter, you can make your oral skills classes more varied, focused, and effective. Giving our students *purposeful speaking practice*[7] means goal-focused study in which they have to step out of their comfort zones, really engage, self-monitor, and digest feedback. For such practice to be effective, students must *buy-in* to what you are providing and continue that buy-in. This can be ensured through ongoing assessment which mirrors classroom activities and clearly shows student progress and achievement.

By getting buy-in, using purposeful practice, and building in repetition with variety, we can get our students talking about themselves, their experiences, and their opinions. It won't always be easy (let's not kid ourselves), and at times, it's going to be frustrating. But, if you are persistent and dynamic, teaching conversation can inspire students and be tremendously satisfying.

Notes

1 Vocabulary target level is set to increase to 1600~1800 in junior high + 600~700 words from elementary school.
2 See Chapter 8 in this *Handbook*, "Real world listening in the Japanese university classroom" for a more detailed discussion of the strategic use of listening to activate speaking.
3 See Chapter 15 in this *Handbook*, "Creating engagement and motivation in the Japanese university language classroom" for more on how to build student buy-in.
4 Taken from *English Firsthand Series* by Marc Helgesen, John Wiltshier, & Steven Brown (Pearson 2018).
5 A discussion, as Penny Ur tells us in her classic book *Discussions That Work* (Cambridge 1981), is "the most natural and effective way for learners to practice talking freely in English" and it involves "thinking out some problem or situation together through verbal interchange of ideas" (p. 2).
6 Our own experience matches what Penny Ur writes in tip number 33 of her useful book *100 Teaching Tips* (Cambridge University Press 2016). Here she emphasizes the need to "stir up" students in the middle of the lesson, since they have often been engaged in more focused learning on new material to that point.
7 "Purposeful practice" is a term used by Anders Ericsson in his book *Peak: Secrets from the New Science of Expertise* (Houghton Mifflin Harcourt 2016, p. 14).

6 The blind spots of reading
Switching on lights in the Japanese university classroom

Gordon Myskow, Paul R. Underwood, and Rob Waring

Reading blind spots

If you ask your students which of the four skills they feel most confident about, chances are they will say "reading." By the time we meet our students at university, their eyes have spent a great deal of time looking at English text. They have bored into complex sentences, laboriously engineering them from English to Japanese. They may have even memorized sample sentences and old sayings. But as they read texts in our classes, some gaps or 'blind spots' in their reading skills soon become apparent.

Much of the vocabulary that students have diligently accumulated, often in preparation for their university entrance exams, is comprised of low-frequency, unsystematically learned words and phrases, which leads to gaps in their word knowledge and fails to provide a solid foundation for comprehending a wide variety of English texts.[1] The instructional focus on decoding complex sentences has left little time for developing reading skills such as predicting, skimming, scanning, and summarizing. Despite an attempted re-orientation of language teaching to communicative approaches for speaking and listening in Japanese secondary schools, the underlying grammar-translation methodology (called *yakudoku*[2]) for reading and writing has left the impression that English texts are structural artifacts to be broken down to their component parts and understood 'completely' before moving on to the next text. Moreover, many of the texts students have encountered are far too difficult for them, slowing reading to a laborious pace and no doubt helping to forge an association between English and failure.

As students take their seats in the orderly rows of our once-a-week, 90-minute university reading classrooms and quietly peruse their English texts on their desks before them, it is no surprise many of them don't share our intellectual wonder with the reading passages we select for them, even those that we choose thinking they are relevant to their lives or invite their imagination. While their eyes have spent a great deal of time processing English text, the various blind spots in their reading studies can make English overly challenging and outright demotivating. This chapter explores the ways we have tried to 'switch the lights back on' in our university reading classrooms.

High-frequency vocabulary and word recognition skills

Studies have routinely shown vocabulary knowledge to be "the single best predictor of text comprehension."[3] This will probably come as little surprise to students, but what they are less likely to know is what vocabulary they should be studying. Students in Japan, even at highly ranked universities, have been shown to have inconsistent knowledge of the most common 2,000 words of English.[4] It is important, therefore, that instruction aims at ensuring they develop a core of high-frequency vocabulary. The New General Service List (NGSL),[5] derived from the Cambridge English Corpus, contains approximately 2,800 words from everyday English. If students know the NGSL, they will understand about 92% of the words in most general English passages—and more in passages written for EFL courses. English for Academic Purposes students will also benefit from the New Academic Word List (NAWL). It is based on academic corpora and consists of 963 words. The developers, Japan-based academics Charles Browne and his associates,[6] have created a dedicated website, newgenersalservicelist.org, providing links to these lists (and the supplementary TOEIC Service List and Business Service List) as well as tools, apps, and resources for students and instructors. A further list worth mentioning is the PHaVE List,[7] which is based on the Corpus of Contemporary American English. It contains 150 of the most frequent phrasal verbs and their key meaning senses. We have found that emphasizing the importance of these lists and simply asking students to review them—providing them with the links and an assignment that requires them to browse through and comment on them—can have a motivating effect.

As for the acquisition of this vocabulary, given their personal learning styles and educational backgrounds, students benefit from a blend of autonomous rote list learning and vocabulary study from course passages. To quickly identify NGSL and NAWL vocabulary in passages,[8] instructors can use online profiling tools such as VP Compleat,[9] Online Graded Text Editor,[10] or downloadable vocabulary profilers.[11] It is also a good idea to provide regular in-class opportunities to monitor and assess vocabulary learning. One classroom activity we have found particularly useful is *Quiz Master*. In groups of four, students take turns being a quizmaster for 90 seconds. To ensure ongoing review, the first three masters ask questions on only previous vocabulary lists, the final master on the current passage's list. Questions can include English/Japanese translations, spelling, or sentence making, and points are awarded for correct answers. The quizmaster keeps a record for each student; a team score can also be awarded. Alternatively, students can exchange vocabulary cards (or notebooks) with a partner and quiz each other.

Of course, vocabulary knowledge is only one dimension of reading ability. Even for advanced-level university students, the reading process can be slow, despite their vocabulary knowledge. Part of the problem is poor word recognition skills. Japanese orthography and phonology differ significantly from English, which is why students might have trouble quickly distinguishing the meaning-forming phonemes in words like *uncontrollably*.[12] An engaging activity we have used to improve word recognition skills is *Hyperlink*.[13] One student reads aloud the passage (studied previously) while the other, looking only at a related vocabulary list, listens for the first word. On hearing it, the listener calls, "Hyperlink!" and asks how to say that word in Japanese. This transports the reader from one process, *reading*, to another process, *noticing*, hence, the metaphor of a hyperlink. The reader answers and continues reading. Students can reverse roles several times before reaching the end of the passage. Developing the ability to rapidly process high-frequency words is an important instructional objective—and one that is a critical part of the more general goal of improving reading fluency.

Reading fluency

If there is one area that all students can improve it is their reading speed. While simply reading a lot of level-appropriate texts over time will almost certainly increase reading rates, there are some classroom activities that are specifically designed to improve reading fluency. Second-language reading expert Paul Nation identifies the following four conditions of a fluency-based activity: (1) Students' attention during the reading process should be directed toward *the meaning of the passage*, not its structural features (i.e., vocabulary and grammar), (2) there needs to be some *pressure to read faster* than usual, (3) all vocabulary and grammar must be *familiar* to learners, (4) there should be *a large quantity of practice*.[14]

Probably the most canonical task type that addresses these rather stringent fluency conditions is *timed readings*. In this activity, students engage in extensive practice by regularly reading short passages that are carefully crafted to include high-frequency vocabulary and thus can be considered 'familiar.' There is pressure to read faster as learners are required to record their times in charts and try to improve on them. Comprehension questions at the end of each passage ensure that students are focused on the text's meaning. Some well-known resources for timed readings by Paul Nation and his associates include the textbook series *Reading for Speed and Fluency*[15] and the free online course *Asian and Pacific Speed Readings for ESL Learners*.[16]

Another way fluency can be cultivated is by *rereading* passages that have already been studied in class. This of course ensures that the language is 'familiar' as students have already read the passages. However, it also means that learners are not likely to be focused much on their meaning as they presumably already understand them. One activity called *Pop-up*, developed by one of the authors of this chapter (Gordon), aims to address this issue. The activity gets its name from the annoying advertisements that 'pop up' when viewing pages on the internet. It works like this: In pairs, Student A is responsible for reading the first half of the reading passage, and Student B the second. Individually, students take some time to prepare several questions they will ask their partners about the part of the reading passage their partner is to read. Student A begins reading aloud her half of the text. When she finishes reading a part of the passage that contains an answer to one of the questions, Student B says "Pop-up!" and asks Student A a question about it. Student A must then look up and try to answer the question without checking the text. If Student A answers the question correctly, the student can continue reading. If not, she or he must start again from the beginning. Students switch roles after Student A reads the first half of the text. The pop-up questions help to ensure that students are not just saying sentences in the text but attending to their meaning. To meet the fluency condition for time pressure, pairs can compete against other pairs to finish first.

Reading skills

Another potential blind spot for our learners is under-developed reading skills. When students are presented with an English text, many of them will just dive into it 'cold'—that is, they don't make use of their background knowledge or visual clues to aid them in understanding it. This may be a legacy of their English exams that have strict time constraints and provide few visuals to aid comprehension. For developing pre-reading skills, prior to reading students can be shown visual images on overhead screens that highlight key points in the reading passage and be asked to make predictions about the content of the passage. Direction-setting and interest-raising questions and activities can also be used to have students discuss what they hope to learn from the passage.

For improving *while*-reading skills, well-developed comprehension questions can be a useful resource. Questions can be designed to promote a variety of skills such as skimming for main ideas, scanning for details, and guessing vocabulary from context. From our experience, having students work together on comprehension questions addresses the specific needs of individuals more efficiently and effectively than instructor-led explanations alone. Naturally, students will also feel more comfortable discussing answers initially in pairs or small groups than in front of the class.

We have found the cooperative learning structure *Think-Pair-Share* especially helpful. To ensure fuller participation, students first work individually on comprehension questions. When time is called, they discuss their answers with an adjacent student and, if needed, again with the student seated behind (*Think-Pair-Square*). To check comprehension and provide accountability, the instructor randomly calls on students to share their answers with the class.

An alternative structure is our variation on *Think-Heads Together*.[17] Students first work individually. In teams of four, they stand and share their answers in turn. Different answers are discussed until consensus is (or cannot be) reached. Students may change the answers they wrote, but if they do so, using a different color pen indicates who changed their answers as a result of discussion and who got it right the first time. We find having them stand increases focus—who wants to be the last team standing? In large classes, sitting when finished clearly indicates task completion.

When students have completed comprehension questions, the instructional focus can shift to *post*-reading skills such as summarizing and evaluating. One activity for summarizing that we call *para-tence* (paragraph + sentence) requires students to reduce the information in paragraphs to single sentences.[18] In a cooperative variation of this activity (*scrambled para-tence*), teachers write a summary sentence for each paragraph in a reading passage. Sentences are cut into strips and each group (usually four students) is given one set of scrambled sentences, which is distributed evenly among group members. The first student reads the first paragraph aloud while others listen and read along quietly. Students then decide individually if they are holding the sentence that best summarizes the paragraph they have just read. If they think they have the correct sentence they put it on the table for other team members to see. When all members have reached consensus on the best sentence, the next student begins reading the next paragraph. The activity continues until the entire reading passage has been read and summary sentences have been selected for each paragraph.

Such highly scaffolded cooperative activities can make reading skills practice more interactive, helping to switch on lights in the reading classroom. It is worth noting, however, that if learners lack familiarity with high-frequency words and common grammatical patterns, skills-based instruction may have diminishing returns. After all, the skill of guessing words from context is dependent on sufficient familiarity with the words that surround the one you are guessing!

Reading intensively, *not* intensely

Few researchers nowadays would disagree that knowledge of grammar (or syntactic awareness and parsing), and the ability to process grammatical information quickly, correlates strongly with fluent reading comprehension.[19] Yet, if there's one thing that students have had enough of by the end of high school in Japan, it's grammar 'teaching.' We are referring here of course to classrooms filled with heavy-eyed students, where grammar is taught deductively through teacher-led explanations and translation. For university instructors, especially those who lack confidence in their own grammatical explanations, this key component of reading can easily become a blind spot in the curriculum.

The challenge then is to address students' grammar needs while maintaining high levels of engagement. One way to achieve this is through a more inductive approach in which students work together to 'discuss, discover, and explain' grammar. Activities can include problem-solving tasks and discussions about structures and functions, information-exchange activities, and more communicative, collaborative output tasks,[20] such as dictogloss, text editing, reconstruction cloze, and jigsaw tasks. One potential issue is when instructors over-rely on students to articulate the grammatical rules. In our experience, a judicial blend of inductive and deductive approaches can usually address this.

Something that students always seem to enjoy in our reading classes is an interactive activity that we've called *Spot the Difference*.[21] The instructor prepares two versions of a short text, each containing grammatical (and/or lexical) differences. To reduce the cognitive burden, students should already be familiar with the content. In pairs, they read aloud each sentence one at a time and try

Student A ①Travel and Leisure broadcast on Tuesday a list of the top 10 destinations. ②The magazine's website notes the Japanese city has been the ancient capital for more than 1,000 years and preserves Imperial history. ③It points out Kyoto has more than 2,000 temples and shrines. ④Charleston, which is the oldest city in the U.S. state of South Carolina, comes second. ⑤Siem Reap in Cambodia, which the Angkor Wat temple complex is located, took third spot, and the Italian cities of Florence and Rome rounded out the top five.

Student B ①Travel and Leisure announced on Tuesday a list of the top 10 destinations. ②The magazine's website notes the Japanese city was the ancient capital for more than 1,000 years and preserves Imperial history. ③It points out Kyoto have more than 2,000 temples and shrines. ④Charleston, where is the oldest city in the U.S. state of South Carolina, comes second. ⑤Siem Reap in Cambodia, where the Angkor Wat temple complex is located, took third spot, and the Italian cities of Florence and Rome polished up the top five.

Figure 6.1 Spot the Difference focusing on lexical and grammatical differences
Note
a The example passage is taken from Kyoto 'Best Travel Destination' (*NHK's* ニュースで英会話, September 22, 2015) cgi2.nhk.or.jp.

to identify the difference. They do not show their sentence to each other. Next, they decide which sentence is correct and discuss why. At the end, the instructor can call on pairs to explain, clarifying with a deductive explanation if needed. Figure 1 shows an extract from an activity created for a beginner's sophomore course, *English in the News*, which one of the authors (Paul) teaches. The mistakes (in gray) are not highlighted in the student's version.

Intensive reading need not be confined to sentence-level language features. Learners' attention can be drawn to how language works beyond the sentence to create textual unity at the discourse level. Halliday and Hasan's work on cohesion in English offers a useful set of categories for explaining how texts cohere or 'hang together' across sentences.[22] These categories include *conjunction* ('so' and 'but' as well as signal words like 'however'), *reference* and *substitution* (pronouns and possessive determiners), *ellipses* (language that is deleted because it is recoverable from context), as well as lexical ties such as *repetition* of words, *synonymy* (weird, nutty), *antonymy* (attractive, repugnant), and *superordinates* (government, president). To raise students' awareness of these features we have them use different colored pens to highlight the various types of cohesion in their reading passages—an activity we call *Colored Connections*. We've found that the simple addition of color helps to bring an otherwise routine language-focused lesson to life. After all, there is something intrinsically fun about working with your classmates to add colorful graffiti to your reading texts! It may also be interesting for students to compare how more challenging academic texts that rely heavily on conjunction and superordinates to connect ideas differ from other more personalized genres such as narratives that make more use of reference and repetition. Using colored visualizations of language features can help to drive home important differences between genres.

Natural reading: reading extensively for interest and pleasure

Extensive Reading (ER)—the fast, fluent enjoyment of masses of comprehended text—has enjoyed a boom in the past two decades in Asia in general and Japan in particular. Yet it is still underutilized in the Japanese university language classroom, which is unfortunate given that the skills and pleasures of ER illuminate the miracle and meaning of reading itself. In an ER program, students typically select a graded reader—a text well within their current reading ability. Since any given page has few words or phrases they don't already know, they can read it smoothly and enjoyably. They can get lost in the text and hardly even know they are reading—much like we do when we read for pleasure in our native language. Because there are over 4,000 graded readers available on the market—covering the full gamut from drama, mystery, and romance to biography, autobiography, and information-based non-fiction—nearly any student should be able to find something of interest to read in an ER library.

In a typical ER program, students have access to a large number of graded readers in paper or online versions; in the graded text at each level, key words and phrases are repeated in different contexts so gaps in the students' vocabulary are filled before they move up to the next level. By scaffolding their language development on previously read material, students develop a solid foundation upon which they slowly but confidently build not only reading fluency but also overall language ability. In an ER program stretching over a term or a year, students should read at least one book a week at their level. This will allow them to repeatedly meet

---

Common Features of Extensive Reading (ER) Programs at Japanese Universities

- Students read at least one book per week.
- Students read quickly, naturally, and without a dictionary as they would in their first language.
- Students choose from a variety of material to read for pleasure, but sometimes are asked to read content outside their immediate areas of interest.
- Students mostly read out of class. In-class reading monitors whether they are reading at the right level and speed.
- Students develop an emotional interest in the library by helping to select materials and by sharing their reading experiences with others to create a reading community.
- Students are typically assessed on their reading indirectly such as by presentations, reports, or the amount they have read (direct assessment, such as tests, isn't necessary).
- The reading program is integrated into the curriculum in order to build general language ability.

Figure 6.2 Summary of extensive reading practices

new and previously met, but as yet unmastered, words and phrases soon enough before they are forgotten. To ensure that students are encountering words and patterns at their appropriate level, they need to consider whether they can READ a text. In short, they should ask themselves if they can

Read the text quickly and

Enjoyably with

Adequate comprehension so they

Don't need a dictionary

Teachers need to be careful when suggesting which texts students should read because a student's test vocabulary size is not the same as their ER reading level. For example, if a student knows 4,000 words as determined by a test, some of these words can be recalled immediately when needed, others might be accessed slowly, and yet others only when deliberately prompted, say on a quiz. The student's fluent reading vocabulary is thus the subset of these 4,000 words that they can access fluently—typically about 25% to 40% of their 'test' vocabulary size. Thus, a student with a 2,000-word test vocabulary might only be able to read a 500–800 level graded reader fluently and enjoyably.

The benefits of ER are enormous. Firstly, dozens of studies report heightened interest in English study in general (since students are able to read pleasurably and learn naturally, this is unsurprising). Secondly, by reading more fluidly, students build a 'sense' of how the grammar and vocabulary that they studied so diligently in earlier English classes fit together: how language is a system of grammaticalized lexis, not just a list of abstract words and concepts and forms to be memorized. Thirdly, ER has positive knock-on effects on the students' speaking and writing skills because of this heightened understanding of language. In general, English learners in Japan are reluctant to speak or write in particular patterns or use specific vocabulary until they have attained a comfort-level awareness of the use of that language item. If they aren't comfortable knowing which word or grammar pattern to use, they will avoid it. The massive reading exposure from ER helps take them beyond the discomfort threshold by giving them enough experience with the language to risk using it. In this way, ER casts light on previously dormant language and activates it; this is a huge enabler for students' overall language development and their personal confidence.

Tips for starting an ER program

1 Read a lot about ER before starting a program—for example, the Extensive Reading Foundation's *Guide to Extensive Reading* available at http://erfoundation.org/ERF_Guide.pdf
2 Think big, but act small at first—start slowly with one or two classes and try out different ideas to see what works in your situation before expanding to other classes, departments, grade levels, or schools

3   Get students to help select books for the library and design a relaxing reading area
4   Make an easy to understand book-borrowing system. Color code books by difficulty level to make them quick to find
5   Make sure all stakeholders understand the reasons for having the ER program (department chairs, curriculum committee members, library staff, and of course teachers and students)
6   Secure long-term support and funding
7   Decide how to integrate the ER permanently into the school curriculum to make the ER program bigger than one enthusiastic teacher. How will you integrate the ER into the courses you have already, for instance?
8   Expect problems and think ahead about how to avoid or solve them
9   Collect data on the reading to monitor how the program is evolving. Share your successes and failures with others
10 And don't forget Extensive Listening too!!!

Conclusion

Five serious blind spots in university reading pedagogy have been highlighted in this chapter: (1) high-frequency vocabulary and word recognition skills, (2) reading fluency, (3) reading skills, (4) reading intensively (rather than intensely), and (5) reading extensively for interest and pleasure. Throughout the chapter, we presented various activities to illustrate ways that we have tried to cast light on these areas in our own classrooms. Most of these activities are interactive and were chosen because we have found that they help bring the reading class to life and promote student engagement. After all, it is only when our students are engaged that the lights will truly 'switch on' in our classrooms.

Notes

1 See Chapter 9 in this *Handbook*, "Teaching and learning vocabulary in the Japanese university" for a detailed discussion of their vocabulary background.
2 See Greta Gorsuch's influential (and controversial) study: "Yakudoku EFL Instruction in Two Japanese High School Classrooms: An Exploratory Study" in *JALT Journal* (1998), 20: 1.
3 John C. Alderson in *Assessing Reading* (Cambridge University Press 2003) pp. 35–36.
4 See Stuart McLean, Nicholas Hogg and Brandon Kramer's article "Estimations of Japanese University Learners' English Vocabulary Sizes Using the Vocabulary Size Test" in *Vocabulary Learning and Instruction* (2014), 3:2, pp. 47–55.
5 Charles Browne, Brent Culligan, and Joseph Phillips in The New General Service List (newgeneralservicelist.org 2013).
6 Brent Culligan and Joseph Phillips.
7 Mélodie Garnier and Norbert Schmitt in *Language Teaching Research* (2015), 19:6, pp. 645–666.
8 The authors are not aware of any online tools for profiling the PHaVE List.
9 lextutor.ca/vp
10 er-central.com/OGTE/
11 Laurence Anthony's AntWordProfiler is available from laurenceanthony.net

12 David Penner in "Linguistic and Contextual Factors that Affect Japanese Readers of EFL" in *The Language Teacher* (2011), 35:1, pp. 23–27.
13 The "Hyperlink" activity outlined here is inspired by an activity of the same name presented by Matt Sparling in a class Teachers at College, Columbia University (2005).
14 Paul Nation in *Teaching ESL/EFL Reading and Writing* (Routledge 2009), p. 66.
15 Paul Nation and Casey Malarcher in *Reading for Speed and Fluency Student Book 1* (Compass Publishing 2012).
16 E. Quinn, I.S.P Nation and Sonia Millett in "Asian and Pacific Speed Readings for ESL Learners" (2014) available from: victoria.ac.nz/lals/about/staff/publications/paul-nation/Speed-reading-whole.pdf
17 For both "Think-Pair-Square" and "Think-Heads Together," see Spencer Kagan and Miguel Kagan in *Kagan Cooperative Learning* (Kagan Cooperative Learning 2009).
18 See also John Swales and Christine Feak in *Academic Writing for Graduate Students* (Michigan University Press 2004), pp. 149–156.
19 William Grabe's *Reading in a Second Language: From Theory to Practice* (Cambridge 2009) provides a comprehensive discussion of the role of grammar in reading.
20 Hossein Nassaji and Sandra Fotos in *Teaching Grammar in Second Language Classrooms: Integrating Form-focused Instruction in Communicative Context* (Routledge 2011).
21 This idea was adapted from one presented by Arieh Sherris in "Integrated Content and Language Instruction" (*CAL Digest* September 2008) p. 2.
22 M.A.K. Halliday and Ruqaiya Hasan in *Cohesion in English* (Longman 1976).

7 Mandatory 'sentencing'
Breaking loose in the Japanese university writing classroom

Gordon Myskow

Building on previous learning

Many freshman students I teach in Japanese universities have little experience writing in English. By 'writing', I don't mean language-pattern practice, or 'sentencing' drills—something they have devoted countless hours to in their secondary school English classes. I mean extended composition beyond the sentence—writing to perform some social activity such as persuading others, conveying information, or expressing feelings. Despite ministry directives for more communicative pedagogy in secondary school, the reality is that for many students, writing in English still means performing highly controlled sentence-level exercises (e.g., translation, phrase substitution, and cloze drills).

In Japanese high schools, assignments that involve writing beyond the sentence are often tacked on to the end of textbook chapters for the purpose of practicing language features covered in the unit—something along the lines of 'Now use present perfect to write a letter to someone you haven't seen in a while.' Students who do have experience with extended composition typically study some variation of 'paragraph writing,' or, more rarely, the 'five-paragraph theme.' But these are often taught with the same rule-based formulas used to teach sentence-level grammar. The enduring sentential logic of *subjects, verbs,* and *objects* is neatly extended to include *topic, supporting,* and *concluding* sentences of a deliciously teachable yet no less rigidly prescriptive 'paragraph grammar.'

Of course, there are some good reasons why writing is taught this way. For one, such approaches conform to common sense. The notion that language can be acquired by building up linguistic bits—from sounds to words to sentences and eventually to paragraphs and essays—is an appealing one, not to mention very teachable (and testable)! Unfortunately, such prescriptive formulas do little to model how language is actually used to perform meaningful social activities. They prioritize form over function—the communication of structures rather than the structuring of communication.

That said, few teachers or researchers nowadays would disagree that form-focused instruction should play a vital role in language courses. Besides, it is always better to build on than to ignore the experiences and educational preferences students bring to the classroom. Using instructional approaches that radically depart from learners' prior experiences can be disorienting and demotivating. The challenge, then, is moving beyond pattern practice or 'sentencing,' while making use of students' previous language-learning experiences and educational preferences. This chapter outlines some of the ways that I and other writing teachers address these challenges and help students break out of 'mandatory sentencing' in our university writing classes.

Meaningful writing tasks

The amount of freedom instructors have to develop their own writing tasks depends on the university and department where they work, but even in highly coordinated, centralized curriculums there is space to innovate by making traditional writing assignments more meaningful to learners. A simple way to do this is to set a clear purpose and audience. In most classrooms, the default audience is the teacher or some generalized academic reader. Of course, there is nothing wrong with this audience, but if it is the only one that students experience, it can reinforce an asocial view of writing—that its purpose is simply to complete assignments for a teacher to grade.

English for Specific Purposes (ESP) courses in fields like business, law, and other 'English for'-type subjects offer fertile ground for developing meaningful, 'real-life' tasks. Students can write cover letters and create resumes for actual companies they want to work for, and when 'hired' (virtually or imaginatively), they can then compose in other genres such as product proposals and sales reports. All the while, the instructional focus can be placed on using these to achieve specific social goals.

Content-based and CLIL (Content and Language Integrated Learning) courses on academic subject matter are also great ways to inject meaning into writing assignments.[1] In an advanced CLIL course I teach on modern US history, students participate in weekly online discussions about the course readings and lectures using the Google Groups application.[2] I emphasize to them that although I read and comment on their posts, I am not the main audience. It is their classmates whom they need to share their ideas with, inform of related areas of interest, and persuade of their viewpoints. To do this, their language must be crafted for that particular purpose and audience.

Even traditional 'paragraph writing' and the 'five-paragraph theme' that encourages students to write highly structured "bland but planned"[3] essays can be adapted to make them more meaning focused. The following task instructions are based on an assignment I used when teaching the academic essay to lower–intermediate university students:[4]

> Choose one place in Japan (or another country) that you enjoy visiting. In 300–400 words, write an essay to persuade your classmates to visit this place. Your essay should be well-organized with an introduction, conclusion, and two to four main reasons including examples and details explaining why this is a good place to visit.

This task is similar to the kinds of essays required for the independent writing section of the TOEFL test. However, it also includes information about the topic and rhetorical mode (persuasion), the audience (classmates), and purpose (persuade them to visit a place). Moreover, it does not specify that students use three body paragraphs. This gives them some degree of rhetorical flexibility, allowing the informational structure of the essay to emerge from the meaning they want to communicate, rather than some predetermined rhetorical formula.

Genre analysis

One thing my students seem to really appreciate is when I provide them with samples of the genre they are writing. It's not hard to understand why. When faced with a new genre, the first thing most of us probably do is go online and look for samples of it. We look at how experts use the genre to get a sense of the kinds of language to use and how best to organize our ideas. But an over-reliance on models in our classrooms can constrain our learners' self-expression, reinforce a formulaic view of composition, and even lead to copying and plagiarism. So how do we make the most of genre analysis while avoiding its pitfalls?

1) *Use multiple samples for analysis activities*: If we provide students with only a single sample, we should expect them to produce singular responses. But by using multiple samples that vary somewhat in their language and rhetorical patterns, we can model a wider range of ways to effectively complete the assignment. This also helps to address the needs of learners with different linguistic abilities. The various language structures across multiple samples provide 'a little something for everyone' that they can borrow and adapt in their own essays.

2) *Use samples at different stages of the instructional process*: Presenting students with samples before they start writing can help them to clearly understand the expectations for the assignment and how to effectively complete it. However, there are also good reasons to wait until later in the instructional process. By handing them out only after learners have had a chance to complete an initial draft, they can compare or 'notice the gap' between their own writing and that of more proficient writers. This can promote deeper cognitive processing and greater language awareness.

3) *Provide samples from a variety of sources:* Essays written by students from previous years are excellent resources for genre analysis activities. My students also seem to really appreciate it when I take the time to do the assignment myself and share my writing with them. I don't always write 'exemplar' essays; I sometimes compose flawed models, which makes for fruitful class discussions about their rhetorical weaknesses. Another benefit of writing a task on my own before assigning it to students is that I have a chance to evaluate whether or not it works. Many times I have thought a writing task seemed straightforward when conceiving it only to realize when I started writing that it was much more challenging than I thought. If we struggle with the tasks we assign students, no doubt they will too!

4) *Use both deductive and inductive instructional techniques:* Inductive techniques require learners to form their own generalizations about the genre's rhetorical organization and language features. They are effective ways to promote deeper cognitive processing and greater learner autonomy. But from my experiences, such methods can also be time consuming and challenging for some learners. In my classes, I try to balance inductive approaches with teacher-fronted deductive explanations of key genre features. Figure 7.1 shows a PowerPoint slide for highlighting how a target language feature (signal words) is used in the persuasive essay. It includes signaling expressions for giving reasons (*one reason, also, moreover*), examples (*such as, including*), and concessions (*although*). Such teacher-led activities can also be useful for showing students *how to* analyze genres, helping instructors transition from teaching genre analysis to developing *genre analysts*.

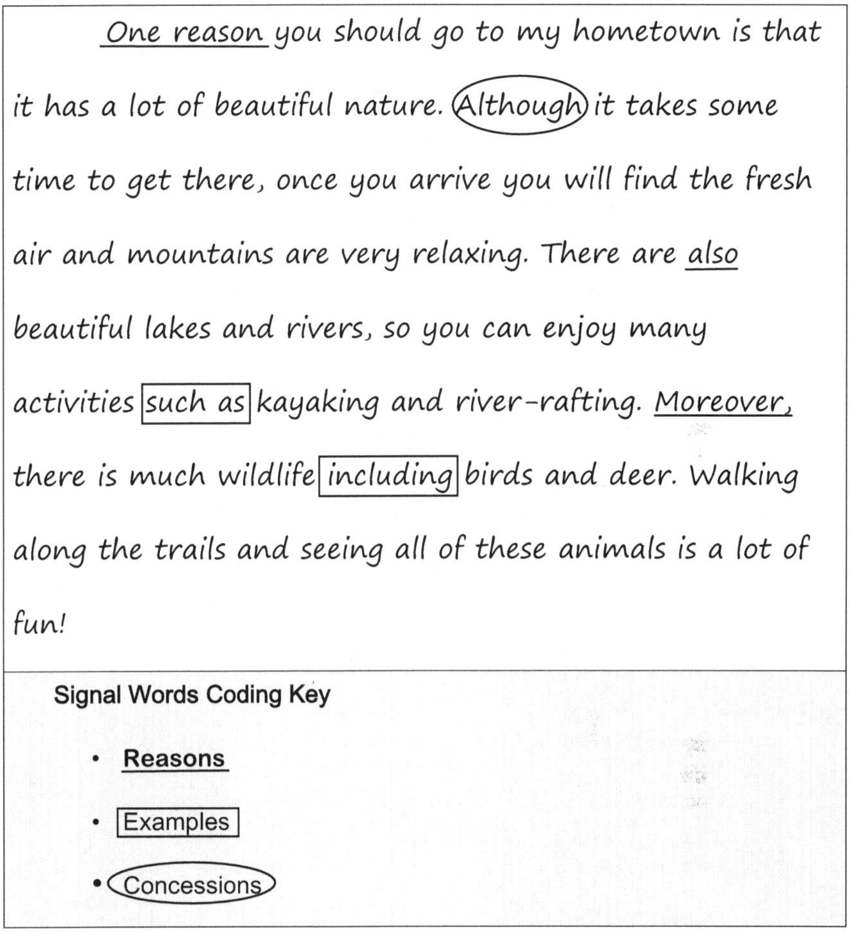

<u>One reason</u> you should go to my hometown is that it has a lot of beautiful nature. (Although) it takes some time to get there, once you arrive you will find the fresh air and mountains are very relaxing. There are <u>also</u> beautiful lakes and rivers, so you can enjoy many activities [such as] kayaking and river-rafting. <u>Moreover,</u> there is much wildlife [including] birds and deer. Walking along the trails and seeing all of these animals is a lot of fun!

Signal Words Coding Key

- <u>**Reasons**</u>
- [Examples]
- (Concessions)

Figure 7.1 Sample genre analysis activity

5) ***Teach techniques for textual borrowing and avoiding plagiarism:*** Encouraging students to borrow from sample texts raises the thorny question of what is considered acceptable textual borrowing. The issue of plagiarism in second-language writing classrooms is complex, and our admonitions to students about it can be confusing and even scary.[5] When dealing with this issue in my own classroom, I try to follow Rebecca Moore-Howard's oft-cited (2001) maxim to "Forget about policing plagiarism: Just teach."[6]

Avoiding Plagiarism
Read the original sentence below about Roosevelt's New Deal from Frieden (2006: 235). Then decide which of the options below (A-D) plagiarize the original sentence and which do not.

Original Sentence by Frieden (2006: 235):
"In 1930 the country had barely three million union members, representing less than 11 percent of the nonagricultural labor force; by 1941 there were nine million union members, and they were 23 percent of the labor force".

Option A
In 1930 the US had barely three million union members, but by 1941 there were nine million union members.
Plagiarism? (Yes)/ No

Reason(s): *No citation, and too much copying from original.*

Option B
According to Frieden (2006: 235), the US had barely three million union members in 1930, but by 1941 there were nine million union members.
Plagiarism? (Yes)/ No

Reason(s): *Citation, but too much copying from original .*

Option C
Frieden (2006: 235) points out that at the beginning of the 1930s the US "had barely three million union members... [but] by 1941 there were nine million union members".
Plagiarism? Yes /(No)

Reason(s): *Citation and quotation...but such sentences don't need to be quoted—should be paraphrased!*

Option D
In 1930, only three million workers belonged to unions, but by 1941, membership nearly tripled to nine million (Frieden, 2006: 235).
Plagiarism? Yes /(No)

Reason(s): *Citation, and paraphrasing.*

Figure 7.2 Plagiarism awareness-raising activity

Note
a The sentence used in this activity is from Jeffry A. Frieden in *Global Capitalism: Its Fall and Rise in the Twentieth Century* (W.W. Norton & Company 2006) p. 235.

Figure 7.2 shows an activity I used in a CLIL course on modern US history with my upper–intermediate students as part of their term paper assignment on the impact of major historical events. In this activity (answers included), students are supposed to compare an original sentence about Franklin Roosevelt's New Deal with four options A–D that restate the information from the original. Students must decide whether the sentences are instances of plagiarism and give reasons to explain their choice. While the subject matter of this particular activity (US political history) would surely be far too challenging for the majority of university students, I have found activities like this one help make clear important strategies for avoiding plagiarism and easing learners' anxieties about this issue.

Controlled language practice

It is usually not enough to just raise learners' awareness of particular language features through genre analysis activities. The pattern practice or 'sentencing' drills that students are already intimately familiar with can also be of much use. Here are a few activities to help make these drills more interactive, and hopefully a little less dull.

Showdown: This activity, developed by Spencer Kagan[7], can be used for highly controlled language exercises that require only multiple-choice or single-word answers. The teacher first distributes a stack of small cut-up bits of paper to each group. Students are told to individually complete each question and privately write their answers on separate bits of paper. When groups are ready to check their answers, one student on each team will say "showdown!" and all team members simultaneously show their answers to the first question. If all students have the same answer, they can then move onto the next question. If they have different answers, they must discuss them until they reach consensus about the answer.

Guess the Fib: This activity, also from Spencer Kagan,[8] works well for less controlled language practice. Students are instructed to use the target language structure to write three to four statements about their own lives or the subject matter they have studied in class. Only one of the statements is false. As students share their sentences with their teams, other members have to reach consensus on which one is false.

Running Dictation: This is a classic ESL/EFL activity. In its simplest form, the teacher writes sentences on strips of paper (one sentence per strip) and tapes them up on the walls around the room. In pairs, one student walks up to the paper, reads and remembers the sentence on it, then returns to say it while their partner listens and writes it down. This activity is more effective when used as a transformation or substitution exercise. Rather than having students simply memorize sentences, they can be tasked with transforming prompts into a target grammatical structure and then saying the transformed sentence to their partners.

The activities described above are not just for lower level learners. I recently used the running dictation activity in an advanced CLIL world history course for students to practice more complex ways of showing causation. Learners were required to change simple causal connections using *then* (*People were angry. Then there were large protests.*) into more complex ones that use nominalizations and causal verbs (*Rising anger led to large protests.*). The three activities outlined here can be used with virtually any sentencing drill to make them more lively and engaging.

Teacher-directed feedback

For many instructors, large class sizes and hefty course loads can make sustained and detailed feedback unrealistic, if not impossible. Yet, there is an unshakable belief among many students, perhaps from their experience of painstakingly learning written Japanese, that the primary job of writing teachers is to *correct* their mistakes—what I call the 'teacher-as-editor approach' to writing. Whatever our approach to feedback, therefore, it is worthwhile taking some time to share with learners our rationale and what we want them to gain from it.

Alternatives to the time consuming and pedagogically questionable practice of simply correcting learners' mistakes (direct feedback) are types of indirect feedback.

Error	Code	Examples
Capitalization 大文字・小文字	**CA**	He woke up early this ~~M~~orning. (CA / morning)
Conjunction / Signal words 接続詞・シグナルワード	**CJ**	Sashimi is tasty. It is good for you ~~but~~ it is low in calories. (CJ Also, / CJ because)
Determiners: articles & possessive pronouns 限定詞：冠詞・所有格	**DT**	~~Yours~~ book is on a table beside you. (DT Your / DT the)
Plural/Singular 複数・単数	**PL**	I love seafoods, especially oyster. (PL / PL oysters)
Preposition 前置詞	**PP**	Most my classmates live at Tokyo. (PP of / PP in)
Punctuation 句読点	**PU**	Moreover exercising is a lot of~~,~~ fun. (PU , / PU)
Spelling 綴り	**SP**	My ~~frend~~ studied abroad in Canada. (SP friend)
Sentence Structure 構文	**SS**	I went to Seoul. ~~And~~ I met many nice people there. (SS , and)
Verb Form 動詞の形	**VF**	He always bring his pencil, but he forget it today. (VF brings / VF forgot)
Word Form 品詞	**WF**	When we are lately for class, the teacher gets annoying. (WF late / WF annoyed)

Figure 7.3 Error code handout with translations and examples

Note

a Thanks to Paul Underwood for the idea of including example sentences in the coding handout and Masumi Ono for help with the translations.

These include underlining or circling mistakes (error location) and using coding symbols or abbreviations to indicate particular types of mistakes (error identification). I have personally had more success in my classes with error identification. Using abbreviations like *sp* (spelling) or *pp* (preposition) and other coding symbols can add a game-like quality to revising because they limit the number of options for revising, but still require some amount of cognitive processing as students are forced to come up with alternatives. Such feedback, therefore, works better with rule-governed grammatical errors than more open, semantics-based choices. Using, for example, the coding abbreviation *ww* (wrong word) will probably not be very helpful to most students. In such cases, I might suggest an alternative word or ignore it altogether, depending on my purposes for providing feedback and the stage in the writing process.

In tagging grammar errors, it also important to keep in mind Dana Ferris's observation that learners "resent cryptic codes they don't understand."[9] Providing translations of codes with clear examples helps address this problem. Also, using larger error code categories such as 'verb form' that subsume other related categories of verb tense and agreement makes the coding system more manageable (see Figure 7.3 for an error code handout with translations and examples).

Peer feedback

One alternative to teacher-directed feedback that is both pedagogically well grounded and less burdensome for teachers is peer feedback. Yet simply having students swap papers with their partners and telling them to give suggestions for improvement rarely ends well. Learners in this context are often highly reticent about giving feedback that could be interpreted as criticism and will opt instead for face-saving but unhelpful comments like, 'Your English is amazing!'

There are a number of ways to address this issue. Having learners focus on particular language features covered in class, such as signaling expressions or verb tense, can shift their attention to clear, observable features of writing rather than good/bad evaluations of it. For content-related feedback, writers can be directed to identify areas of their partners' essays that they don't understand or that require more explanation and elaboration. This softens any perceived 'criticism' because the feedback is related to the reader's desire to understand rather than the writer's lack of ability. In argumentative prose, learners can be tasked with identifying potential counterpoints to their partner's claims, which can then be incorporated into subsequent drafts in the form of concessions (e.g., *although . . .; of course . . .; however . . .*). This can help to make academic writing more meaning focused because it requires writers not only to consider the views of an imagined audience, but also to actually integrate those of a real one into their texts. Finally, writers may also self-select areas of feedback. But such open-ended approaches assume students possess well-developed metacognitive skills and self-awareness as writers, which may need to be modeled for learners and developed over time.

I have personally found peer feedback to be most effective when used as part of the later editing/proofreading stage of the drafting process when students' writing is more elaborated. I ask them to bring hard copies of their final assignment to class on the day it is due. I then draw their attention to a list of points that they are to check in their classmates' essays.[10] I usually structure this activity cooperatively by dividing the checklist into four parts and having each student in teams of four responsible for a different section of the checklist. One student might, for example, review the use of references and citations, while another checks for grammatical errors such as verb tense and prepositions. This ensures students are getting feedback from multiple students on a range of areas.

For this activity to be effective, it is important that students clearly understand the categories they are examining in their teammates' work. Prior to the feedback session, therefore, it may be worthwhile creating 'expert groups' where all students in the class who are responsible for the same part of the checklist gather together to confirm their understanding, possibly by completing error-identification activities developed by the instructor. When finishing this session, students are often surprised to find out how unpolished their 'final products' are. I then generously give them the option to revise and resubmit the following week (it is very rare for students not to choose this option). I have found that using these 'false deadlines' as opportunities for peer feedback greatly improves students' assignments, and importantly for me, reduces the range of feedback I have to provide!

Assessment

If there's one thing that seems to annoy students most about their English classes it's when they don't understand their teachers' expectations and grading systems. Compared with the discrete-point tests of English grammar, there is a subjectivity in teachers' judgments of their written work that can be a source of mystery and frustration. A well-designed rubric that is explicit about task requirements can go a long way to addressing this issue. The use of analytical categories such as 'organization' and 'accuracy' can help to communicate teachers' expectations and provide greater transparency for their assessment decisions.

It is important, however, to distinguish rubrics that are highly explicit from those that are overly prescriptive.[11] An explicit rubric specifies the characteristics of a successful piece of writing while giving the writer the rhetorical room to approach the task in a novel way. An overly prescriptive rubric constrains the writer by mandating the use of particular rhetorical or grammatical features that are optional but not essential for completing the task. For example, it is probably not possible to write an effective argumentative essay without first orienting the reader to your topic in some way, providing support for your position, and using signaling expressions to guide the reader through the essay. However, the task may be performed perfectly well in six rather than five paragraphs and without the use of a particular grammatical feature such as present perfect or the fourth conditional. Mandating the use of optional language features in extended pieces

	Complete	Extensive	Moderate	Limited	Absent
Orientation					
Appropriate orienting information that makes the audience want to continue reading.	4	3	2	1	0
Effective argumentation that persuades the audience of the writer's position.	16 14	12 10	8 6	4 2	0
Appropriate concluding section that summarizes the essay's main points.	2		1		0
Appropriate use of signaling expressions to guide the reader through the essay.	4	3	2	1	0
Occasional minor mistakes do not interfere with the reader's understanding.	4	3	2	1	0
Total	/30	%		Grade:	

Figure 7.4 Rubric for an argumentative essay assignment

of composition can change a potentially communicative, meaning-focused task into a language-focused one.

Figure 7.4 shows a rubric for an argumentative writing task based on one I have used in my own classes. It uses a five-point scale (0–4) with different weightings for each descriptor, which include information not only about the required features of the essay but their purpose and function. The category *Orientation*, for example, specifies its rhetorical function to *make the audience want to continue reading*. By writing the reader into the rubric, so to speak, it helps to ensure that students are attending to the message they are conveying rather than the structure they are producing.

The *Accuracy* category contains the specific descriptor *appropriate use of signaling expressions* because these were considered an obligatory feature of the genre and were a learning objective in the course. The scaling descriptors *complete, extensive, moderate, limited, and absent* are used to focus my rating on the extent to which particular features are present or not in essays. I recommend avoiding overtly evaluative descriptors like "*excellent, average, needs work*". These conflate evaluation (the essay is good/bad) with assessment (the essay has/does not have this or that).

In conclusion

The outset of this chapter framed the teaching of writing as a challenge—that of moving beyond pattern practice or 'sentencing,' while building on students' language-learning experiences and educational preferences. Throughout the chapter, I shared ways that I and other colleagues in Japan have tried to take up this challenge in our own classrooms by looking at issues in task design, genre analysis, language-focused instruction, feedback, and assessment. But of course, the techniques I have presented here are possibilities, not solutions. Devising new ways to help learners move from sentencing to meaning is both the challenge and the fun of teaching writing in the university.

Notes

1 See Chapter 11 in this *Handbook*, "Teaching subject content through English: CLIL and EMI courses in the Japanese university" for a detailed discussion of CLIL and English-medium instruction (EMI) in Japanese higher education.
2 This writing task is inspired by the use of Google Apps for writing assignments outlined in Chris Hale, Gordon Myskow, Reiko Takeda, Ethan Taomae, Megan Burke, and Joël Laurier's "Catastrophe, Community and Google Apps: Reflections from a TESOL Graduate Course" in *JALT 2011 Conference Proceedings*.
3 Thomas E. Nunnally in "Breaking the Five-paragraph-theme barrier" in *The English Journal* (1991) 80:1, p. 67.
4 A similar writing task is outlined in Gordon Myskow, Paul Underwood and Takahiko Hattori in *EFL Writing in Japan: Theory, Policy and Practice* (Media Island 2012) p. 41.
5 See Alastair Pennycook for a detailed discussion of these issues in "Borrowing Others' Words: Text, Ownership, Memory and Plagiarism" in *TESOL Quarterly* (1996) 30:2, pp. 201–230.
6 Rebecca Moore-Howard in "Forget about Policing Plagiarism: Just Teach" in *The Chronicle of Higher Education* (2001).
7 Spencer Kagan in "Kagan's Articles: Structures Optimize Engagement" kaganonline.com/free_articles/dr_spencer_kagan/ASK28.php
8 Spencer Kagan in *Cooperative Learning* (Kagan Publishing 1994) p. 10:14.
9 Dana Ferris in *Treatment of Error in Second Language Student Writing* (University of Michigan Press 2002) p. 69.
10 For a sample self- and peer-evaluation checklist used in the Japanese EFL context, see Paul Wadden and John Peterson's "Best Practices for Teaching Academic Writing: A Guide for University Teachers in Japan (and Elsewhere)" in *NU Ideas*, 6 (2017).
11 See also Gordon Myskow, Paul Underwood, and Takahiko Hattori in *EFL writing in Japan: Theory, Policy and Practice* (Media Island 2012) p. 65.

8 Real world listening in the Japanese university classroom

Chris Carl Hale

Listening in the Japanese university curriculum

Teachers in the Japanese university classroom are lucky that their students come with significant experience listening to English, but then comes the shock when they discover that what they've been listening to is like nothing they are likely to hear in the real world. I remember the first time I played a short clip from a U.S. travel program for my students. At the end of the clip, the students were silent, sitting with stunned looks on their faces. This brief "authentic" clip seemed to be in an unknown language—certainly not one they had been studying for years. Fortunately, the shock passes, and during a well-designed course students gradually gain confidence in their listening skills, eventually being amazed at their ability to listen to (and understand) authentic texts.

While the stand-alone listening course is not as common at Japanese universities as it used to be (now often replaced by the ubiquitous and nebulous "English Communication" course), the typical curriculum still includes courses targeting listening skills, such the test-prep classes focusing on the TOEFL, IELTS, and TOEIC listening sections. In fact, standardized tests like these that largely assess receptive listening and reading skills are starting to replace the English component of some universities' entrance exams. They are also being adopted as "exit exams" to demonstrate English achievement. Further, they are more and more required of job applicants (most company positions now require a minimum TOEIC score from applicants). As a result, many universities are adding listening-intensive, test-prep courses to their curricula to better enable their graduates to get jobs. Finally, as some universities include more subject-specific and EMI (English-medium instruction) courses in their curriculum, the need for courses that prepare students to comprehend academic lectures has grown. Since the importance of English listening ability has increased across the board in Japanese universities and professional workplaces, listening skills should be cultivated in English courses across the curriculum. Therefore, the discussion that follows should be of keen interest to English teachers at many different levels in many different departments.

Unknown knowns

Japanese students arrive in university having spent six years studying English in junior and senior high school, with their contact hours set to increase and lengthen in 2020 with the formal introduction of English instruction in primary schools.[1] For the university teacher, this may lead to the expectation that students will come to the classroom with fairly advanced listening ability. This expectation is, unfortunately, dashed when the rubber hits the road on the first day of classes. Many new teachers have to significantly revise their syllabus after the first class—oops!—realizing that they have overshot what their students can comprehend and therefore cover in course content. Though one might assume that the experience at an elite university would be different, this is usually not the case (their second-language skills have not kept pace with their other educational development).[2] Confoundingly, their low comprehension level is not necessarily due to a lack of English vocabulary, because one benefit of all those years of English education is a rather sizable vocabulary (even if it is spotty for academic words). The problem, rather, is with their listening ability—they seem unable to recognize the words they "know" when they hear them spoken at a "normal" speed and with proper (that is, non-Japanese inflected) pronunciation. Thus, the challenge of the listening teacher is to sharpen students' sense of a sound system which has little in common with their own.

Research on the listening comprehension challenges of Japanese college students reveals three areas of particular concern: speech rate, pronunciation, and unknown vocabulary.[3] Any listening course—or any other course with a meaningful listening component—should be developed keeping these three difficulties in mind.[4] Here, I will examine mainly the first two (see Chapter 9 in this *Handbook* on vocabulary for discussion of the third), and offer suggestions for overcoming them. To begin, I briefly discuss listening as a cognitive process to contextualize the unique problems Japanese second-language listeners face.

Bottom-up, top-down, and integrated listening

When language learners are exposed to listening input, they tend to process in two ways: *top down* and *bottom up*. Top-down processing refers to the ability to "intuit" the gist of a phrase, or use contextualization cues (in the form of visual input, paralinguistic clues, and even prosodic features of the talk itself) to generate understanding. This process relies heavily on the learner's "knowledge of the world" that creates a context in the brain that results in comprehension. Bottom-up processing, on the other hand, is when the listener focuses on specific linguistic features of an utterance, such as the parts of speech to which individual words belong, affixation, and other syntactic and morphological features. There is a large body of research showing that Japanese learners have been exposed to listening tasks in secondary school that favor bottom-up processing (such as quiz questions which focus on grammatical/lexical features and translation). Thus, it follows that lower level learners in our university classes are overemphasizing their bottom-up processing and have become hung up on trying to understand every. word. they. hear. Yet counter-intuitively, lower level learners actually tend to overemphasize top-down processing, excessively trying to rely on context clues to understand as a way to compensate for not having the language proficiency to comprehend the input. It is actually the more proficient learners who use bottom-up processing most effectively, and the most advanced learners tend to effectively integrate the two.[5] Our goal as teachers of listening, then, is to maximize the opportunities for our learners to integrate top-down and bottom-up listening.

However, this is only half of the job. By enhancing the top-down and bottom-up processing skills of our learners, we improve their ability to comprehend input (which is fine if the only goal of our teaching is to prepare them for the listening section of the TOEIC); however, in order to actually boost the communicative competence of our learners (the reason we become teachers in the first place), we need to be sure that our learning activities also enhance their overall language proficiency. This means creating opportunities for students to notice something in the listening text that they did not know before, or at least, were not aware of before. This "metacognitive" process, where students reflect upon what they are listening to, and how they are interpreting it, enables students to "notice" what they know and, more importantly, what they do not. Raising this awareness ultimately leads to improved overall proficiency and increases the likelihood that students will not only understand a segment of connected speech, but also know how to respond to it productively. Traditional comprehension-type listening activities can be restructured to enhance this noticing element, such as through pair-reading, sentence-completion tasks, and role-plays.[6] In other words, students should be asked to *do something* with the language they are listening to, which engenders more cognitively complex levels of comprehension. Essentially, we need to think of the traditional "comprehension-check" activity as the starting point, not the end in itself.

Addressing the challenges of the Japanese learner

The listening challenges of Japanese learners are primarily tied to their difficulty in parsing out words in connected speech. To address this, teachers need to build learners' ability to comprehend English spoken at a natural speed and to grasp the pronunciation of (non-Japanese) speakers of English. Japanese has a very predictable phonology, where syllables are clearly demarcated, even in connected speech. There are no "unstressed" vowels, glides, or diphthongs. Therefore, it can be challenging for even a proficient Japanese learner of English to recognize the individual words comprising the phrase *"alavwacheravin,"* spoken at normal speed, by a native English speaker. Where the bottom-up processing might fall short, learners can utilize their top-down processing powers to understand the utterance from context. (We're at a restaurant, he looked at what I'm eating, points at it approvingly, and says, *I'll-have-what-you're-having*). But what of utterances spoken in unfamiliar contexts, without visual cues, or spoken in an accent unlike the audio CD that accompanies their listening textbook? Part of the problem is that language learners in Japan, while having been exposed to potentially hundreds of hours of spoken English by the end of secondary school, have gotten their input primarily from "graded" sources—that is, from level-appropriate audio files included in domestically published textbooks authorized by the Ministry of Education. As any former JET or ALT in Japan can attest, the language on these CDs is slow and inauthentic. The end result, therefore, is learners with listening comprehension that leaves them underprepared for real world listening. As Vivian Cook has said, they seem to be "handicapped by never hearing authentic speech in all of its richness and diversity."[7]

Keeping it real

Exposing a listener only to graded material is like feeding a child exclusively on baby food and then wondering why the child cannot cope with an adult diet.[8]

John Field's quote perhaps overstates the point, but only slightly. In the Japanese higher education context, students are coming to class having spent years studying largely inauthentic English materials. Their considerable experience has been with graded listening texts expressly designed for learners at a particular level of proficiency. As students move higher through school, the complexity of these listening texts increases correspondingly. What does not change is that the texts seldom reflect real world input and, having been sanctioned by the Ministry of Education, they aren't very interesting either. Here, it is helpful to define what is meant by authentic. According to most researchers, "authentic" refers to texts that are created with the native (or "native like") speaker in mind. That is, they *were not* designed for the purpose of second-language learning. It is also important to note that authentic does not mean only "conversational" listening texts. Speeches, presentations, and lectures are also "authentic," provided they are not designed (and therefore "graded") according to the needs of second-language learners. That said, it is hard to find contemporary university teachers who have not used a TED Talk or two in their classes. Such materials expose learners to speech as it naturally occurs. With proper adaptation and scaffolding by the teacher, these authentic materials can augment existing course materials or even serve as the main content for listening courses.

Deceptively difficult

Effective listening comprehension skills are the basis of second language learning. Learning to speak a language begins with comprehension.[9]

Just because the listening texts are authentic, doesn't mean they have to be difficult. Real world listening texts are often at the students' comprehension ability, yet natural pronunciation and speed render the texts incomprehensible to the students' untrained ears. Looking at many transcripts containing authentic talk reveals how relatively simple the language actually is. The challenge for the

> When you're at a bar or a lounge, always bring your camera. It's a great ice-breaker. When you walk up to a guy that you might be interested in because you like the way that he looks, ask him to take a picture of you and your girlfriends. After he takes a couple of snaps, ask him to jump into the picture and then get his e-mail address and send him the photos. It's a great way to start a dialogue.

Figure 8.1 Sample authentic listening text: *Looking for Love in the Big City*

a This text is taken from the video series *1st Look*, which is a lifestyle video program produced by NBC in New York introducing places and activities of interest in New York City (and most recently, Los Angeles). Videos tend to be three to five minutes in length, perfect for focused listening activities. While not all topics covered will be of interest to Japanese university students, several, including those dealing with love, dating, and exotic food tend to be quite popular. Videos can be found at nbcnewyork.com

listening teacher is guiding students to successful comprehension of pronunciation and connected speech in the texts. For example, in my courses, I often find 80 to 90 percent of the text contains vocabulary known to my students, with the remainder being idiomatic, metaphorical, or culture-specific expressions that do require explicit teaching. Once this fact is revealed to students through repeated listening and through focused comprehension activities, motivation sharply increases. They realize that their language ability isn't as bad as they thought. For example, after reading a printed transcript of an authentic three-minute video one of my classes had just seen, describing how New Yorkers "find love in the big city,"[10] a student looked up from the transcript and declared, almost euphorically, "We learned all this vocabulary in junior high school!" Student confidence in the authentic course materials, and of their own English ability, was never an issue after that shared realization. A sample from this transcript is in Figure 8.1.

Short and sweet

In the university classroom, authentic materials should either serve as the primary content of the listening class or at least heavily augment the prescribed graded materials. The next step is to decide what materials are most appropriate. This is where it can get time consuming for teachers because they must preview and select the materials that best fit their particular learners. Using authentic materials effectively is not as simple as choosing a movie to watch, relaxing for two hours, and ending the class with some light discussion of the film's themes. Chances are that students wouldn't understand enough of a full film to be able to discuss it (and would also see through your blatant laziness). Instead, materials have to be *carefully* screened and selected. Think of your job as a curator of content, and with an infinite amount of content now available on the web, this is no small task. To somewhat narrow your focus, it is best to have an overall theme to each "unit" of the course, such as "Health and the Environment," "Comparative Cultures," and so on, and to look for audio and video clips that support your theme. Once a clip has been identified, you will want to isolate *no more than* three to five minutes of actual audio or video for students to listen to at a time. Longer than this will overwhelm the students, particularly if there is video accompanying the audio. Keeping the clips short also allows students to listen to them several times.

Rinse, repeat

One of the benefits of learning to read in a foreign language is the ability to re-read passages again to support comprehension. With listening in the classroom, students get one shot at understanding an utterance (unless they aren't too shy to ask their teacher to replay or repeat it). Therefore, listening materials should be accessible to students to independently manipulate (replay, slow down, pause, come back to later). With contemporary technology, it is possible to instantly share links to audio and video clips through a class email list or the university's LMS; students can then play the clips as many times as they want to on their computers at home or on their smartphones commuting to and from campus. As this repeated listening naturally takes time and can be done individually, it is perfectly suited for homework, partnered with a simple comprehension activity students can bring to class to show they have done the listening. Class time can then be spent on further comprehension and expansion activities.

Listen for it: types of activities

Once you choose a clip, you will need to create appropriate and *clear* tasks for students to engage the content. In addition to content comprehension, tasks can focus on a particular point made by a speaker, listening for gist or speaker's intention (paying attention to prosody or intonation), or even identifying a particular grammatical construction. These comprehension tasks will depend on the level of your learners, with more advanced learners performing more complex tasks with the segment. Students should also be asked to *do something* with the language they are learning—to create and complete their own cloze exercises, design a dialogue with a partner utilizing similar language patterns, or use the script to practice the text and invent their own variations of it. At all stages of the instruction, students' attention should be drawn to the speed and connectedness of the speech in the listening materials. And while it is no longer in vogue to engage students in choral repetition practice, when it comes to naturally occurring speech, having them repeat or "shadow" the language can be an effective way to draw their attention to and notice these difficult features of authentic speech.

Three phases of listening activities

It is important to consider the three phases for effective listening comprehension when designing tasks: pre-listening, while-listening and post-listening.

Pre-listening activities help students activate their knowledge schema (the top-down processing) and should be designed to contextualize the content and subject of the listening before they actually listen to it. Activities in this phase can include

- brainstorming about the topic when looking at pictures related to the text
- introducing vocabulary that will appear in the text and asking students to predict what they think text will be about
- enhancing students' metacognitive listening strategies by deciding in advance what particular features in the text they should be listening for

While-listening activities are completed as the students engage with the listening text, and they should contain specific foci for the learners. The focus could change in repeated listenings, such as moving from general understanding of the text in the first listening to paying attention to specific aspects of the text in further listening, such as vocabulary, connected speech, and accent patterns. It is important, though, that the while-listening tasks do not contain too many additional exercises that can cause cognitive overload, such as too many comprehension questions, or written responses, or paired reading passages. In the end, teachers need to make sure students are focused on building their listening comprehension, not displaying their reading or writing abilities (those can be demonstrated elsewhere). In addition, it is helpful to give students a chance to check their understanding and their answers with classmates prior to each subsequent hearing of the text. This allows them to see (notice) what they already know (and thought they did, but perhaps did not), and focus next on segments of the text that they are less confident with. Activities in this stage can include

- checking true or false statements about the text as they listen
- numbering the events in the text in the order in which they occur
- drawing a line from a point in the text to a picture that represents something contextually connected to it (the contextuality of which is only apparent if the listening text was comprehended)
- taking brief notes as they watch a video or listen to a text

Post-listening activities are where teachers can introduce other skills to the lesson through expansion activities, such as

- writing a summary of the text
- creating an alternative script
- debating an issue in the text
- making and performing a skit

Teachers can also, of course, invite student requests to elaborate on specific features or areas of the text that were particularly challenging for them but were perhaps not the focus of the while-listening activities. They can also lead group discussions related to the topic of the text.

Deferring to the experts: listening course textbooks

For the busy university teacher (and especially the part-timer hurriedly criss-crossing the city), designing a course entirely around originally curated materials and pedagogically sound activities to support them can be very time consuming. Instead, listening textbooks can serve as the primary class content, while the teacher-sourced authentic materials are supplementary. Major ESL publishers are now integrating their graded materials with authentic clips, such as from NPR, BBC, CNN, and other mass media. One benefit of using these materials is knowing that they will be organized thematically and that activities (the critical *doing* something with the language) will have been thoughtfully considered by experts in second-language acquisition.[11] These texts can also serve as excellent templates and exemplars when you design and create your own listening materials.

Conclusion

Improving the listening skills of students can significantly boost their overall language proficiency, and in many cases, it mainly requires "unlocking" language they already possess by helping them focus on comprehension of connected speech and pronunciation. By designing a course around authentic materials as outlined here (or augmenting a coursebook or test-prep text with authentic materials), teachers can cultivate students' cognitive processing of language, boost their confidence, improve their performance in other English courses, and prepare them for real world listening beyond the university classroom.

Notes

1 See Chapter 17 in this *Handbook*, "English language policy in Japan and the Ministry of Education (MEXT): emphasis, trends, and changes that affect higher education" for more details on the curricular changes outlined by the Ministry of Education (MEXT).
2 See Kensaku Yoshida (*The Modern Language Journal* 2003) for a rather frank assessment of how second-language education at the secondary-school level has never fully aligned with the lofty (some might argue, "unrealistic") language policies of the Ministry of Education.
3 In a study published in the *Annual Review of English Education in Japan*, Takuji Noro (2006) looked specifically at the difficulties faced by Japanese college students in English listening comprehension, which is very helpful for our context here.
4 Tomoko Kurita wrote a very accessible chapter looking at these three aspects of teaching listening in the Japanese context called "Teaching Listening in Pre-tertiary and Tertiary English Education in Japan" in the book *Asian English Language Classrooms: Where Theory and Practice Meet*, Handoyo Widodo, Alistair Wood, and Deepti Gupta (Eds) (Routledge 2017).
5 When teaching listening courses to new teachers, John Field's (2004) very readable article for *System* titled "An Insight into Listeners' Problems: Too Much Bottom-up or too Much Top-down?" can be helpful.
6 See Jack C. Richard's (2006) "Materials Development and Research—Making the Connection" in *RELC Journal*, 37(1) for an accessible treatment of materials development for the second language listening classroom teacher.

7 Vivian Cook's perspective on SLA is typically as enlightening as it is entertaining. His book *Second Language Learning and Language Teaching* (Routledge 2013) is no exception.
8 Not to be outdone by Vivian Cook, John Field also has some colorful opinions about second-language listening. This one is from *Listening in the Language Classroom*, p. 271 (Cambridge 2010).
9 Jack Richards, a major contributor to listening theory and pedagogy in particular and SLA in general, has always placed importance on listening in second-language learning. This quote is from *Key Issues in Language Teaching* (Cambridge 2015). I am grateful to Jack for generously providing me with this text (as well as other helpful advice and comments) as I drafted this chapter.
10 The materials in this vignette come from an online listening course I designed while a graduate student in New York (called *Listening NYC*). After 10 years, I'm humbled to see this freely available course still being used around the globe: listeningnyc.blogspot.jp/
11 Two excellent series with a mix of graded and authentic listening clips that have proven popular with Japanese university students are the *Northstar* series (Pearson) and *Developing Tactics for Listening* series (Oxford University Press). Both provide a good mix of listening materials spoken in a variety of accents.

9 Teaching and learning vocabulary in the Japanese university

Paul Wadden, Charles Browne, and Paul Nation

The learning challenge

The typical Japanese student enters university with an English vocabulary of 2,000 to 4,000 words. While this provides a foundation for further language learning and initial academic study, it challenges the classroom teacher because

1. it is the bare minimum needed for reading authentic texts and comprehending academic lectures (and knowledge of roughly 6,000 to 8,000 words is required for higher level language courses and subject-specific study);
2. beyond the initial 1,500 or so words the students have learned in elementary and middle school, individual students have not acquired the same core vocabulary, and research shows there are significant gaps in their basic vocabulary;
3. few students have yet to systematically learn the all-purpose academic vocabulary most useful for English-medium and subject-specific courses—for example, words included in the Academic Word List (AWL) and New Academic Word List (NAWL);
4. due to their prior instruction, students' word knowledge tends to be receptive rather than productive.[1]

Despite these limitations, Japanese students bring a number of strengths to the classroom. Individually, they understand—even more so than some of their teachers—how crucial vocabulary is for their language learning and their academic study. Culturally, they follow directions, study diligently, complete assignments, and work well in pairs and groups. In addition, many are interested in creating short-term, word-learning goals and long-term vocabulary plans because they know a better knowledge of English will be an asset not only during their college study but also throughout their professional lives.

In this chapter, we first identify the vocabulary most useful to Japanese university language learners (based upon corpus research analyzing millions of pages of text), describe from personal experience effective ways of teaching it, offer suggestions for conceptualizing vocabulary instruction across courses and curricula and, in conclusion, ask—and partially answer—some additional questions on vocabulary pedagogy in the Japanese university classroom.

Learning words that matter

Not all words are of equal value to the learner. With more than 60,000 word families in the English language, knowledge of the most common few thousand can be incredibly useful. The 2,800 headwords in the New General Service List (NGSL), for instance, provides up to 92 percent coverage of typical English newspapers, magazines, and books, and an even higher coverage of spoken English.[2] The JACET 8000, a vocabulary list based on the British National Corpus plus a subcorpus of Japanese university entrance exams and secondary school textbooks, also provides a sound basis for vocabulary study.[3] Research indicates that learners need a basic understanding of roughly 95 percent of the words in a text before they can confidently comprehend it and successfully guess unknown words from context; therefore, unless a few thousand of the most commonly occurring words in English are learned, it is linguistically and mathematically impossible to reach this comprehension threshold. In reality, these high-frequency words are so prevalent in our daily lives that they form a core vocabulary that is essential for students to master before tackling less common and more technical words.[4]

The first step, then, is to identify what words the students in your class already know. The Vocabulary Levels Test and the New Vocabulary Levels Test, both available online, diagnose how well students have learned the five most frequent 1,000-word bands. Paper and online versions of the New General Service List Test (NGSLT) and New Academic Word List Test (NAWLT) are also available to evaluate word knowledge of these important word lists, to identify where a student's significant gaps are, and to later assess progress in vocabulary learning. These instruments—used as pre- or post-tests, or both—take 30 minutes or less to complete.[5] For academic English classes, including subject-specific and EMI (English-medium instruction) courses, the tests can identify what vocabulary students know, the gaps in their high-frequency and academic vocabulary, and the next band of vocabulary they should focus on.

For subject-specific and EMI courses, technical vocabulary makes up a much larger proportion (20% to 30%) of the words in texts. Subject areas differ greatly in the proportion of technical words largely unique to that subject area.[6] Some fields such as economics and applied linguistics use many commonly known words as technical words; their secondary and tertiary meanings must be learned for that field. Fields such as medicine and botany have specialized technical vocabulary which are a learning burden for both native and non-native speakers. However, underlying all of these fields are common academic vocabulary (words such as "approximate," "deficient," "empirical," "proportionate") particularly valuable for students in classes across the curriculum, including their courses for general requirements and courses in their majors. The two word lists which best identify these are the AWL with 570 headwords and the NAWL with 963 headwords.

Effective teaching and learning strategies

The most important job of the vocabulary teacher is to plan what vocabulary students learn—depending on the course and the students' level—which may be high-frequency general vocabulary, mid-frequency general vocabulary, academic vocabulary, or field-specific vocabulary. The first choice a teacher faces is whether to select a course text that includes targeted vocabulary, to instead opt for a supplementary vocabulary text, to draw target vocabulary directly from other course materials, or to create a parallel program focused on high-frequency or academic vocabulary. Following are descriptions of some of the hands-on approaches to teaching this vocabulary the authors and their colleagues have taken in their courses.

Scenario 1: the general English class (Charles Browne)

The typical Japanese university course meets for 90 minutes 15 times per semester. In most general English classes, and other English courses as well, teachers don't usually have much extra time for direct vocabulary instruction. Yet since vocabulary underlies all four skills and is crucial for proficiency, I recommend devoting a lot of out-of-class study to it. Because Japanese students have significant gaps in their knowledge of high-frequency words, my starting point is having them take the NGSLT (New General Service List Test) and NAWLT, which are available online. The first checks students' knowledge of the 2,800 most commonly used words in the English language, and the second tests their knowledge of the most common 900 or so words used in academic texts. The results of both tests are broken down into frequency bands to show the students' knowledge level. A sample of the readout can be seen in Figure 9.1

After identifying which bands students have significant gaps in (NGSL Band 4 for the student in Figure 9.1), they are then directed to learn the unknown

New General Service List Test Results
Name:
Instructor: Charles Browne
Class: Eigokakyoiku
This is a test of the New General Service List, a vocabulary list that covers around 2,800 of the most useful English words for language learners
There are 5 levels in the test, each covering around 560 words. You should aim for a score between 80% and 100% in each of the levels

Vocabulary level		Score
First 560 words	Level 1	86.67%
Second 560 words	Level 2	80.00%
Third 560 words	Level 3	80.00%
Fourth 560 words	Level 4	53.33%
Fifth 560 words	Level 5	93.33%

Figure 9.1 Sample readout showing NGSLT results

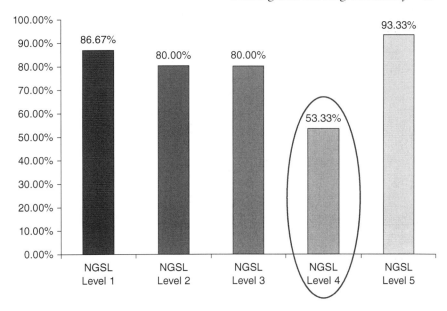

Figure 9.1 (cont.)

words using the free Quizlet.com flashcard site, where the NGSL and NAWL have already been uploaded in bands of 50, 100, and 560 words (the 560-word band groupings correspond to the results of the NGSLT). Quizlet offers six different word-learning activities for each set of words, and I am able to easily track students' progress on their free LMS (learner management system). Next are some screenshots of what the student in Figure 9.1 would see on Quizlet.com when he or she tries to learn Band 4 words of the NGSL.

Students who instead prefer learning via their smartphones I direct to my free iPhone or Android flashcard apps: NGSL Builder or NAWL Builder.[7] Each of these apps allows students to study words via a spaced-repetition flashcard system. Figure 9.3 some illustrations of NGSL Builder.

Use of these tools and resources helps students build a personalized vocabulary program ideally suited to their current level of vocabulary proficiency. I actually take this same approach to building vocabulary in my Teacher Training and Applied Linguistics courses, too. It is an approach that can be used across the entire curriculum for English skills courses and subject-specific classes. It boosts essential word knowledge and promotes fluency by first closing the gaps in students' basic high-frequency vocabulary and then focusing on high-value general academic vocabulary.

Scenario 2: the listening class (Paul Wadden)

For lower level academic listening courses, our required English textbook features one 10-minute lecture per chapter. I lobbied hard for several years to get

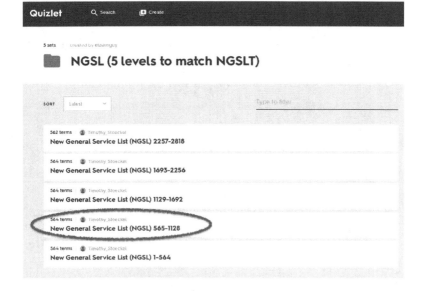

Figure 9.2 Screenshots of student feedback from Quizlet.com

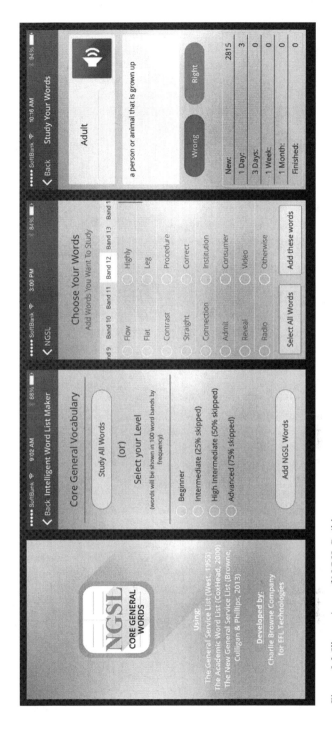

Figure 9.3 Illustrations of NGSL Builder

the program to adopt this text which highlights vocabulary from the AWL and includes exercises that activate and pre-teach vocabulary needed to comprehend the talks featured in the textbook. During the course, I ask students to keep a vocabulary journal of the targeted words they don't know but want to learn, and I set aside time in class for them in pairs to share with each other the words they focused on the previous week. This helps them review, reinforces their vocabulary learning through teaching their classmates, and makes it more communicative. My higher level listening courses are based on Ted Talks. For each class, I run the transcript through the LexTutor vocab profiler[8] so I can identify the words from the NAWL on the students' copy. At the top, I make a list of about 20 NAWL words for every lesson. Depending upon available time, energy level, and class size, I have students write down and annotate the vocabulary in their class notebooks (handed in later for assessment), or if they vote to, they make online flashcards individually or collectively as a class (Quizlet.com even adapts these cards for a variety of self-administered quizzes on students' smartphones). From these, I myself compose a brief quiz on the previous week's vocabulary that students then take in class (sometimes, instead, I assign teams of students to create the quizzes as part of their vocabulary learning). The minor portion of their course grade based on vocabulary is half from their class notebook (or personalized or group flash cards) and half from their quiz scores.

Scenario 3: the extensive reading class (Kimberly Klassen)[9]

At the beginning of my two-term extensive reading course, I test my students' vocabulary using the Vocabulary Levels Test,[10] and then share and interpret the test results with them. I explain that extensive reading with graded readers, combined with personalized word cards, is an excellent way to improve their vocabulary knowledge. I show them Nation's chart, which indicates how much time they need to spend reading in order to achieve the 3,000-word level (10 minutes per day, five days a week).[11] Then I set a reading goal of 200,000 words for the spring term and 300,000 for the fall term. (To build fluency, the spring term also includes a speed-reading component of brief passages at the 1,000-word level.)[12] Word counts during the course are tracked using the free extensive reading software Mreader.org. In the first few weeks of the spring term, training is done in class: in particular, Sustained Silent Reading (SSR) and the making and revising of word cards. While reading, students have their blank word cards on their desks so they can add words as they read. Their goal is to note down seven unknown words in a 20-minute SSR. After a few weeks, students do the extensive reading and word card note-making out of class. They are expected to carry their cards with them: if they finish a task in class before other students, they review their cards. I opt for physical rather than online cards because it's easier to see students are on task (learning vocabulary rather than texting with friends); also, students are able to adapt the cards to their own learning styles (e.g. using English definitions, Japanese equivalents, example sentences, collocations). They can also regroup the words as they learn them and reshuffle them for spaced repetition. I find that students are very receptive to setting concrete goals in numbers. For example, "*I want to increase reading speed to 200 wpm, so that I can read 200,000 words this term in order to learn the 3,000 word list over the spring and fall.*"[13]

Scenario 4: TOEFL, IELTS, and overseas study classes (Paul Wadden)

For the courses I teach to prepare students for TOEFL, IELTS, and overseas study, the English monolingual test-prep books don't offer good vocabulary coverage or vocabulary-building exercises, so I use a supplementary Japanese–English academic vocabulary text I wrote called TOEFL® TEST究極単語 (きわめたん) 5000 [roughly translated, "Complete Vocabulary for the TOEFL Test: 5,000 Core Words"]. The book has 31 lessons covering 3,500 general academic vocabulary, starting with high-frequency words and proceeding to lower frequency; it also includes common idioms as well as subject-specific vocabulary for 24 fields. Depending upon their own self-perceived vocabulary level, my mixed-proficiency students choose one of three sequences of lessons to study: Lesson 1–13 (basic vocabulary), Lesson 10–23 (mid-level), or 19–31 (advanced). The publisher has a 20-item quiz available for each lesson, so for 10 minutes at the end of each weekly class, students take a quiz to check their vocabulary comprehension and assess their learning for that lesson. It's a small part of their grade, but it gives them feedback and motivation. The 31 lessons provide them with an English sample sentence of each word in context and unlike monolingual texts also include the word's Japanese equivalent (research shows that access to students' native language boosts vocabulary learning, particularly for academic and technical vocabulary). On their phones, students can also download audio files to hear definitions, sample sentences, and the pronunciation of each word. Even though we can't cover the entire book during the course, it is a great resource for students to continue their vocabulary study when the class ends. Students who start with the initial chapters proceed onward to more challenging lessons; students who start with later chapters return to earlier lessons to fill gaps in their high-frequency vocabulary. In addition, the book provides students with access to core vocabulary from 24 different fields—from economics to biology to art history—which gives them a valuable boost when taking subject-specific courses abroad or EMI courses in the university.

Scenario 5: TOEIC and business English classes (Charles Browne and Paul Wadden)

The business English classes we teach build students' English skills for company employment as well as improving their TOEIC scores so they can be hired in the first place. Many Japanese companies now require a minimum score of 600, or higher, to even apply for a position. Reading business-related texts (emails, invoices, product descriptions) and listening to business-related talks and conversations are the main focus of the course. Critical to improving both their reading

1. Read the information and words in the box.
   Words with *pend*
   Example: **suspend**

   | Pendulum | pending | depend | suspend | pendant | appendix | penthouse |

2. **Completing the sentence**
   Use the words in the box to complete the sentences below.
   1. You can_____on Mary. She's a very reliable worker.
   2. That old clock has a long_____
   3. The light is_____from the ceiling.
   4. The doctor removed the patient's_____
   5. Vivian is wearinq a beautiful_____
   6. Mr. Williams lives in a_____with views of the river.
   7. Paul's application to join the golf club is_____

3. **Pair work**
   Work with a partner. What do you think *pend* means? Write your guess in the box below. Then check your answer with another partner.
   I think *pend* means_____

Figure 9.4 Sample word-part activity

and listening comprehension—and raising their TOEIC scores—is acquisition of business vocabulary. Even students whose English skills are high but who don't know the common vocabulary of business tend to underperform on the TOEIC exam. In our courses, we focus on developing knowledge of the words on the TOEIC Service List (TSL), which is only 1,200 words long, corpus-derived, and, when combined with the words of the NGSL, offers up to 99% coverage of the reading and listening sections of the TOEIC. This means that students can recognize and will potentially understand nearly every word on the test. Most of our students already know the majority of the NGSL words and about half of the TSL words so the learning burden is not too heavy (knowledge of the NGSL is established by giving students the New General Service List Test mentioned in the first scenario on p. 86). We begin by developing receptive knowledge of all TSL and NGSL words through the use of free, spaced-repetition flashcard apps like NGSL Builder and Word-Learner as well as the free NGSL and TSL word-learning activities on Quizlet.com; this also helps students to develop other aspects of word knowledge such as spelling and pronunciation. Students use quizlet stacks and other apps to learn the vocabulary. The TSL words are then highlighted in authentic business readings, which helps to contextualize students' understanding of the words including collocational knowledge. Learning these essential business words has value long after the course is finished. In addition, for students who want to move beyond learning "test English" and who have goals related to understanding and using business English in real settings such as for their future jobs, we teach the words on the Business Service Lists (BSL). These 1,700 words are also corpus-derived and offer up to 97% coverage of authentic business texts. Like the TSL, the BSL is designed to provide the next most important words to learn after mastering the core NGSL words.[14]

Scenario 6: helping more advanced learners (Charles Browne)

Once students have mastered most of the important high-frequency and common academic vocabulary (4,000–5,000 words in total), it becomes less practical for them to try to learn new lower frequency words since it takes so many more new words to add significantly to their coverage (learning 1,000 new words at this level often adds less than 1% additional coverage). At this point, the study of word parts (prefixes, suffixes, and roots) can be a good use of their time since a single word part can occur in scores of other words, helping students with the strategy of guessing the meaning of an unknown word by analyzing its word parts. Rather than have students memorize lists of word parts, I prefer to have them work inductively in groups, discussing several examples and first trying to reason out what the word part means. Figure 9.4 shows one of the activities I developed for my students to help them come up with the meaning of the word part themselves.

Scenario 7: subject-specific and English-medium instruction courses (Paul Nation)

EMI courses provide ideal opportunities for vocabulary learning if they are focused on a narrow subject-specific area. This narrow focus reduces the vocabulary load, builds up useful background knowledge to support incidental vocabulary learning, and provides good opportunities for repetition and varied use of the same vocabulary. EMI, content-specific, and CLIL courses should all include a deliberate vocabulary-learning component:

1. *Teachers should make target lists of subject-specific vocabulary for their students (since the students themselves can't identify the higher value field-specific words).*
2. *If possible, teachers should over time include English definitions and Japanese translations in these lists. The Japanese translation is especially valuable for specialized and technical vocabulary since it often allows the student to immediately and clearly grasp the meaning of the term.*
3. *The lists should reflect the frequency and range of the subject-specific words in the course so that there is the best return for learning effort.*

Providing this kind of supportive vocabulary will help students better focus on the content, a principal purpose of such courses.

Because vocabulary learning is a formidable task, an important component of a tertiary-level language course should also involve training the learners in *how to learn vocabulary*. This training should include:

- developing an awareness of the nature of vocabulary distribution and vocabulary levels (high, mid, low) so that the learners can prioritize which vocabulary to learn;
- confirming the importance of deliberate vocabulary study using L2–L1 flashcards and the nature of the retrieval process;
- training in word-part analysis and elaborated dictionary use to help words stick in memory;

- understanding how to get suitable meaning-focused input and output to complement deliberate learning;
- being aware of the importance of going back over old reading and listening materials to get repetition and to help develop fluency.

The individual classroom and beyond: vocabulary instruction across courses and curricula

When university teachers have the chance to teach intensive English courses that meet several times a week, or the chance to design curricula across courses in a department, they can more broadly plan opportunities for vocabulary learning. A useful way of doing this is to consider the four strands of meaning-focused input, meaning-focused output, language-focused learning, and fluency development. Although it is a challenge, the four strands can even be applied to narrowly focused courses, such as speaking, listening, and reading. For example, if a course is focused on the teaching of reading, then around 50% of the course time should be devoted to meaning-focused input, specifically reading. Meaning-focused output can be largely ignored except where there are clear and pressing related needs to speak or write about what was read, or where producing output would greatly improve the reading skill. Similarly, meaning-focused input through listening could be largely ignored, although activities like reading-while-listening might be a small part of the meaning-focused input strand of a reading course. Around one-quarter of the course time, for example, 20 minutes per class, should involve deliberate language-focused learning such as intensive reading, strategy development (including inferring vocabulary from context), and vocabulary teaching. The remaining quarter of the course time should be spent on fluency development, which should include a vocabulary-controlled speed-reading component and reading of relevant relatively easy material. Conceptualizing language learning and vocabulary acquisition across the four strands allows departments and programs to more effectively offer high-quality language courses for their students.[15]

Conclusion

There are many aspects of vocabulary teaching and learning we would like to explore here but are unable to due to space limitations. In closing, though, we would like to ask—and briefly answer—several of the many questions we have so far ignored.

How can I help my students make their receptive vocabulary more productive? Make use of linked skills activities where the same material is focused on through three different skills; for example, read about it, listen to it, and then talk about it. If the last activity in the sequence of three involves productive use of the language, the two previous steps will support this productive use. For courses with a writing component, have students use a certain number of newly learned vocabulary in each writing assignment.

What are some good resources for teaching students vocabulary useful for listening and speaking classes? Base your listening and speaking activities on what learners may have already read in English. This gets repetition and encourages more thoughtful processing through varied use. For words frequently used in spoken English, you can draw upon the New General Service List-Spoken (NGSL-S). Another list of high-frequency spoken English words is included in Geoffrey Leech, Paul Rayson, and Andrew Wilson's *Word Frequencies in Written and Spoken English* (Longman 2001) and can be accessed on the volume's companion website ucrel.lancs.ac.uk/bncfreq.

My students tend to cram vocabulary using rote memorization. What are some ways I can make my vocabulary instruction more communicative? First, be aware that rote memorization is useful and initially a powerful word-learning strategy. However, this rote learning needs to be linked to meaning-focused use, through reading and speaking, for example (yes, reading is also a communicative activity!). In fact, the linking can be from rote learning to use, or from use to rote learning.

How important is "context" in learning words? Very important. Generally, about three-quarters of the course time should be spent on meaning-focused language use. However, around one-quarter should involve deliberate language study, including rote learning and decontextualized attention. It is not an "either/or" proposition but "both/and" practice.

I teach my courses in English. Should I also insist on "English only" in my vocabulary teaching to keep my students "in English"? If both you and your students can manage an English-only class, then you are making very good use of the class time for meaning-focused input and output. Using Japanese translation to convey and learn the meanings of words is fine, but if enough of that is happening outside of class, then using just English in class provides much needed meaning-focused input. Giving students access to L1 (Japanese) translations for vocabulary is particularly effective for subject-specific and higher level academic vocabulary since such words are often difficult to convey in simple English, and the Japanese term may instantly convey understanding.

Should I set regular vocabulary-learning goals, for example, so many words per week? If so, how many words per week? Because there is so much vocabulary to learn, it is good to be systematic and principled about learning it. Twenty-five words per week is a modest but worthwhile goal (this works out to be 1,000 words over 40 weeks), and this matches native-speaker learning rates. For a class focusing on the same general or academic vocabulary, this might actually mean presenting students weekly with around 50 targeted words, since students may already know half or more of the words. One further advantage to goal-setting is that motivated students can continue to learn vocabulary during the four to five months each year when university classes are not in session, keeping their momentum going and developing autonomy in their language learning.

Notes

1 See Stuart McLean, Jeffrey Stewart, and Brandon Kramer's "An Empirical Examination of the Effect of Guessing on Vocabulary Size Test Scores" in *Vocabulary Learning and Instruction*, 4(1) 2015 and Charles Browne and Brent Culligan's "Combining Technology and IRT Testing to Build Student Knowledge of High Frequency Vocabulary," *The JALT CALL Journal*, 2(4) (2008) for some of the background research behind these points.

2 For the coverage provided by the New General Service List, see Charles Browne's "A New General Service Vocabulary for 2nd Language Learners" in *The English Connection*, KOTESOL, *13*(3), (2013) pp. 10–12.
3 The JACET 8000 combines the British National Corpus with a subcorpus drawn from English texts in Japanese secondary school textbooks, university entrance exams, children's literature, and American newspapers, magazines, TV programs, and films.
4 One of the impediments to students' mastery of high-frequency vocabulary is the backwash effect from entrance exams. Exam passages often include low-frequency and specialized vocabulary which leads students to focus, dictionary in hand, on learning low-frequency words that appear on the test, leaving them with significant gaps in their knowledge of core vocabulary words. Charles Browne and Brent Culligan discuss this harmful blowback in "Using Portable Technology to Build Student Knowledge of High Frequency Vocabulary: A New Era of CALL" in *The Journal of English and American Literature and Linguistics*, Number 121, Meiji Gakuin University (2008).
5 To access the Vocabulary Levels Test and the New Vocabulary Levels Test, Google the tests or go to victoria.ac.nz/lals/about/staff/paul-nation#links or lextutor.ca/tests. To access the New General Service List Test (NGSLT) and New Academic Word List Test (NAWLT), do a web search or log onto newgeneralservicelist.org/ngsl-levels-test
6 For discussion of the proportion of technical vocabulary in academic fields, see Teresa Chung and Paul Nation's "Technical Vocabulary in Specialised Texts" in *Reading in a Foreign Language, 15:2* (2003).
7 Search key words "NGSL Builder" and "NAWL Builder" or go to newgeneralservice list.org/ngslnawl-iphone-apps/
8 See the most useful vocabulary profiler at lextutor.ca/vp/eng/ and the general site and its various apps at LexTutor: lextutor.ca/
9 Kimberly Klassen completed her PhD in applied linguistics at Cardiff University and teaches in the English for Liberal Arts Program at International Christian University, Tokyo.
10 See LexTutor for the tests and Schmitt, Schmitt, and Clapham's article "Developing and Exploring the Behaviour of Two New Versions of the Vocabulary Levels Test" in *Language Testing, 18*(1) (2001) for explanation of the tests.
11 See the chart "Amount of reading input and time needed to learn each of the most frequent nine 1000 word families" in Nation's "How Much Input Do You Need to Learn the Most Frequent 9,000 Words?" in *Reading in a Foreign Language, 26*(2) (2001).
12 For excellent downloadable extensive reading materials for a variety of levels, go to Sonia Millett's website: victoria.ac.nz/lals/about/staff/sonia-millett. For the speed reading passages mentioned in this scenario, go to victoria.ac.nz/lals/about/staff/publications/paul-nation/Speed-reading-whole.pdf or search for Elizabeth Quinn, Paul Nation, and Sonia Millett's "Asian and Pacific Speed Readings for ESL Learners: Twenty Passages Written at the One Thousand Word Level" in *English Language Institute Occasional Publication* No. 24 (2007).
13 These targets and rates are based upon Paul Nation's "How Much Input Do You Need to Learn the Most Frequent 9,000 Words?" in *Reading in a Foreign Language, 26*(2) (2014).
14 For the TOEIC Service List (TSL), go to newgeneralservicelist.org/toeic-list/ and for the Business Service List, go to newgeneralservicelist.org/bsl-business-service-list/, or use "TOEIC Service List" and "Business Service List" in a keyword search.
15 For comprehensive discussion of applying the four strands to language-learning courses and curricula, see Paul Nation's *What Should Every EFL Teacher Know?* (Compass Publishing 2013).

10 Teaching presentation in the Japanese university

Curtis Kelly

Stop a moment. Jot down the *three most important things* Japanese college students need to be taught for making presentations. We'll compare our lists later.

Your first presentation class

To begin, let me tell you how I first taught presentations. I'd assign a topic, such as "Compare Tokyo and Kyoto," correct manuscripts and then have students, one by one, give their presentations to the entire class. Then, I'd do it all over again with another topic. I was lucky to get one set of presentations done every four classes. The monotone droning was painful for everyone. Worse, my suggestions afterwards—such as "speak louder," "more eye contact," "be more dramatic"—had virtually no effect. After all, the students were struggling so hard with language and memorization that they had few cognitive resources left for style. I came to consider a presentation that was not read, no matter how incomprehensible or boring, a success.

What went wrong?

I was focusing on the wrong things: writing, English, and teaching the product. Now, after 20 years of teaching presentation, as well as making over 400 presentations myself, I've come to understand that virtually everything I did during those early years was wrong.

To start with, I allotted too much time for manuscript checking. By assigning long speeches, especially those on impersonal world issues, the processes of drafting and memorizing became the main tasks; too little attention was given to delivery. In fact, as I learned over time, memorization *is* important, a prerequisite for excellent presentations, and perhaps the single most important criterion in a presentation class. The reason is that unless the students can deliver a talk smoothly without reading, they cannot use the other presentation techniques. Delivery becomes flat, their voices drone and become hard to hear, and even you, the English expert, have trouble following.

In addition, commenting on performance *after* delivery is the worst way to get students to improve. Instead, we must intervene in the *process* by having students learn delivery techniques *before* and *during* their preparation for presentation. Just as in teaching writing, responding to the final product creates a system whereby they internalize the wrong way first, and it is wishful thinking to expect your suggestions after one final presentation to influence the next one. Even if a student remembers that you told her to work on eye contact, she just won't have the mental resources at delivery time to work on that skill.

Good presentation comes from learning a myriad small techniques

Another mistake I made was trying to teach everything for each presentation. Good presenting requires learning 20–30 small techniques, and mastering just two or three at a time. Some of these techniques are physical, such as posture, voice projection, where to place hands; some are related to writing, such as using spoken rather than written English and making the audience care; and some are interactional, such as using rhythm, pauses, and voice variety. To teach these skills, it's best to assign short and easy presentations whose contents require less energy to draft and memorize so that students can focus on several key delivery techniques.

However, memorization itself is one of the first techniques you must teach, since it precedes the ability to use most others. While most Japanese already know numerous ways to memorize, they often don't know the important ones.

First, have students *use a "memory card"* for their presentations. A memory card is a piece of paper, small enough to hide in your hand, that has a list of one or two key words for each sentence. Cards serve two purposes: helping students memorize their speeches at home and then offering support during their presentation. However, you must be insistent on their use. Learners will avoid using them at first, unaware of the advantages they offer. Alternatively, if visuals are important for the talk, interspersing images with key phrases can play the same role, although in this case presenters will need to learn the skill of not gazing backward at the screen. Note that forgetting part of a talk does not mean that the student-presenter did not practice. Anxiety can cause us to blank out. Blood and energy go to the limbic emotional system instead of the sensory cortices and other areas involved in language processing. The memory card can help get students back on track after their mind suffers a blank out.

Another technique for memorization is the first of my own *three most important things*. It is to **practice with your body**. When asked to practice, students usually just sit in a chair reciting silently. Learning is fundamentally situated, which means learning something in one situation is hard to recall in a different one. (How many times have you run into students you know, but outside of class could not recall their names?) Memorizing something while sitting and looking down makes it harder to recall when standing and facing an audience.

Furthermore, quiet memorizing works for words, but it does not give students practice in the other things that must be memorized: eye contact, voice control, stance, gesture, and other aspects of delivery. Instead of sitting, students should practice with their whole body: they should stand in the same way they will stand when presenting, speak out with volume, work the imaginary audience with their eyes, and do the same things they will do in the real presentation.

Just telling students to practice with their bodies at home is not enough. Give them a few minutes to stand up and do so before each in-class presentation so that it becomes a habit.

Other body-related techniques to teach early on

The very first thing I do in a presentation class is give each student a short proverb to memorize and deliver verbatim before a video camera. I don't give any coaching, and as you can expect, their first presentation is pretty miserable. Good. That is just what I want because I record them delivering the same proverb six classes later, after they have mastered delivery techniques, and I put together a before-and-after video for them. You'd be surprised how well that works to show them their progress.

As soon as the proverb is delivered the first time, I start teaching body-oriented techniques. These include:

Posture: Stand with balance, not leaning on anything, such as one leg. Feet should be slightly apart.

Hand position: Hands at your sides is the natural position. Nervous students tend to put their hands behind their backs, which gives the message, "I am hiding something from you." Clasping hands in front transmits humility, but works against establishing authority.

Gestures: They should appear unconscious and natural, not practiced and pretentious. Gestures should be muted and generally stay in "the box," a 50 cm × 50 cm square in front of the chest and abdomen. Have them practice with short utterances: "This train goes from Kyoto to Osaka to Kobe." [*Slight hand motion downwards and then to left, reflecting physical location.*] Or "This is my opinion. Now what do you think?" [*Slight gesturing toward self and then audience.*]

Walk, Stop 3, Talk, Stop 2: I teach this the first day, right after students have finished the proverb, and it has a huge effect on making them look confident as speakers, and what's more, actually *being* confident. Instead of jumping in front of the camera and blurting out the proverb, I have them get in position, take three seconds to scan the audience and *then* speak. It is amazing how effective this little technique is for gaining attention. Then, pausing two silent seconds before leaving the podium magnifies impact.

Voice projection: Telling them to "speak more loudly" rarely works. Sometimes it leads to shouting, which is neither good for their throats nor our ears. Instead, teach them how to project their voices from their abdomens, using their diaphragm muscles to push words out.

Eye contact: Teach eye contact after mastering the previous techniques. While some trainers say, "Find friends or smiley people in the audience and speak to those individuals," I find that for myself as a presenter that approach takes too much conscious thought. Instead, I teach the learners to just "work the audience," looking left, right, and center every few seconds.

Here is a great way to teach that technique I learned from Joseph Britton, a speech trainer: Put students in groups of four. Have each one deliver an easy presentation to the other three. The other three stand facing the speaker, representing the right, center, and left sides of the audience. Their right hands are raised. The speaker will face one and present until that student, after silently counting to five, lowers his or her hand. The speaker must speak to another student for five seconds. After one round of timed practices with raising and lowering hands, have them do it again but allow the speakers to change facings freely, according to word flow.

Next work on content

The next set of techniques is related to drafting and content. I usually teach them from the second presentation on. The first is another of my three most important things. It is, paraphrasing Carmine Gallo, "Make the audience care."[1]

> ***Make the audience care***: In fact, this might be the single most important thing to teach in your class. Most students do presentations "briefing" style, which means just explaining something. Research has found that you can't really attend to something unless it has emotion, which means it must be personally relevant.[2] Cold cognition, thinking removed from emotion, doesn't work. So the first duty of any speaker is to answer the question in every listener's head, "Why should I care about what you are going to tell me?" In other words, the topic to be discussed must be made relevant to the audience. Even in cases where the relevance is already obvious, such as in "Classes You'll Absolutely Love," accenting that relevance increases interest.

There are many ways to make the audience care. A presenter might start out with a touching image, a thought-provoking question, or a story, but the key is to connect the topic to the audience's own unsolved problems: what to do when X happens, how Y works, why Z can help you. Most people skip the problem and just explain a solution. But making the problem clear first is far more effective.

For example, the first presentation I assign is to have students talk about products they like. I give them a prescribed six–sentence format where they explain what the product is, what it does, where to buy it, and how much it costs. "This is my favorite hair spray. It is good for . . . You can buy it at . . ."

These presentations are generally pretty dull, as intended. I then explain that they first need to make the audience care and then I have them do it again with a problem–solution format. "Have you ever woken up late and your hair is a mess? So what do you do? You put on a hat. It's so embarrassing." Only after the problem is fully established do they introduce the product, which is the solution. "Well, let me tell you how to solve that problem, and it only takes 7 seconds . . ."

Use speaking words: This is the third of my *three most important things,* and like the others, rarely mentioned in presentation books. Most students make the grave error of writing their speeches and memorizing them verbatim. Written English, though, is far more complex than spoken English. It is longer and uses complex structures. If a presenter delivers written English, you have to hold the entire sentence in memory to process it, and if you miss even one word, you get lost. Spoken English is made of short phrases, questions, lots of repetition, and works best when the original terms are used instead of "it" or "that." How many times have you heard someone going on and on with "It is . . .," It has . . .," and you had no idea what "it" referred to?

Using stories: I am always tempted to add stories to my list of *most important things,* but lists of three have more sticking power. The power of stories is already fairly well known. We learn information in narrative form faster and retain it longer than information in factual explanations. Stories can also arouse us emotionally. Every presentation should include stories.

Quick review: my *three most important things* to teach are **(1) practice with your body, (2) make the audience care,** and **(3) use speaking words.** How does this compare to your list? I have found these hold the secret to fixing most of the problems student presenters have. Even if you take nothing else from this chapter, I hope you incorporate those three.

In addition to spoken language and volume, some of the other vocal aspects to focus on are:

Phrasing: Long, unbroken sentences are poisonous. Teach students to compose their sentences with short, medium, and long pauses: "One day . . . . . a man . . and his child . . . . . went out . . for a walk . . . ." Phrasing does a lot of the grammar processing for the listeners.

Dialog voice: Tell them to use direct speech instead of indirect, and make different voices for each character. This also reduces the listener's processing load.

Voice change: The human brain is built to notice change, not stasis, so a monotone voice causes zoning out. Changing volume, speed, pitch, and tone keeps attention.

Long pauses: I consider a long pause, three seconds or more, a presentation "super bomb." The voice style before and after the pause should be different. "So who is responsible?" (high and fast) . . . 3–5 seconds . . . "We are!" (low and slow).

PowerPoint, Q–A, and making vows

Here are some other techniques:

PowerPoint design: The audience can only listen or read, not both, so as Garth Reynolds advises, presenters should avoid making "sliduments."[3] I suggest no more than seven words per slide and just keywords to serve as anchors. (The exceptions are when poor pronunciation or difficult content makes content hard to understand.) You should also suggest using only one picture per slide, cover the whole slide with that image, and avoiding animations other than simple "appears."

Make numbers meaningful and look for wows: Numbers need metaphors to express their meaning. For example, rather than say, "There are over 2 billion active Facebook users," say, "What are the three largest nations in the world? Number 3 is India, number 2 is China, and number 1 is . . . Facebook. Facebook has over 2 billion users." In this way, important data is able to "wow" the audience.

Q-A strategies: The question–answer segment of a speech contest is often where students falter. Having them generate potential questions, putting them into groups, and then preparing six or so "bucket answers" that cover each group is a great way to improve their Q–A skills. They also need to learn how to compliment the questioner, "That's a great question," and deal with questions they cannot answer ("I don't have that information now, but give me your email address and I'll get back to you").

In conclusion

There are more techniques I'd like to describe, such as using taglines, using body movements for punctuation, joint speaking, debate moves, and so on, but all techniques serve a single deity: passing on the passion. As Carl W. Buehner said, "They may forget what you said, but they will never forget how you made them feel."[4]

Notes

1. For some great ideas for teaching presentation see Carmine Gallo's *The Presentation Secrets of Steve Jobs: How to be Insanely Great in Front of Any Audience* (Prentice Hall 2009).
2. See Mary Helen Immordino-Yang's *Emotions, Learning, and the Brain: Exploring the Educational Implications of Affective Neuroscience* (WW Norton & Company 2015).
3. From Garr Reynold's amazing *Presentation Zen: Simple Ideas on Presentation Design and Delivery* (New Riders 2007).
4. Attributed, with some controversy, to Carl W. Buehner (1971). See quoteinvestigator.com/2014/04/06/they-feel

11 Teaching subject content through English

CLIL and EMI courses in the Japanese university

Howard Brown and Annette Bradford

Questions, questions, questions

So, you've been asked to teach a subject-content class in English at a Japanese university. You might be an English-language teacher making the transition to teaching subject-content classes or a content specialist coming to Japan to teach your specialty. Either way, you probably have some questions. Well, we have some answers.

What kind of class will I be teaching?

That depends on your program and curriculum, and to some extent, how you want to approach the class. At the risk of oversimplifying, there are two basic approaches depending on the roles of content and language in the class. You might teach a content and language integrated learning (CLIL) class. This fairly new approach is becoming popular in Japan. Classes have a dual focus. The teacher and students work toward both language and content learning outcomes: both are planned for, both are assessed.

Another approach is English-medium instruction (EMI). Here, there are no primary language-learning aims. You might hope for some language development and you will probably assume that a course taught in English provides what language teachers call comprehensible input for your students. However, there are no specific language-learning goals for the class. The students' uptake of content is the priority. This kind of class really is just a subject-content class taught in English.

Are classes taught in English common in Japan?

Hard figures for how widespread CLIL is in Japanese higher education are unavailable, yet anecdotally the number of universities offering CLIL classes appears to be steadily rising. And the tracking data for EMI shows that it is rapidly expanding. The number of universities that offer content classes taught in English is growing and the size and variety of EMI programs at those universities is also increasing. Nevertheless, EMI is still not a part of mainstream university curricula. According to the latest available figures, just over 40% of universities in Japan have undergraduate EMI classes (as of 2015). However, many EMI programs serve fewer than 10% of the student body, so EMI is not something that most university students in Japan will experience. That said, government policies and market forces are aligning to encourage more classes taught in English. The Japanese government is now financially supporting EMI initiatives through grants to a number of universities, first with the Global 30 Project, then with the Go Global Japan Project, and more recently with the Top Global University Project. The adoption of EMI in Japanese universities follows the worldwide trend toward internationalizing higher education. Universities view EMI as a way to attract foreign students and increase diversity. It also gives their campus an allure of internationalization and academic rigor to appeal to domestic students.

Who will the students be?

Depending on your school, there could be a wide range of students. Most EMI students are domestic Japanese students taking a few EMI classes as part of their otherwise Japanese-medium degree program. They might have graduated from a run-of-the-mill secondary school in Japan, or they might be returnees coming back home after a long stay abroad. Your EMI classes might consist of only domestic students, but in many cases, there will be more diversity.

Universities often offer several different EMI programs simultaneously. This is especially true at larger, comprehensive universities. They might have an English-taught program where both international and domestic students can earn their entire undergraduate degree by taking courses taught in English. Or, they might have a short-term program for visiting or exchange students from abroad. They might also offer domestic and international students a limited number of EMI classes as part of, or as a supplement to, their mainstream Japanese-medium program. A given EMI class may be positioned as part of any or all of the programs. Therefore, your class could be made up of students taking EMI for a variety of reasons and bringing with them diverse backgrounds, both cultural and academic.

What level of English proficiency do my students need before they can take classes taught in English?

You may or may not have the freedom to set a language-proficiency prerequisite for your courses. If there is a prerequisite, your program may use any of the common proficiency tests, including IELTS, TOEFL, TEAP, or EIKEN exams, or there may be an in-house test developed by program stakeholders. There has been little research on the question of language prerequisites in Japan, but in Europe, the findings are fairly clear. A Common European Framework for Languages (CEFR) level of B2 is widely regarded as a threshold for success in EMI. This is the level at which learners are considered proficient for most framework goals and able to express themselves on a variety of topics. Below that level, there is a fairly direct link between students' language proficiency and their academic success in EMI. At or above B2, though, variations in language proficiency are only a minor factor in the students' overall academic performance. If the students are receiving effective language support in addition to their EMI program, such as through parallel English for Academic Purposes classes, a writing center, or other support mechanisms, the slightly lower level CEFR B1 may be an appropriate starting point. Of course, if you are teaching CLIL classes, language learning is part of the purpose of CLIL so the students' starting point is less of a factor.

Can my students really learn as much in an EMI class as they would studying in Japanese?

The answer here is a qualified yes. Assuming that the students have the language proficiency, academic skills, and support they need to be successful in EMI, there is no reason for their learning outcomes to suffer. In fact, EMI students can even do better than their peers in classes taught in their first language. EMI students tend to need more time to complete homework and assignments, especially reading tasks, and dedicating that time leads to better academic outcomes. EMI students also make fewer assumptions about what they are learning and are less likely to be satisfied with a vague or half-formed understanding than when they study in their first language.

However, it is also important to recognize that there is often a lag in academic outcomes in EMI. Students' uptake of the academic content is often lower than first–language peers at the early stages of EMI programs. But with sufficient exposure to EMI, their performance catches up to, and often exceeds, their peers.[1] Unfortunately, at present, we do not have a clear sense of how much exposure to EMI is sufficient.

Who usually teaches these classes?

This is a difficult question because there is little data on the national trends of who is teaching what. Early indications show that in university-level CLIL classes, the teachers are more often than not foreign faculty members with a language-teaching background. EMI classes are taught by both foreign and Japanese faculty, although it is somewhat more common to have EMI classes taught by Japanese faculty. Among the foreign faculty in EMI, some are language specialists taking on one or more EMI classes in addition to their language-teaching duties, and some are content specialists hired directly to work in EMI programs. Among the Japanese EMI faculty, many are younger professors with graduate school qualifications from, or work experience at, universities abroad. Some Japanese faculty are hired directly to work in EMI programs, but many are already teaching in the mainstream Japanese-medium program and add EMI courses to their teaching load.

However, it is important to remember that the national trends may not necessarily tell the story of what is happening in your local context. Established EMI programs at larger universities tend to have more full-time tenured Japanese faculty, with foreign faculty hired on short-term contracts or as adjuncts. Both groups tend to teach classes in their specialist area. These larger programs have fewer professors teaching outside their field of specialty. Programs at smaller universities, or small programs within larger universities, tend to have a more mixed faculty group with both full- and part-time Japanese and foreign teachers, and perhaps more faculty members working out-of-field.

What kind of materials can I use? Can I find a good CLIL or EMI textbook?

Some new high-quality CLIL textbooks are becoming available on the Japanese market. However, it is important to make sure that the content is at a sufficient level of intellectual challenge to be a legitimate part of the students' curriculum, and not simply a vehicle for language practice. Some publishers simply insert the word CLIL in the title of a standard reading or general-skills language textbook, so look for CLIL materials written, or at least co-written, by authors with expert knowledge of the field. Many CLIL teachers who cannot find appropriate commercially published materials write their own or adapt authentic materials to make them more suitable for their local context.

For EMI classes, a common approach is to use western materials: books or articles written for students at western universities, often those in the U.S. These have the expert-level content expected from EMI and, short of developing an entirely original set of class materials, this approach may be the best solution. However, there are a few things to note. First, western materials tend to be written with underlying assumptions about what the students already know, background knowledge that students in Japan may not share. You may end up having to explain examples or cultural references that the writers take for granted. Also, as these texts are written for native-English speakers, you may find it beneficial to scaffold the students' learning, perhaps by supplementing with readings designed for English learners or by providing the students with outlines, summaries, lists of key terms, and study questions that guide them through the text. Finally, pay attention to the length of the materials. Texts written for a western market conform to a western academic calendar, where students are likely to take fewer individual classes but spend more time on each. Students in Japan have many more classes with less time for each. A first-year student in a general education program in Japan could, for example, have as many as 15 to 18 separate classes per week, *each for a different subject with a different professor*. If you choose a western textbook for your EMI class, you may not be able to cover every unit or chapter.

I am not teaching subject content in English, but my colleagues are. How does that affect my language classes?

If your students are enrolled in EMI classes now, or preparing to take them later in their degree program, it may impact the language classes they take.

If you teach English-language classes for these students, the most important thing you can do is understand their needs. EMI students benefit from a much more focused approach to language learning than is typical in undergraduate English classes in Japan. They have a clear and immediate goal and they may also have a language-proficiency benchmark they are aiming for. Most EMI programs in Japan do not have a fixed entry benchmark for language proficiency yet, but it is becoming more common. In fact, your students may be preparing for one of the more well-known English proficiency tests like TOEFL, TOEIC, or IELTS.

In addition to general language proficiency, your students will need to develop their academic skills and discipline-specific language. Based on outcomes at programs across Japan, we can say that most students entering EMI need better input skills, especially increased reading speed and better lecture comprehension. They particularly need vocabulary coverage. At a minimum, students should have a solid understanding of Browne, Culligan, and Phillips' New Academic Word List (NAWL),[2] and you will want to systematically build their discipline-specific vocabulary as well. For a discussion of how to help students develop these skills, see Chapter 9, "Teaching and learning vocabulary in the Japanese university classroom," which includes a section on vocabulary for subject-specific and English-medium instruction courses and Chapter 6, "The blind spots of reading: switching on lights in the Japanese university classroom."

However, even this kind of targeted English for Academic Purposes (EAP) class may not meet all of your students' specific needs. EMI classes are often very context-dependent, so we recommend finding out for yourself what they need. Talk to your colleagues who are teaching EMI classes and find out what they expect in terms of student skills and performance. Will the students have to do timed writing in a final exam, or will they need to write term papers, or both? Do the EMI teachers prioritize discussion in their classroom or listening to lectures? Will the students need oral presentation skills? How much, and in what genres, will they have to read in a given week? Finding out the answers to these and other questions can inform your teaching and make it more effective. Reaching out like this also facilitates collaboration between the language classes and the EMI program, a connection often lacking at universities in Japan.

Moving forward

The number of subject-content classes offered in English is currently accelerating. If you are starting to work for a Japanese university, it is probable that you will be asked to teach one. In fact, many institutions are asking that all new faculty hires, both foreign and Japanese, be willing and able to teach at least one subject-content class in English. As universities continue to strive to become more internationally competitive and to offer their students a globally relevant education, it is likely that CLIL and EMI are here to stay. So as you prepare for this new challenge, here is a set of questions and points to consider.

At the planning stage:

- Do you have explicit language-learning goals for your students—is your class a CLIL or an EMI class?
- If you have explicit language-learning goals (CLIL), how will you balance language and content learning in your classes?
- How are you going to assess your students? Does that assessment actually fit the language/content goals of the class?
- What types of English-language classes have your students previously taken? What is their incoming language proficiency?
- Will you set a language-proficiency prerequisite for your class?
- How does this class fit into your students' degree program—is it a general elective, or does it build upon other courses within their major?
- How does this class fit into the university's overall international strategy? What goals are you meant to be accomplishing?
- Who will your students be? Domestic? International? A diverse group? How will this affect your teaching?
- Check CLIL textbooks carefully to make sure they are not merely English-language textbooks masquerading as CLIL texts.
- Look for support and inspiration from colleagues in academic associations. The Japan Association for Language Teaching (JALT) has a growing number of members interested in CLIL and EMI, and the Japan CLIL Pedagogy Association (J-CLIL) is an active group of like-minded professionals. You might also want to check out the annual Conference on Global Higher Education at Lakeland University, Japan. Looking internationally, consider the ICLHE Association (Integrating Content and Language in Higher Education).

During the class:

- How will you manage a mix of cultural and academic backgrounds and language-proficiency levels in your classroom?
- Will you permit any Japanese to be spoken in your classroom to aid the discussion of content?
- Be aware of the cultural assumptions present in many textbooks written for the native-English speaking market. You may need to adapt materials and explain cultural references.
- Do your students need extra language support to complete your classes? How will they get it? Will you provide language scaffolding?
- How will you support the students' development of discipline-specific vocabulary and general academic skills?

Notes

1 For details on students' academic outcomes in EMI, see the Interlica Project at the University of Madrid at ucm.es/interlica-en/
2 For more information about the NAWL, check the project homepage at newacademicwordlist.org

12 Using technology in the Japanese university classroom (and beyond)

Dan Ferreira and Joachim Castellano

What uses of tech will engage, enliven, and enhance my students' learning? What tools will make my teaching more efficient and my courses more effective? What applications do my students already know and how can I teach them others that might be beneficial without taking up too much class time? What principles should guide my tech practices and my students' use of learning technologies in and beyond our classroom?

While tech tools, applications, systems, and even hardware continually change, these questions remain constant. They also form the basis for our discussion of ways to use technology in the Japanese university classroom. In this chapter, we will provide an overview of the "technology landscape" the teacher is likely to encounter, punctuated with real-life anecdotes from an early technology-in-education adopter, Joachim, and observations from a current e-learning specialist, Dan, and conclude with some possibilities for extending the classroom in space and time.

The lay of the tech land

A good place to start is an inventory of the resources in your assigned room and more broadly at your institution. The tech affordances of university classrooms in Japan range from computer labs with the latest bells and whistles to glorified broom closets without much more than a soiled whiteboard and a marker that has already dried out. That said, most schools have a tech support department somewhere. Find out if there is Wi-Fi, how robust it is, whether connected classroom-computer rooms can be reserved, what tools can be borrowed (laptops? hotspots?), and most importantly for administrative staff, what paperwork and process is needed.

> *Joachim*: I departed for Japan thinking I was landing in a technological oasis. Wrong. As anyone who's been to a local city hall realizes, only certain segments of Japan are cutting-edge. Back home, I had been spoiled by my university's open-network Wi-Fi which provided access across the entire campus. Now I was punished with a network the size of three living room sofas. My vision of an innovative curriculum fizzled. However, instead of falling into despair, I found that the tech desert at my first Japanese uni

taught me key lessons. First, persistence. Any tech that I used in a lesson was likely to encounter a problem. But by preparing "work-arounds" and especially testing the lessons as I expected my students to experience them often preempted potential pitfalls. My favorite work around for limited Wi-Fi access was to pre-download content for my lesson, for example, download YouTube files and embed them within my slideshow. This proved even more valuable later when certain YouTube videos were deleted yet I had permanent copies. Another valuable lesson was that most Japanese institutions are willing to listen to ideas and proposals if offered with tact, patience, and cultural sensitivity. Instead of complaining and demanding more Wi-Fi like an entitled Westerner, I collaborated with the university's tech department, faculty, and staff. For instance, after several meetings about Wi-Fi, I convinced them that access was necessary throughout the university. After two years, the school expanded the Wi-Fi network to the entire campus. But I still used my pre-downloaded files because I knew they would work every time.

Ask tech support about the e-resources available to students as well. These could range from a one-device-per-student policy (for only a few hours or a whole day) to just basic Wi-Fi on personal phones to nothing at all. Finally, it never hurts to think outside the box; the bring-your-own-device concept is about making the most of what is already there. Consider how you can incorporate the tools the students carry with them (the typical smartphone has many magnitudes the power of the NASA computer that sent the astronauts to the moon), in addition to the personal hardware you are willing to use. Even *one device* could enhance the learning experience if used innovatively.

> *Joachim*: Wake up call #2 involved my own Japanese students' digital literacy. This was the country that gave birth to the Walkman and the thousand-buttoned remote control. So everyone, especially the young, must be tech ninjas. Yet many of my students have no idea what a Google Doc is or that the "blue program" actually has a name: Microsoft Word. The fact is most Japanese youths have had limited exposure to technology for educational purposes in secondary school.[1] Thus, before engaging in a tech-related task, ask yourself, "How simple will this be for a complete beginner?" And check with the academic affairs office to find out whether students have had technology orientation workshops in Japanese as part of their freshman orientation. If no such program exists, suggest they create one. From my experience, many students can pick-up new programs and applications swiftly; however, don't assume that they have experience with programs as basic as Microsoft Office or Google Apps.

CALL in the classroom

Different learning objectives may not only require creative use of resources, they may also call for a complete change of learning environment. Early enthusiasm for the potential of technology to enhance learning saw many educational institutions invest heavily in computer-assisted language laboratories (CALL). Although prohibitive costs for infrastructure and a shift in teaching methodology are some of the reasons behind the current trend away from the traditional CALL classroom, it is still a good idea to find out if you have access to this type of tech environment, even for a one-off lesson. Many CALL classrooms are well equipped but sit unused for most of the school day.

The traditional CALL classroom is usually arranged so a central teacher's console can control all the resources, including students' computers and the big screens at the front of the room. Knowing the extent to which your CALL classroom can be controlled and manipulated is useful for lesson planning. For example, the ability to directly project information on students' computers or on shared monitors at the front or to prevent users from using their equipment in particular ways is useful when there is a need to draw attention away from individualized work.

> *Joachim*: In my years of training teachers inexperienced with educational technology, I have noticed several patterns. First, guilt. We can add "teaching with technology" to the list of things we *should* be doing, along with eating vegetables and voting in local elections. Next, fear. Every day there seems to be a hot new app, hardware upgrade, or buzzword (mobile learning! augmented reality!) to intimidate the uninitiated. Actually, I see such teachers as ideal candidates to use technology most effectively in the classroom in contrast to stereotypical gadget-wielding early adopters whose classes might be innovative only in appearance. Technology should serve our teaching; it should extend and amplify opportunities for language learning. It is irresponsible to simply impose apps or require tablets in our classes without effective pedagogy. Before Googling "Top 10 language learning apps," do your homework. Familiarize yourself with the writings of CALL experts such as Mark Warschauer and Carol Chapelle. Read Ken Beatty's *Teaching and Researching Computer-assisted Language Learning*. Browse the *JALT CALL Journal* online for ideas and recent research and maybe browse through *CALICO Journal*. Short on time? Find an infographic on Ruben Puentedura's SAMR Framework. A responsible use of technology in the language classroom depends on informed choices supported by a theoretical framework and empirical research. Look before you take the technological leap.

The traditional CALL classroom will also be running a Learning Management System (LMS). There are several questions you need to ask whenever you come across such a system: Is the interface of the instructor's console bilingual? If not, are there commercial or in-house translations of the training materials available? Are they accurate? Does tech support provide training on how to use the system? If not, find the "tech-savvy" colleagues who can give you a run-through. Are the user computer interfaces bilingual? Is there a help phone available to contact tech support in the event something goes wrong in the middle of a lesson? To what extent can you connect your own devices to existing networks? Are there any accessories available either in the CALL classroom or at tech support that are compatible with your personal devices? It is always a good idea to test out any equipment before the term starts. And it is never a bad idea to play around with other devices you could use as a contingency should the main device not work.

Frustrated with your institution's tech facilities? Remember, many universities use grants to purchase new equipment once every five or more years, and during the years in between those across-the-board purchases they will only marginally upgrade systems and hardware. Therefore, your school will likely make do with what's available and blend new technology with old, resulting in a hybrid CALL-like learning environment. Such an arrangement may require ingenuity on your part. While it may be convenient to push the "almighty stop switch" in the traditional CALL classroom, which freezes students' computers so that you can gain their attention, not having that feature will require a different behavioral strategy. A simple gesture such as the instructor ringing a bell as a cue for all to momentarily stop working and listen may do the trick.

> *Joachim*: I must admit, for the record, that I used to be the early-adopter teacher-geek lampooned in the previous scenario. However, I have evolved into a self-described tech curmudgeon. Perhaps I grew tired of the mushrooming start-up companies releasing app after app, angling to profit from the education sector. Or perhaps it's simply aging. Anyway, recently I had the opportunity to take a break from teaching and returned to the classroom with fresh eyes. I decided to try teaching without ANY technology. Then, over time, I observed which tools I simply *had to* re-incorporate into my lessons because not doing so would impair student language-learning opportunities. Six months into my experiment, here is my own list of ELLT ("Essential Language Learning Tech"—just made up that acronym, as if we needed another one in educational technology!):

1 Slideshows: Teaching merely through textbooks or handouts limits content to printed material. Slideshows (created by PowerPoint, Keynote, Google Slides, etc.) enrich the classroom with projected images, audio, and video. Slideshows are also useful as classroom management tools to start class sessions with a few bullet points previewing the "flow" of the lesson and to end the class with a slide illustrating the homework. I encourage students to take a photo of the homework slide with their smartphones, so they don't forget it!

2 Photos: Visual images are probably the most effective media to elicit student output. Less proficient students struggle through dense text and get lost in a stream of unknown words from videos. An image, diagram, or even a painting can be worth a thousand words, and much faster.

3 The Internet: Yes, I tried teaching without Wi-Fi for a while. However, I missed the ability to do a quick Internet show-and-tell. For example, it was hard to explain what Airbnb was without a brief tour of the actual website.

4   Videos: The shorter, the better (60 seconds or less). Advanced students can handle content such as TED Talks, but it's better to flip the classroom. In this case, have them watch videos for homework, and discuss the content in class. (Note: Although video production in the classroom is time-consuming, it is engaging and highly beneficial when your students collaborate in English as they create and edit footage.)

For further flipping the classroom, the final three suggestions on my list are best used outside class time as these technologies are ideally suited to an individual student's own pace:

5   Audio: My first go-to activity with audio is students recording their own voices in preparation for a presentation. Here they can reflect on their own output and improve it before they stand and deliver. Gap-filling with audio files such as podcasts and songs are classic language-learning tasks as well.
6   Digital flashcards: I encourage students to make their own digital flashcards (alone or in pairs or groups) with apps such as Anki or Quizlet. Reviewing vocabulary on a mobile device is highly efficient.
7   A dedicated LMS: Valuable to share classroom content, remind students of homework, post assignment grades, and open communication channels outside of class. Without an online presence, you are limiting learning to contact hours in your classroom.

A general tool, which bundles some of these together, is a Virtual Learning Environment (VLE)—meaning, the use of an Internet-based platform for educational purposes. Sometimes synonymous with LMS but not limited to a discrete system, it extends into a virtual learning space independent from your physical classroom.[2] If there is a general-purpose VLE in place at your university, find out what access you and your students have to it, what support and training can be arranged for you and for them, confirm your students' current proficiency levels, and be aware that the administrators may have placed some restrictions on the system's use (such as disabling features in order to control the flow of information). Some tech-savvy teachers develop their own independent VLEs using the Google platform, but if you can adapt the one in place at your school it may be more efficient, particularly if students are already signed up on it and familiar with it.

Tech beyond the classroom after the term ends

While the main focus of this chapter is technology in the classroom, one unparalleled advantage of tech is that it vastly multiplies the possibilities for personalized self-directed language study. The use of video, audio, and digital tools discussed above—at home, in the classroom, on the train, and before, during, or after the term—are all examples.

Moreover, given the proliferation of language apps, as well as the increasing availability of hybrid and completely online courses, it is important to recognize these trends will expand. In fact, digital resources might even be more relevant *after* our students graduate from university. Over time, it is likely our edu-sphere's virtual space will be devoted less and less to passive learning such as information-posting, drilling, and media consumption. As educational organizations begin to master VLEs, active learning opportunities will accelerate. Perhaps the best way to prepare our students for a future beyond the classroom, and encourage lifelong language study, is to help them become discerning users of tech, by yes, turning them into tech curmudgeons!

In particular, students should learn to ask themselves whether the tech they utilize to extend and transcend the classroom

- encourages real communication
- promotes active learning
- provides rich faculty-to-student and student-to-student interaction
- offers useful feedback
- suits their preferred learning style
- helps them achieve their own language-learning goals
- supports claims of "improvement" with actual second-language or CALL research

With students having limited time in language classes during their university years (as little as 90 hours),[3] and so much of their lives ahead of them, one of the lasting impacts teachers can have on their students is to give them experience in online learning. Using tech, a teacher can point students toward digital resources that they can harness for their purposes, at their own pace, for the rest of their lives.

Notes

1 For an introduction on Japanese university students' previous experience with CALL, read the Thomas Lockley and Lara Promnitz-Hayashi article "Japanese University Students' CALL Attitudes, Aspirations and Motivations" in the *CALL Electronic Journal* (2012) available at callej.org/journal/13-1/Lockley_Promnitz-Hayashi_2012.pdf
2 For further ideas on using technology outside the classroom see Chapter 13, "Homework in the Japanese university classroom: getting students to do it (and then evaluating their performance)" in this *Handbook*, and Chapter 8, "Real World Listening in the Japanese University Classroom."
3 As pointed out in Chapter 17, "English language policy in Japan and the Ministry of Education (MEXT): emphasis, trends, and changes that affect higher education" of this *Handbook*, "In general, freshman students are required to take 90 hours of English in total to graduate (two *koma* a week for two 15-week semesters)."

13 Homework in the Japanese university classroom
Getting students to do it (and then evaluating their performance)

Thomas N. Robb

Why the attitude (and homework)?

Many students regard their years in university as a much-deserved break between the grueling ordeal of high school and the dawn-to-dusk lifetime job that awaits them upon graduation. They studied hard while in high school, and perhaps even a year or two afterwards in college-prep cram school, to get into the school of their choice. Once in the university, they feel they have earned the right to relax, make friends, earn some spending money at a part-time job, and enjoy life a bit. But then the villain steps into the classroom, asking them to do—homework!

The students' attitude is, to some extent, understandable. In Japanese universities, there are many courses where casual attendance at lectures, a brief term paper, and an "all-nighter" just before the examination will produce a passing grade. What most students don't realize, however, is that the subject matter in courses in languages and sciences cannot be mastered so easily. A school-wide survey at my own university, for instance, showed that the students majoring in foreign languages and in sciences attended classes much more faithfully (and reluctantly?) and spent considerably more time daily on homework than their fellow students in economics, commerce, and law.

The need for homework is clear—not just to absorb and apply what students are learning but also to prepare for life after college. For example, to arrive at a TOEIC proficiency level of 600+ that is required by an increasing number of employers in Japan, students with a starting level of 300 on the TOEIC will need around 500 hours of *efficient* study and practice with the language, yet a single year-long language class meeting once a week will yield only 45, often inefficient, hours of in-class time.

Stoking motivation

There are a number of ways that students can be motivated to study outside of class. Obviously, the most desirable is for them to have an inherent interest in the subject. The stronger their desire to learn the English language, the less you, as a teacher, have to do to encourage them to study. Teachers can, through the content of a course and manner of presentation, try to heighten their self-motivation.[1] Educational theory favors this kind of approach, looking upon the teacher as a sort of beneficent facilitator whose job is merely to guide highly motivated students in their effort to learn. While there are, indeed, many Japanese university students who are highly motivated, for the vast majority it might be better to adopt a more pessimistic philosophy: If the students can get away without doing much work, they will.

When students are not highly motivated to begin with, perhaps the next most common method of motivation involves teacher coercion. This normally takes the form of grades on assignments and penalties for work not done. The big stick is, of course, failure. Be advised, however, that there are schools, particularly smaller colleges that are hurting for enrollment, where the administration will not permit students to be failed so long as they have attended class for a minimum number of class hours, often two-thirds. If this is the case at your school and students know they probably cannot be flunked, then the school's administrative policy may take some of the teeth out of your threats, but you can still try.

Yet another approach to motivating students is through "peer pressure." Particularly in Japan, where the society tends to be group oriented, students will feel greater obligation to do their homework if doing it will have a positive effect on their peers (i.e., they will be able to share it) or if they're not doing it, it might have a negative effect (i.e., their partner in pair work will be inconvenienced or receive a lower grade). The following techniques are useful for encouraging students to do homework but do not necessarily produce so much student work that it would place an undue burden on the teacher to check it. Take it from me, these suggestions work, and so will your students!

Inform students that their homework is important

Lay down the law on the first day of class. Tell them that their homework will account for a specified percent of their final grade, for example, 30 percent. If you will be discussing the answers in class, do not accept late work. Homework assignments need not always be returned to the students (especially if you explain that handing back papers takes up too much class time). For assignments that you elect not to return, you might point out to the students some of the common errors that you found in them. However, returning assignments every so often, particularly ones deemed not to be well done, will suggest that the instructor is reading and evaluating all their submitted work and considers it important.

If you do not want to personally keep accurate records of each assignment, then have the students themselves keep a portfolio of all their work, which you can then collect at the end of the term. To their portfolios, they can attach a summary sheet of their assignment grades (on a standardized form of your own design) which will save you the trouble of compiling them. I even have them tally the total number of As, Bs, and Cs so they fully recall and understand their grades while reducing my administrative work. It may be the case, particularly if you are teaching seniors who have to be absent for job interviews or teaching practice, that you will let them skip a given number of assignments at their own discretion, although beyond that number, their grades will suffer. Yet another approach is to present an entire semester's schedule of homework, with assignment descriptions, in advance, Thus, if students know they will be absent, they can hand in an assignment early.

Assign homework which is relevant

Make sure your assignments either prepare the students for the next class or consolidate what was covered in the previous one. Remember, the more interesting the assignments, and the more relevant they appear to what the students themselves perceive to be their needs, the more likely they will do the work. Beware, for example, of choosing composition topics which might only be of interest to you. A modicum of democracy and freedom will go a long way, and offering some options in topic and approach will improve the quality of the homework. You might hold a class vote on types of assignments, or even have students design their own assignments. All other things being equal, they will be more willing to do homework if they have had a say in what they will study.

Make sure they understand what they are supposed to do

It is often difficult to find out if the students understand what they are supposed to do until one brave student comes to you after you have let the class out, or when you discover that most have not done the homework in the way you intended. If a significant number of students misinterpret the homework assignment, take the blame yourself. One way to head off this sort of misunderstanding is to heed the early warning signs: Look around the room after you have finished your explanation, and if you see students talking to each other, most likely they are trying to figure out your instructions. Take this as your cue to elaborate further, or call on one of the students who is talking and ask what it is that he or she does not understand. Write your explanation on the board (or post it online) so they can *read* it, also specifying how long you expect it will take.

Frequently, a model, example, or diagram can save a long explanation. Model assignments, especially excellent work done by students in a previous year or different class, can give your students both a high standard to aim for as well as an idea of what you expect; but be sure to get permission from the students and to remove their names first. If time permits, having students begin their homework shortly before class lets out will allow them to ask questions more freely, allow you to circulate and see that they are on the right track, and allow them to get some momentum going on it.

If you assign homework, at least look at it

Homework will appear completely irrelevant if you don't even look at it. That does not mean that you have to collect or correct it. It might be better, depending on the assignment, just to walk around the room with gradebook and pen in hand and glance at each student's work. Mark an "X" by the name of each person who has not prepared the homework. Students need not know what you will do with the Xs; they will fear the worst. The importance of checking cannot be overstated; students commonly believe that if the teacher does not check the homework they have done, they have "wasted" the time they spent doing it

Make sure there is visible proof that the homework was done

Writing assignments generate hard proof, but practice in listening, reading, and speaking may not without techniques such as the following:

a   Reading: Have students

- write a short summary;
- write their reactions to what they read;
- make a list of new or interesting words and phrases they come across.

b   Listening: Have students

- transcribe a portion of what they hear (give them the first and last words of a segment of appropriate length);
- do an in-class dictation of a segment;
- do a cloze test of a segment while you play the audio to the class;
- draw intonation contours for sentences they hear.

c   Speaking: Have students

- memorize part of a dialogue;
- prepare a cue card from which they must reproduce the homework dialogue;
- turn in an audio file in which they have recorded the dialogue with a partner using the school's LMS or a shared folder on Google Drive or DropBox.

Discourage copying

Any assignment for which an entire class is expected to produce exactly the same work invites copying. With assignments from a textbook, there are usually some open-ended questions that should elicit a variety of answers. When roving the class to check homework, glance at one such item. Because students who inappropriately share work usually sit together, it is easy to find suspiciously identical answers. Even when students are sitting apart, it is surprisingly easy to spot two identical answers; then compare the rest to see if the other answers coincide.

If you find identical assignments, give all involved an "X" in your gradebook since even the student responsible for the original work is guilty as a collaborator. (Also, practically speaking, it is often impossible to know who is, in fact, the original author.) While such marks need not have any bearing on final grades, the recording of the misbehavior has a remedial effect. Here again, peer pressure puts the person who copied in an embarrassing position because the person who did the homework also got a bad mark. One or two instances of this in a class are enough to deter students from even asking their classmates to allow them to copy assignments.

Keep in mind, however, that similar answers can sometimes be the result of students sharing information on aspects of the assignment they have not understood. Such discussion should be encouraged. Be sure to make clear to the class what you consider to be legitimate forms of collaboration, such as explicitly co-authoring an assignment or exchanging ideas before writing individual essays, and what you consider to be illicit, such as transcribing a classmate's answers

Have students critique each other's work

For writing classes, students can attach a checklist to their compositions and have classmates evaluate the assignment against the criteria listed thereon. Criteria can include matters of mechanics (margins and paragraph indentations) or content (interest, relevance to topic, etc.). Other specific criteria can be added to the checklist to adapt it to each assignment. (See Chapter 7, "Mandatory 'sentencing': breaking loose in the Japanese university writing classroom" for discussion of writing feedback and rubrics.) Students may also pencil in comments. Swapping compositions (or collecting and re-distributing them randomly) not only allows students to give each other feedback, but also lets them see how others have handled the same topic. It motivates them to improve their writing because they have a larger audience—their peers as well as the instructor. Further, if they have not done the assignment, they have nothing to trade with the others and cannot participate—an embarrassment they can avoid only by coming to class prepared. For conversations, substitution drills, and similar assignments which the students have prepared at home, have one student of a pair elicit the sentences from the other.

Textbooks with digital components

It is increasingly common for paper textbooks to come with an online workbook, or at least a set of self-access materials to complement the textbook content. Some of the material is excellent, but you will also find that although some material sports a snazzy interface, the pedagogical content is mediocre. The opposite can also be true: the content is well thought out but the interface is clumsy for both you and the students to navigate. If you are considering using such online material,

1 look over one or two representative chapters. The rest will follow the same pattern.
2 determine whether you feel that the material will enhance the course objectives.
3 check whether the site has a login system. If you cannot track what the students are doing online, most stop doing the work. As a check, of course, you can prepare follow-up activities in class that rely on having done the outside work prior to class.

Other online study sites

There is a plethora of online study sites these days that focus on one or more of the basic language skills. Many of them, however, are meant for the independent learner and do not have the tracking function that is required for a large class of less-than-motivated learners. Before adopting any of these as part of your out-of-class study program, ascertain whether there is a viable way for you to assess your students' use of them. If there is no registration system or teacher page, screenshots of results brought into class, or a quiz that you have prepared on the contents, or perhaps an "online access record sheet" will help keep the students on task.

Don't worry about giving them too much work

Students will invariably complain that they have too much homework, but experience shows that the more you expect from them, the more they will do. In an experiment that the author did with a colleague, two student groups were required to do vastly different amounts of homework; however, both groups responded with no significant difference to the question, "I felt that there was too much homework." It is quite reasonable to expect one hour of homework for each period of class time, depending of course, on how you perceive the students' homework load from their other courses. In fact, this is generally the amount of homework the Ministry of Education, Culture, Sports, Science and Technology (MEXT) expects!

Evaluating performance

When it comes to overall assessment of students for their final grade, it is hard to state a set of hard-and-fast rules since there is considerable variation from school to school in how much freedom is afforded to teachers. Some might do impressionistic grading and give students the grade they intuitively felt they deserved (with no hard numbers) while others base their grades entirely on a mid-term and final exam (or only final exam) with no consideration of class participation or even attendance. Over the past two decades, the Ministry of Education has exerted soft pressure on universities to use more transparent, accountable, and cumulative grading (for example, not basing a grade exclusively upon an exam or two).

Below is some general advice to help you determine the best policy for your class.

- Ask your colleagues about how they go about grading. If there is a general consensus, then it would be wise to follow suit.
- Are you supposed to write a syllabus for your own class? If so, you might have been asked to provide a breakdown on how you intend to assess your students, such as "40% participation, 20% homework, 20% in-class quizzes, 20% final examination." How strictly you must follow your breakdown depends upon your school. Many students don't bother to read course syllabi but they might if they are facing failure.

- If you are teaching one of many sections of the same course, the course coordinator may have written the syllabus on behalf of all of the instructors. It should be available on paper or online for you to read and check.
- Some schools expect all students to pass if they have attended most of the classes, although the number of schools with such a laissez-faire policy has been decreasing in recent years. Often there is either an explicit rule or a general consensus that missing one-third of the classes can result in an automatic failure.
- Still, the general student mentality is that attending class regularly is sufficient reason to pass the course. Thus, it is imperative that you disabuse your students of this notion at the onset of the class. Detailed requirements in the syllabus that you can point back to later or an initial class handout outlining your expectations will stand you in good stead.
- Students usually have the right to appeal their grade. Be sure to keep accurate records of attendance! Students might claim "But I came to every class! Show me the days I was absent." Curiously, some schools actually forbid attendance to be listed among the criteria for evaluation, but naturally, the "participation" mark will be low for those who don't attend.
- Some schools have rules on the average grade for your class. In some cases, even if you have two classes of vastly different ability for the same subject, you still might be expected to have the same grade average or grade distribution for both classes.
- Some schools frown upon giving high grades to too many students. Others frown on failing too many. What is the school's general policy on failures? Sometimes there is no explicit policy but just a common "understanding." Will the administration back you up when you fail someone and have clear evidence that they deserve to fail? Discreetly talk to your colleagues to find out.
- Some teachers are reluctant to fail poor students because they know that they will simply end up with the same student again, adding to the number of students they have to teach the following year.
- It is a good policy to keep your gradebook handy so that you can make quick notes on student behavior that should be either rewarded or penalized in the final assessment. You might find a mobile app handy for these notes, as well as for taking attendance.

Finally, for all aspects of evaluation and grading, be aware of the Japanese concept of *honne* and *tatemae*. There could be a significant difference between what the official policy states (the *tatemae*) and the unsaid understanding of how rules are applied (*honne*). Choose quiet comfortable moments to ask your colleagues what they base their grades on and how they have handled difficult situations in the past.

Note

1 See Chapter 15 of this *Handbook*, "Creating engagement and motivation in the Japanese university language classroom," for a detailed discussion of theory and practice.

Part 3
The classroom

14 Nails that still don't stick up
Revisiting the enigma of the Japanese college classroom

Fred E. Anderson

> *Anyone who has dropped into a Japanese* karaoke *bar late at night—where drunken businessmen, accompanied by pre-recorded background music, croon into a microphone—or anyone who has listened to the interminable speeches at a wedding reception, attended a six-hour faculty meeting, or paid a visit to a clamorous first-grade classroom knows that the "Japanese are silent" stereotype is hardly accurate. Japanese do talk, and at times they talk a lot. But the contexts in which talk is culturally sanctioned, and the types of talk that occur in these settings, do not correspond to those of the West. Just as languages differ in their rules for grammar, cultures have rules for when, where, and how one talks. This is no less true in the university classroom than in other social settings.*
>
> Fred E. Anderson (1993)
> "The Enigma of the College Classroom:
> Nails that Don't Stick Up"

Introduction by Paul Wadden

This chapter thoughtfully extends one of the most influential analyses to date of the interpersonal dynamics of the Japanese university classroom. In the original "The Enigma of the College Classroom: Nails that Don't Stick Up," Fred Anderson drew upon existing scholarship and his own anthropological fieldwork as a sociolinguist in a groundbreaking study of cultural communication styles and classroom dynamics. It was the most widely cited chapter in the Oxford University Press 1993 volume *A Handbook for Teaching English at Japanese Colleges and Universities*, a book which itself had a major impact on language teaching in Japanese higher education.

In this new chapter, Anderson revisits his original analysis 25 years later, reflects further on it, and updates it taking into account his subsequent research and experience. He again explores his original thesis, "The widely held perception that Japanese students prefer to be silent, and that little can be done to pull them out of their shells, is for the most part a result of western instructors' failure to see beyond their own cultural bounds." And he again poses the question underlying his previous inquiry, "The question is not simply why Japanese do not talk in class, but rather, in what situations do they talk and why?"

The earlier "Nails that Don't Stick Up" presented several key concepts and cultural patterns to understand classroom dynamics; among these were group-mindedness, consensual decision-making, formalized speechmaking, listener responsibility, and the combined role they all play from elementary school onwards in forming Japanese students' communicative styles. Anderson contrasted these with the predominant "dyadic" interaction pattern of western classrooms in which the teacher asks an individual student a question, often evaluates the answer by saying "good" or "okay," and then proceeds to another individual student. The teacher controls the classroom discourse and students who want to speak to classmates must do so through that central authority, otherwise they risk being scolded for "talking." This style of interaction differs fundamentally from ones in which Japanese students are acculturated. These include the *happyo* (a brief formal answer which from the first years of their schooling students are taught to "stand and deliver"); the "consensus check" in which students consult with peers seated around them before making a response from the safety and collective wisdom of the group; the *hangakushu* or "small group study" in which students collaborate to complete assigned tasks; and the *gakkyukai* or "class meeting" in which students themselves hold a whole-class discussion to perform or plan an activity with minimal teacher involvement.

The original chapter deployed these concepts and posited these dynamics to suggest principles and practices for more effective pedagogy in the English-language classroom. "Nails That Still Don't Stick Up: Revisiting the Enigma of the College Classroom" continues that effort and invites readers themselves to creatively develop teaching strategies that build bridges between cultural patterns and that harness their learners' previously acquired habits and aptitudes rather than "pit their own culture against that of their students."

When I wrote the original incarnation of this chapter for *A Handbook for Teaching English at Japanese Colleges and Universities* published in 1993,[1] I was still fairly early in my career. At that time, I was a full-time, contracted English teacher at a small national teachers college in Kyushu. I was also finishing my PhD at the University of Hawaii at Manoa, and my dissertation was based on my study of classroom interaction in a Japanese lower elementary school classroom. On a personal level, I had married into Japanese society and was the father of two boys, one born in Hawaii and one born in Kyushu, and both growing up in Japan and transitioning into the public school system. The combination of my professional, academic, and personal experiences was a major factor that piqued my interest in classroom interaction, and continues to influence how I see the classroom.

Fast forward to the present and a lot has changed in my life, both professionally and personally. After the publication of the original *Handbook*, I spent time back in Hawaii writing my dissertation, a few summers teaching in a graduate program on the US mainland, and some years as a lecturer and researcher at two universities in Sweden. But for myself—and, I imagine, many of the contributors to this book—all roads lead back to Japan. I am now a tenured professor of English linguistics at a large, private Japanese university in Osaka. As I write this, I am rapidly approaching retirement age. And I am a grandfather.

Paralleling the changes in my own life in the quarter-century since the publication of the original *Handbook* have been a number of changes in the Japanese educational establishment, some related to English education. One prominent change during this period—at least on the surface level of language education policy—has been the enactment of multiple curricular revisions by the Japanese Ministry of Education, Culture, Sports, Science and Technology (MEXT) aimed at promoting the teaching of "communicative" English, from elementary through secondary school and even at the university level. This alleged turn away from grammar for grammar's sake and toward a more communicative paradigm was first associated with the launching of the Japan Exchange and Teaching (JET) program in the late 1980s. Over the following years, the JET program placed thousands of native or near-native English speaking "Assistant Language Teachers" (ALT) in secondary school classrooms throughout the country. ALTs also came to be hired directly through the schools where they were employed and sometimes even by dispatch companies which then placed them in schools. The net result has been a large increase in the number of non-Japanese, mostly western, instructors employed to teach English in Japanese junior and senior high schools. One would in turn expect this to have significant influence on the English abilities and learning styles of incoming university students.

While it is debatable whether the supposed "changes" in curricula, and the increased presence of ALTs, have been successful in upgrading the overall level of English communication skills (many observers would say no), my own feeling is that they have led to somewhat higher levels of ability to listen to natural English, if not better speaking proficiencies. More importantly, the fact that a large percentage of incoming university students have now been taught by a non-Japanese instructor at some point prior to college means that foreign instructors, particularly Westerners, are viewed with less curiosity—and anxiety—in the classroom than they once were. This alone would seem to create an environment where natural interaction can occur and where students are comfortable being steered into a western style of interaction preferred by their non-Japanese instructors.

However, deeply rooted cultural patterns do not easily change. For the most part, the students who seemed silent in the classroom in 1993—those who may in fact be actively listening, but who prefer to consult with classmates or wait to be called on rather than offering their response publicly—behave in much the same way today. Or, to revisit the metaphor from the earlier chapter, "the nails that don't stick up" still do not stick up. In what follows, I would thus like to review and update my 1993 arguments in light of my more recent experience, research, and thinking.

The enigma revisited

"Nails That Don't Stick Up" generated favorable response from teachers in Japan, as well as from TESOL professionals in other countries. Most notably, many acquaintances in Japan—especially those who were new to university teaching—conveyed to me that it helped them better understand the teaching context and overcome their classroom frustrations. It is fair to say, therefore, that the chapter was successful in accomplishing its primary purpose: to serve as a general guide for practicing teachers of English at Japanese colleges and universities. Indeed, this is a purpose that it shares with all of the chapters in the 1993 *Handbook* as well as with the chapters in the present volume.

But despite whatever success I achieved with the chapter, it also generated the sole piece of hate mail I have ever received: a disjointed, profanity-laced diatribe, which had been scribbled out on a postcard and mailed to my university address shortly after publication of the original *Handbook* (if it were today, I might expect it to be a midnight tweet). The angry writer took issue with my contention that one did not necessarily have to socialize students into the norms of Anglo-American culture in order to teach them English and that, in fact, Japanese students in the future would increasingly use the English language to communicate with other nonnative speakers. The writer went on to accuse me of being the reason why more Japanese do not learn English, and told me that I had been in Japan too long. Although I had not thought that I had written anything especially controversial, it was obvious that I had struck a nerve, inadvertently challenging the writer's core beliefs about teaching and learning in Japan and especially about the "culture" of the English language. I will return to this point toward the end of the chapter.

Fortunately, I received no other angry outbursts. Most criticism was thoughtful and professional, some of it in refereed journals and university working paper volumes; such criticism is expected and welcome. One legitimate critique was that my analysis drew too much on a cultural dichotomy between Japan and the West. Moreover, some of the characteristics of Japanese culture that I singled out, such as "groupism," downplay individual differences among students and thus risk essentializing Japanese culture as a monolithic entity. As critics pointed out, this type of analysis may in turn lead to the perpetuation of stereotypes of Japan and contribute to "othering."[2] In fact, from a purely academic point of view I completely agree with this line of criticism; clearly, one cannot lump Japanese people together as having all of the same traits, nor can one assume that members of all western cultures share the same values or behavior patterns. But the earlier chapter, as well as the present one, are written with practicing teachers in mind—especially western teachers whose experience with Japanese students may be limited—and I believe that the constructs introduced previously, however artificial or simplified they may be, still bear utility for understanding university classrooms.

My original piece began by exploring the concept of "silence" as it applies, or does not apply, to Japanese society. Western English instructors in Japan are often puzzled, even frustrated, by the atmosphere of silence that they perceive in university classroom settings. "Why don't the students talk more?" they wonder. As I pointed out, there are other Japanese settings where there is no shortage of talk: for example, karaoke bars, interminable university faculty meetings, and clamorous first-grade classrooms. "Just as languages differ in their rules for grammar," I noted, "cultures have rules for when, where, and how one talks."[3] So the problem for instructors should not be seen as silence per se but the functions of silence and talk in particular situations, in this case, the university classroom.

I went on to outline two aspects of classroom verbal behavior that conflict with western notions of how classrooms should operate. The first was a type of talk that western instructors would expect in university classrooms but often find lacking in Japan: that is, students seldom initiate discussion or volunteer answers. Students tend to avoid raising new topics, challenging the instructor, or even asking questions, preferring instead to seek clarification by consulting with a classmate (during class) or the instructor (after class). Many instructors find that students answer questions only when called on directly, and even then may be uncomfortable responding if they cannot offer a clear answer. In some cases, the class may perceive the instructor's solicitation of talk as merely a polite way to close out a topic, rather than a genuine attempt to open discussion.

The second problematic aspect of verbal behavior was a type of talk that instructors generally find unwelcome but is common in the Japanese classroom. This is the propensity for students, when called on, to turn to a neighbor and discuss their response before presenting it formally to the instructor and the class. This "consensus checking" process may, even for a brief answer, burn up considerable class time and can therefore be a source of irritation, especially for western instructors.

The overall pattern of classroom interaction was thus described as one where collective action takes precedence over individual expression, and where students feel most comfortable presenting opinions after they have been sanctioned by their peers so as to leave themselves less vulnerable as individuals. This brought to mind the well-known Japanese proverb that served as a metaphor for the chapter: "The nail that sticks up gets pounded down."

I argued that the classroom dynamics could best be understood as a part of a broader system of sociocultural norms that operate on communication style throughout the society and the individual's lifespan. These norms develop over time, as a part of the socialization process from childhood through to adulthood. My analysis then focused on four characteristics of Japanese communicative style that I saw as providing keys to understanding interaction in the college classrooms of English teachers.

The first characteristic was the propensity toward "group-mindedness." Alternatively, some researchers interpret this as "conformity training," "social relativism," or another label, but it has been widely described both anecdotally and empirically, and the basic idea is the same: There is a tendency for individuals to derive their identities from the groups to which they belong, and to moderate their actions in relation to others in their group. This contrasts with the western ideal of individuals as autonomous beings acting according to their own agency. Group-mindedness in Japan is first evident in caregiver–child interactions in the home. For example, studies have shown how Japanese mothers tend to socialize their children by calling their attention to outside forces that may be judging their behavior: invoking concepts such as *hazukashii* ("ashamed") or *okashii* ("strange"). The group-mindedness continues to be promoted through collective activities and cooperative tasks in which children are expected to participate in preschool and elementary school.[4]

Second was the Japanese tendency toward decision-making through consensus. Many westerners have experienced this directly, including those who participate in formal Japanese meetings, such as the university *kyojukai* (faculty meetings), which can continue seemingly forever until a consensus is reached. What is less transparent is how this pattern of behavior develops earlier in life. In my own research on classroom interaction in Japanese first- and second-grade social-studies lessons,[5] I was able to document an incipient form of the consensus-building practice that is implicit into and throughout adulthood: In their first year of elementary school, students in my ethnographic study were taught to comment directly on each other's responses to the teacher's questions by choosing from among several explicitly taught Japanese formulaic phrases: "That's good," "I have something different," or "I have something to add." The teacher would put off evaluating individual student responses until peers had commented on, and sometimes modified, the response. At the end of an interactional sequence, the teacher would provide a blanket evaluation of whatever collective response had emerged from the classroom interaction. I labeled this style "interactional umbrella," which contrasts with the "dyadic" style that researchers have described for American and British classrooms, where a dominant speaker—the teacher—engages in question-and-answer sessions with secondary speakers—the students—on an individual basis.

The third characteristic was the ritualized style of speechmaking valued in Japan, marked by honorific language and formulaic phrases. This is indispensable in business meetings, wedding reception speeches, welcome ceremonies, and other formal speech activities. University students often attempt to adapt this style to their learning of English, particularly those participating in extracurricular recitation and speech contests, traditionally through so-called "English Speaking Societies" (ESS) and now through TED Talk groups, which are popular club activities. My research in elementary school classes also suggested that there is an incipient form of this style: an interactional sequence where student responses to a teacher's elicitation were structured as mini-speeches. Rather than simply responding to a question casually from their seat as one would expect in a western classroom, the student would stand and present an answer in a formal register of Japanese that was more akin to the Japanese written style than to everyday talk. Educational anthropologist Merry White is another researcher who has described how early school life in Japan emphasizes ritualized public performance, which she views as a confidence-building prerequisite to personal expression.[6] Form and function are thus inextricably bound together during classroom performance.

The fourth characteristic that I singled out was the crucial role of the listener in Japanese communication. In contrast to most western cultures, where speaking is central and speakers are expected to transmit their messages clearly, Japan is said to tag the listener with the main responsibility for making sense of a message. Haru Yamada, a sociolinguist whose research focuses on cross-cultural business discourse, has detailed this phenomenon in her book *Different Games Different Rules: Why Americans and Japanese Misunderstand Each Other*.[7] Significantly, the Japanese translation of Yamada's book is 喋るアメリ

力人聴く日本人 (*Shaberu amerikajin kiku nihonjin*), or "*Speaking Americans, Listening Japanese.*" My own research and a similar study by Haruko Minegishi Cook present hints into how the culture of listening develops among students in elementary school classrooms: Data from both of our studies showed teachers emphasizing in their speech how important it was to listen carefully to one's classmates.[8] Seen at the university level, this culture of listening means that a listener who has not completely understood the speaker (even if the speaker is the teacher) may feel too embarrassed to ask for clarification, which contributes to the seeming reticence of Japanese students.

In all aspects of communication style described here, there is a progression of development running from the home through the school years and into adulthood, during which young people are systematically socialized for interaction in the wider society. This socialization happens largely outside of normal consciousness. It is embedded in the way that more experienced members of a society coach younger members on the appropriate use of language; and it is also implicit in the everyday speech activities in which the younger members participate.[9] Over the years, language behavior, including conversational style, becomes second nature as an element of one's culture. This acquired behavior also creeps into one's second language as a "discourse accent" in much the same way that phonological features of one's native language affect pronunciation in a second language. One can thus not expect students who find themselves in a western-style classroom in Japan, after 12 or more years of experience in Japanese classrooms, to interact like western students (although a few might) simply by virtue of having studied English. Non-Japanese English teachers who radically try to alter the existing patterns are usually those who become frustrated and do not last long in the country.

The nails still don't stick up

I have already implied that the dominant classroom interaction pattern of Japanese students has changed little since the publication of the original *Handbook*. This claim is supported not only by anecdotal observations of myself and others working within the Japanese system,[10] but also by recent empirical studies of Japanese classrooms, especially with regard to the role of silence. UK-based researcher Jim King, for example, conducted a study based on 48 hours of recorded data from nine Japanese universities which aimed to quantify the use of silence in English classes in Japan.[11] Although King seemed doubtful at the outset of his research about whether student silence was really as prevalent as often claimed, his analysis showed that it was indeed a significant element of the class: Talk was completely absent in over one-fifth of the class time that he recorded, and of the talk that did occur, *less than one percent was initiated by students.*

Another recent study focusing on silence, a qualitative case study by Japanese researcher Mika Tamura, provides evidence that there has been little change in classroom interaction patterns, including the use of silence. As a part of a larger ethnographic study of scientific English teaching at a major Japanese research university, Tamura combined classroom observations, questionnaires, and interviews to document the struggles of a visiting American biochemistry professor. In particular, the professor was having trouble dealing with the general non-responsiveness of his students, including their hesitancy to ask questions. While showing an understanding of the cultural gap, the professor was nevertheless frustrated by the situation. "I understand that there is a cultural gap," he is quoted as saying. "It's like, uh, hooking up to the Internet. You are logged in but still wireless. Then, you finally see the bars go up. Wireless say, 'Okay, I'm connected.'"[12]

Interestingly, not only the instructors but also Japanese students are sometimes aware of and bothered by the communication gap. Some of the students interviewed in Tamura's study indicated that they understood the instructor's expectations but were nevertheless hesitant to express their ideas openly because they were obsessed with "how they look to other students," suggesting that the norms they learned from their mothers about "outside forces" that might be "judging their behavior" were still operative.

In my own experience, I have found that students returning to Japan after a period of study abroad may be especially sensitive to the difference in communication styles. One student, whom I will refer to as Kohei, had returned to Japan after a year of exchange at an elite American university where he was enrolled in a business program. He approached me one day after class—a lecture class in sociolinguistics with a fairly large number of students—wishing to discuss the reverse culture shock that he had been experiencing. In the US, Kohei explained, much of his class activity had consisted of analysis and discussion of case studies, a style of learning that was virtually absent from his experience in Japan. He retained a desire in Japan to participate actively in class as if it were an American university, and felt that he should be able to do so in my class as I was an American professor. Not surprisingly, he was one of only a few students in the class who attempted to initiate conversation; yet he felt somehow conflicted about his behavior, knowing that he was violating implicit norms for interaction that operated in most Japanese classrooms. By taking speaking turns too willingly and too often, he wondered, was he somehow being unfair to his classmates, whose English was less proficient than his and who were more self-conscious about speaking out?

Another student in the class, whom I will call Yumi, had spent a year at a Canadian university and was eager to discuss her experiences with Kohei and me when she caught wind of our conversation. Like Kohei, Yumi was acutely aware of differences in classroom communication style, and said that she enjoyed participating in discussions actively while in Canada. Unlike Kohei, however, she was not bothered by the more passive style that she found upon returning to Japan, and in fact indicated that she was content to sit and listen most of the time. Both of these Japanese students had adapted to a different mode of classroom communication while in North America, but they displayed divergent patterns for dealing with the Japanese mode once back in their home country; Kohei seemed to be having more difficulty than Yumi in re-socializing to it.

Living with the enigma

The cultural dynamics that operate in the Japanese university classroom obviously pose constraints on English instructors. But as I have argued in my earlier work, there are things that one can do to harness the energy that exists below the surface. In my 1993 chapter, I proposed three general approaches to the classroom, all of which benefit from first recognizing the gap between one's own expectations for how a classroom should operate and the norms implicit in the students' behavior. I summarize these again below, not as strict prescriptions but as general guidelines. As I stated in my earlier chapter, this is in order to help instructors "build on the Japanese styles of communication rather than striking out against them."[13]

The first approach that I outlined was "lecturing," which is a classroom style that Japanese students are fully prepared to accept. No one in the language-teaching business, however—especially in the business of teaching anything akin to communicative language—is likely to believe that lecturing alone is an effective strategy for teaching. However, in required university "general English" or "English conversation" classes with over 50 students meeting only once a week (probably a less common scenario today than it was in the 1990s), one can certainly make a case for some sort of lecturing, for example, connected with content-based language teaching where the focus is on listening comprehension.

The second approach was "pulling the nails up." This referred to the strategy employed by some instructors to encourage students to speak out—either through the clever use of non-threatening devices, such as games or imaginative point systems, or through more direct coercion, including negative evaluation for those who don't speak out. I argued that coercion is almost always counterproductive, as it works against the students' cultural grain and is only likely to exacerbate the instructor's frustrations. Working with the differences, and not against them, is almost always a more reasonable and effective strategy.

The third approach—which I offered as the "one with the most potential"—I called "blending in." I suggested that non-Japanese instructors of English in Japan step into the role of teacher-cum-anthropologist and attempt to observe the foreign culture around them in terms of the culture itself rather than from their outsiders' framework. In other words, what are the contexts—in Japanese society in general, and in the classroom specifically—where people feel comfortable talking? And how is language used in those settings? Adapting aspects of the local sociolinguistic culture to the classroom, even partially, can be a powerful tool in the struggle to get students to feel comfortable using the foreign language.

With the "blending in" approach in mind, I suggested a few ways to structure activities that I saw as culturally sensitive, and which, from my experience, lead to more talk. One was the use of tightly controlled pairwork and groupwork tasks where specific roles—"group leader," "secretary," "spokesperson," etc.—were assigned to group members for task management. If groups are asked to report their ideas back to the class, the fact that the spokesperson would be representing the group as a whole reduces the sense of individual risk that the student may feel. Another effective activity type, especially for lower level students, was games that combine competition across teams with cooperation within teams. The fact that students are encouraged to cooperate with team members to find answers to questions allows students to carry out consensus checks "legally" before anyone answers for the team. I also suggested bridging cultures through activities that created a smooth transition from the students' norms for interaction to those of the instructor. For example, in discussing topics in pairwork situations, students could refer to pre-prepared scripts during a first round of discussion (harnessing the *happyo* of a formal response), then, after a few changes of partners, put away the scripts and depend on their memories and imaginations. A transition is thus made from the formalized Japanese speechmaking style to a more spontaneous, western conversation style.

Negotiating habitus: beyond East and West

Classrooms present a paradox in cultural interaction, at least in the type of EFL situations with which readers of this book are most familiar: those where the students and instructor bring to the classroom different sets of culturally constructed values and attitudes, what followers of French sociologist Pierre Bourdieu might refer to as different *habituses*. The notion of habitus is related to processes of acculturation and socialization that operate at home and at school. Discourse scholars Ron and Suzie Scollon have defined it in simple terms as the way in which a "lifetime of personal habits come to feel so natural that one's body carries out actions seemingly without being told."[14]

In the classroom, then, we are confronted with two competing sets of habits: that of the non-Japanese instructor and that of the students. Which one, we might ask, should take precedence? On the one hand, the teacher's habitus would seem to be the crucial one since it is the teacher who sets the rules for the class and who is ultimately in charge of organizing class activities. But on the other hand, the classroom is embedded in the wider society beyond it, where the students' habitus rules and where the vast majority of students will spend the rest of their lives. This dilemma is compounded by the fact that English—more than any other language in the history of the world—is an international language, used both across and within national boundaries as a lingua franca.

These dilemmas bring me back to the irate postcard reacting to my chapter in the 1993 *Handbook*. The writer objected especially vehemently to my assertions about the role of English as an international language and my contention that Japanese learners of English would have more chances in the future to interact with other non-native speakers, particularly Asians; and because of this teachers should not make assumptions about which communication style will best serve students' needs in the future. Over time, however, it has become even clearer to me that my original assertion was correct, and is increasingly so: In recent years I have had students who communicate on a regular basis in English—because of their experience studying abroad, friendships made in Japan, relatives in foreign countries, and even romantic relationships—with Filipinos, Indians, Chinese, French, Swedes, and Brazilians, among other national and ethnic groups. The age where

Anglo–American communication styles are the only ones acceptable in the use of English has passed. The angry postcard writer, however, asserted that "language *is* culture," implying that one can teach English effectively only by attaching to it the cultural baggage characteristic of Anglo–American cultures, including the interactional norms. But while this kind of tightly delineated language–culture relationship may be applicable to smaller, spatially bounded languages with limited numbers of speakers, contemporary English—with its estimated one to two billion users, where the non-native speakers easily outnumber the natives—is a different matter. As the late Larry Smith, co-founder of the International Association for World Englishes and one of my mentors in Hawaii, often contended, "Language and culture are related, but English (in the contemporary world) cannot be tied to any *particular culture*." What in fact makes English the only truly "global language" in the history of the world is its flexibility; that is, the fact that it can be used to reflect and express diverse values. Larry was also fond of pointing out that "English as an international language" is something that not only non-native speakers, but also native speakers, needed to learn.[15]

So in the end, it is my belief that the successful English class, or English-medium class, will not necessarily follow either the habitus of the instructor or that of the students. Depending on the personalities of the teacher and the students, as well as the students' academic needs and desires, the direction that the class takes may be negotiated more toward the culture of the instructor or toward that of the students. But in any case, it is likely to be somewhere in between: not "East vs. West," but "East meets West," and vice versa.

Notes

1 Fred E. Anderson, "The Enigma of the College Classroom: Nails that Don't Stick Up," in *A Handbook for Teaching English at Japanese Colleges and Universities*, ed. Paul Wadden (Oxford University Press 1993), pp. 101–110.
2 See Bernard Susser, "EFL's Othering of Japan: Orientalism in English Language Teaching," *JALT Journal*, 20(1) (1998), pp. 49–82. Also see Arthur Allan Bailey, "Moving Beyond 'Groupism' and Other Cultural Myths in Japanese University English Classes," 立命館経営学 40(6) (第 40 巻 第 6 号) (2002), pp. 171–185.
3 Fred E. Anderson, "The Enigma of the College Classroom: Nails that Don't Stick Up," in *A Handbook for Teaching English at Japanese Colleges and Universities*, ed. Paul Wadden (Oxford University Press 1993), p. 102.
4 Socialization of children in the home is discussed by Patricia M. Clancy, "The Acquisition of Communicative Style in Japanese," in *Language Socialization Across Cultures*, Bambi B. Schieffelin and Elinor Ochs (Eds) (Cambridge University Press 1986), pp. 213–250. Preschool socialization is taken up by Matthew Burdelski, "Socializing Politeness Routines: Action, Other-Orientation, and Embodiment in a Japanese Preschool," *Journal of Pragmatics*, 42(6) (2010). Social relativism as the ethos of Japanese culture is a major theme in Takie Sugiyama Lebra, *Japanese Patterns of Behavior* (University of Hawaii Press 1976).
5 Fred E. Anderson, *Classroom Discourse and Language Socialization in a Japanese Elementary School Setting: An Ethnographic Linguistic Study*, unpublished doctoral dissertation, University of Hawaii at Manoa (1995). Some of the data and analysis from the dissertation appear in a much abbreviated form in: Fred E. Anderson and Sylvia Wolfe, "Under the Interactional Umbrella: Presentation and Collaboration in Japanese

Classroom Discourse," in *Creating Classroom Communities of Learning: International Case Studies and Perspectives*, Roger Barnard and Maria E. Torres-Guzman (Eds) (Multilingual Matters 2009), pp. 15–35.
6 Merry White, "Elementary Schools: Harmony and Cooperation," in *The Japanese Educational Challenge: A Commitment to Children* (Kodansha International 1987), pp. 110–133.
7 The original, English, version of Haru Yamada's book was published by Oxford University Press in 1997. The Japanese translation appeared in 2008.
8 Haruko Minegishi Cook, "Language Socialization in Japanese Elementary Schools: Attentive Listening and Reaction Turns," *Journal of Pragmatics, 31*(11) (1999).
9 Bambi B. Schieffelin and Elinor Ochs, linguistic anthropologists who have been at the forefront of language socialization research since the 1980s, describe these processes as "socialization to use language" and "socialization through the use of language" (Schieffelin and Ochs, Eds, *Language Socialization Across Cultures*, Cambridge University Press 1986).
10 Other authors who have approached this problem include, for example, Timothy J. Korst, "Answer, Please Answer! A Perspective on Japanese University Students' Silent Responses to Questions," *JALT Journal, 19*(2), pp. 279–291 (1997); and David L. Greer, "'The Eyes of Hito': A Japanese Cultural Monitor of Behavior in the Communicative Language Classroom," *JALT Journal, 22*(1), pp. 183–195 (2000).
11 See Jim King, "Silence in the Second Language Classrooms of Japanese Universities," *Applied Linguistics, 34*(3), pp. 325–343 (2013).
12 See Mika Tamura, "The Sound of Silence in Chemistry Lecture" (p. 73) in *Ethnography of Scientific English: Towards the Development of a Curriculum of Scientific Communication for Graduate Students in Japan*, unpublished doctoral dissertation (Kyushu University School of Social and Cultural Studies 2016).
13 Fred E. Anderson (1993), p. 107. With regard to the role of culture in classroom interaction and English-language teaching, readers may also wish to consult Adrian Holliday's edited collection of studies from various countries, *Appropriate Methodology and Social Context* (Cambridge University Press 1994).
14 Ron Scollon and Suzie Wong Scollon, *Nexus Analysis: Discourse and the Emerging Internet* (Routledge 2004), p. 13. Scollon and Scollon mention that in their own work they actually prefer the philosopher Kitarō Nishida's term "historical body" to refer to this phenomenon, because "it situates bodily memories more precisely in the individual body." Habitus, however, seems more generally applicable to cross-cultural studies such as the present chapter.
15 Danish sociolinguist Karen Risager, in her book *Language and Culture: Global Flows and Local Complexity* (Multilingual Matters 2006), presents a related take on the non-congruent relation between language and culture, arguing that "languages spread across cultures and cultures spread across languages." Belgian linguist Jan Blommaert, in *The Sociolinguistics of Globalization* (Cambridge University Press 2010), similarly argues for a "sociolinguistics of mobility" focusing on "language-in-motion" to counteract the traditional view of languages and cultures being bound in space and time.

15 Creating engagement and motivation in the Japanese university language classroom

Bill Snyder

Many English teachers who come to Japan to work in universities bring with them a stereotype of Japanese students as lacking motivation to learn English. At best, these students are dutiful but barely participatory; at worst, they are indifferent to homework and exams, often tardy, or absent altogether. This stereotype is hardly the complete story, but the students who match it are a frequent source of frustration for instructors who wish their students were more active participants in class.

Japanese learners and motivation: what are the facts?

Many Japanese students do come to university reporting low motivation to study English. Their English classes in high school have demotivated them through emphasis on preparation for entrance examinations.[1] The focus on learning grammar rather than communicative use of language has left many feeling English is only for achieving high test scores. Students who do not achieve those high scores feel their time studying English has been wasted. Along with the focus on language form and exam results, teacher-centered instruction and boring materials contribute to students' negative attitudes. In short, English in Japanese high schools is done *to* students, not *with* them.

Students respond with disengagement. One high school teacher I worked with reported her students frequently ate cup noodle or chatted with friends rather than following her instruction. Some students, signaling how truly unimportant English class was for them, voted with their eyelids and slept. Yet when probed more closely, many students acknowledge a continuing interest in learning English. Another teacher polled his students at a low-level high school on whether they ever had any interest in studying English and was surprised to learn that more than 90 percent indicated specific times when they did. But these moments of motivation were unconnected to their classroom experience. Some of these students did try to take advantage of these moments of inspiration but often lacked effective strategies for turning their interest into successful learning.

So, Japanese university students often remain motivated to learn English; they just aren't motivated to study English *in the classroom*. They disengage because that environment has not served their interests in the past. Perhaps, then, the problem teachers face in the university classroom is less building motivation than getting students to re-engage in their classrooms.

Motivation and engagement are not the same

This is good news for teachers because creating engagement in the classroom may be easier than creating motivation (there are fundamental differences between the two).[2] Students' motivations for learning are often deeply personal. The teacher who was surprised to learn how many of his students were at times motivated to study reported a variety of causes that motivated them: one had a family member married to a non-Japanese and he wished to talk with this person; another wanted English in order to participate in gaming communities online; a third was intrigued by the English words she noticed in public places and wanted to know what they meant. Differences in motivation can be found across all the students of a class. We should not assume that our students are motivated only by grades or future jobs, even if they initially say so.

Compared to motivation, engagement is explicitly public, observable to the teacher as she looks around the classroom. The various properties that help create engagement—including, for example, curiosity, interest, and challenge—can be common across students. Because engagement is more visible, it is more accessible to teacher enhancement than motivation. Also, while motivated students may be disengaged in particular environments, students who become engaged in particular environments often become more motivated overall.

Two different theories from psychology offer some insight into how we can create greater engagement in language classrooms. Flow theory[3] holds that certain activity conditions are more likely to result in greater engagement, along with greater desire to persist and to develop greater skills within the activity. These activity conditions include clear goals, immediate feedback, and balance of challenge and skill. Self-determination theory[4] is a humanistic theory of motivation that posits that all people have three basic psychological needs—autonomy, competence, and relatedness—and that when these needs are supported, people are more likely to be intrinsically motivated and more likely to adopt values associated with that support. Taken together, these six conditions provide a roadmap to designing classes that have higher levels of engagement and which will promote greater motivation to learn.

Getting with the "flow" in task design

Flow theory suggests that engagement can be promoted through the proper design of activities, with three major factors being essential: clear goals, appropriate level of challenge, and immediate feedback. For your students, considering these factors in the design of tasks you ask them to carry out can have a strong impact on their level of interest and willingness to engage in learning English. Various forms of task- or project-based language teaching[5] provide ways to bring these factors into the class design.

Rather than mechanical activities, presenting your students with problem-solving tasks[6] that have personal relevance, multiple possible solutions, and a clear communicative goal to achieve, such as writing a plan or making a report, is one of the most effective ways to do this. The personal relevance creates emotional engagement with the task. The multiple possible solutions means that students can't be wrong in their solution as long as it meets task requirements. It is important students know what kind of outcome is expected of them and what they need to produce in order to satisfy your expectations for the task.

It is also important that what your students are asked to do is manageable for them with the linguistic resources they have, that the challenge of the task is well-matched to their skill level. A task that is too difficult for them can increase their anxiety, result in a sense of failure, and lead them to avoid similar activities in the future. Finding tasks exactly at your students' level can be difficult, especially if you have a mixed proficiency classroom. Ideally, your students should be challenged by your tasks but able to complete them with the support provided, whether that be language (words and phrases) to help complete the task; models of the task outcome; or a template or checklist to guide them in their work. They should know what they need to do at all times in the task, and how to use the support you've provided so they can adjust the task to their level, or be able to consult with you for feedback that helps them progress toward the desired outcome.

To you, perhaps, the idea of teaching this way is the norm. But for your Japanese students, it may be very different from their previous experiences. And so, you may find some difficulty initially in getting students to commit to this approach. For this reason, especially at the beginning, you may want to include a wrap-up at the end of tasks, during which you make students aware of what they have accomplished with English, and have them reflect on what they have just learned. Once students see that the tasks are not just fun but also helpful for learning, greater engagement and more aspiration toward achieving course goals should occur.

Self-determination theory and course design

Flow theory provides a way to think about creating engaging tasks, but those tasks take place in the larger context of your language course. In designing your course, building support for the basic needs posited by self-determination theory into your teaching practice and course design will help support the possibilities for engagement in activities. The three components of self-determination theory are autonomy, competence, relatedness.

Supporting autonomy

Japanese university students are coming from teacher-centered high school classrooms where teachers generally have authority over everything that happens in the room and make all pedagogical decisions. High school English teachers could be sources of language for students alongside the textbook but they often teach predominantly in Japanese. The students in their classes have little autonomy and are seldom able to take charge of their own learning. Naturally, many university students expect the same classroom conditions to continue. One step to change this is to practice autonomy-supportive teaching.[7]

Autonomy-supportive teaching involves a number of practices but the foundation that underlies all of them is building a positive teacher–student relationship. I would argue the basis of this relationship is trust. You need to demonstrate that you trust your students to put forth their best effort at the work you ask them to do, and at the same time, show that they can trust you to help them learn and achieve the goals of the class. This mutual trust is built through communication.

One activity that I have all the teachers I work with carry out is asking their students questions, usually a single wh- question, to be anonymously answered at the end of a class meeting. The question can be about anything but should be one that the teacher doesn't know the answer to and that all the students can offer an answer to. Some questions that teachers have asked their students include "What did you learn today?" "What activity that we've done this week helped you learn the most?" "How did you do the homework last night?" "When was your first encounter with English and how did you feel about it?"

What is essential to building trust through communication is the next step in this process. The teacher needs to read student responses and set aside time in the next class to report to the students on what she learned from reading them and how it will affect her teaching. The teacher who asked about student learning from class activities found out that a large number of students felt that a short pronunciation practice activity that he sometimes used as a "filler" really helped them improve their speaking. He acknowledged to students that it was not his favorite activity, which is why he didn't use it often, but because so many students liked it, he would include it more regularly. This simple act of communication can give your students a voice over how they are learning in the classroom, something that they may never have had before. When they see that you have read and responded to what they say, it lets them know that you care about what they think, take their views seriously, and can be trusted by them.

For many Japanese students, autonomy-supportive teaching is unfamiliar, and they may initially be surprised to encounter a teacher who acts like this. They may also think that you do not know how to teach or try to take advantage of what seems like a lack of discipline. Maintaining standards while also maintaining a supportive tone will help students see that autonomy support does not mean that "anything goes." Hopefully, more successful results will convince students that this kind of teaching helps them learn.

Supporting competence

A frequent comment from Japanese students about why they do not participate in class is that they do not feel confident enough in their English. Their lack of confidence is often the result of experience with assessment that has not been transparent or provided them with feedback that allowed them to perceive their own learning. Instead, assessment has often been punitive, focused on showing students what they do not know, especially in comparison to others. A large part of supporting competence involves changing how you assess your students to support learning and create a positive learning environment.

Giving students tasks they can accomplish in class and assessments that let them show what they can do helps build their sense of competence. A transparent assessment system contains no surprises for students and allows them to be reasonably prepared for an assessment. Testing students on material they haven't studied yet (common enough in high school) is unfair to students, and can break trust and derail efforts to engage them. Students should know from the start of class how and when they will be assessed. They should also have rubrics for speaking, writing, and project assessments so that they know how they will be evaluated and what they should prepare for. Reviewing after assessments and providing an answer key can help students see what was expected and what they need to learn from their mistakes.

A classroom with transparent assessments makes learning visible to students and helps them gain confidence in their improving abilities. It is important that students know that you only compare their performance on any assessment mainly to their *own* previous performances, not to other students' performances, as happened to many in high school. When a classroom is less competitive, it can become more collaborative, a community of learners working toward common goals, a point that will be the focus of the next section.

Supporting relatedness

Japanese students have spent many of their high school years in competition with one another for higher class rankings. In high school, it is customary for students in a class to have to compete for a set number of As and Bs that teachers are allowed to allocate per class. This pursuit of high individual performance continues to college entrance exams, where schools place pressure on students to get into highly ranked universities—thus enhancing the reputation of the high school. This competition did little to build community in the classroom, but neither did regular teaching practice, which generally saw students sitting in isolation from one another and working individually on exercises. The students might know each other as "classmates," but they were not formed into a community of learners that could take advantage of their social relationships to become more proficient at English.[8]

In self-determination theory, relatedness refers to people's basic need to interact with others and feel connected to them. You can support a sense of relatedness and community among your students in a number of ways. Building a class identity starts with reducing the competitive approach to education your students were subjected to in high school, and having you and your students get to know one another as people. When I taught in Korea, I developed the habit of having students make nameplates from index cards on the first day. These nameplates would sit on their desks during class so I could call students by name from the first day. I would hand them out and collect them at the start and end of each class so that I learned names quickly. One of my professors in university used a name quiz based on student self-introductions in the second class meeting to get all of his students to know each other's names and something about each other. The quiz, which was deliberately easy ("Who is from Iowa and loves the Rolling Stones?"), counted only for a few points in course grading but enough to convince everyone to take it seriously. Preparing the quiz taught him every student's name and something about her or him. I've continued this practice throughout my entire teaching career and found it works especially well in Japan. Don't forget to include yourself in the community you are building. Along with learning all your students' names and something about *them*, you should let them learn something about *you*.

From this basic knowledge, you can start to build a community by sharing course goals with students and having them think about how they can help each other achieve them. Having students work together on this and on other tasks in class shifts the classroom away from the competitive, teacher-centered model that they are used to and creates possibilities for them to collaborate and become more engaged as a class. A master's student that I worked with in Turkey examined student engagement under different conditions in classes at her university and found that students were most engaged when they worked in pairs or groups and least engaged when the teacher taught to the whole class. (It also helped engagement if they had some choice over what they were doing in their group.) Students working together can manage a task they can't do individually, learn more, and enjoy it more than when just listening to you.

The ultimate goal: a collaborative classroom community

You should design your course and the tasks within it to engage your students as individuals and as a collaborative class learning English together. Doing this will mean ceding some of your authority and responsibilities to students as the course progresses. From the beginning of class, you should talk with your students and entrust them with increasing responsibility for managing the class and their own learning. From taking attendance to (if you are really daring) writing tests and quizzes, students will take responsibilities of self-management seriously in an environment of trust and community. In order to do something like write a test, for example, they will have to have studied the material, right? You, the teacher, retain final responsibility, but students who are supported in being autonomous, who are connected to one another, and who feel confident about their learning can take on more than you (and even they) might have thought possible when you first met them.

Notes

1 Kikuchi, K. *Demotivation in Second Language Acquisition: Insights from Japan* (Multilingual Matters 2015).
2 Reeve, J. "A Self-Determination Theory Perspective on Student Engagement." In S. L. Christenson, A. L. Reschly, & C. Wylie (Eds), *Handbook of Research on Student Engagement* (Springer Science & Business Media 2012), pp. 149–172.
3 Csikszentmihalyi, M. *Finding Flow: The Psychology of Engagement with Everyday Life* (Basic Books 1997).

4 Ryan, R. M., & Deci, E. L. *Self-Determination Theory: Basic Psychological Needs in Motivation, Development, and Wellness* (The Guilford Press 2017).
5 See Dave & Jane Willis' *Doing Task-based Teaching* (Oxford University Press 2007) for more on task-based teaching, and Legutke, M., & Thomas, H. *Process and Experience in the Language Classroom* (Longman 1991) for more on project-based teaching.
6 Chapter 3 of Paul Nation's *What Should Every EFL Teacher Know?* (Compass Media 2013) provides a good guide to designing problem-solving activities.
7 Reeve, J. "Autonomy-supportive Teaching: What It Is, How to Do It." In W. C. Liu, J. C. K. Wang, & R. M. Ryan (Eds), *Building Autonomous Learners: Perspectives from Research and Practice Using Self-Determination Theory* (Springer Science & Business Media 2016), pp. 129–152.
8 For various aspects of community formation, see Dörnyei, Z., & Murphey, T. *Group Dynamics in the Language Classroom* (Cambridge University Press 2003).

16 The Japanese student and the university English teacher

Donna T. Fujimoto

One thing many teachers will agree on is that discussions about students and teaching almost never take place in faculty meetings. However, when teachers get together, stories about what happened (or didn't happen) in their classrooms often crop up in conversations. While an eavesdropper may dismiss these as rants and complaints, actually this type of interaction has some valuable functions: it allows teachers to release stress *and* by relating their experience, they are in essence objectifying the story, making it understandable to a different audience. Oftentimes, the other teachers will say they have experienced exactly the same thing, and simply sharing sympathetic comments can be a boon to the frazzled teacher. In some cases, teachers will share success stories of things that worked in the classroom. This sharing of both positive and negative experiences can be the starting point to explore solutions. This type of outcome could certainly be considered 'informal' professional development.

In this chapter, I would like to share some teacher experiences which can contribute to our informal professional development. The focus will be on helping us understand our students' perspectives, which in turn can help us improve our teaching. It should be noted that the participants in the composite discussions that follow included *both* Japanese and non-Japanese teachers of English. In other words, the teacher voices represented here were not essentializing the Japanese students, but they were talking about real students in their classrooms.

My students are so passive. During class time, they tend to stay silent, or make the most minimum of comments. They look down at their desks because if they make eye contact, then they might be called upon. They hope others will do the talking. I often wonder why they waste time in class when they could be learning so much.

Rather than getting frustrated, it might help to back up and consider what our students' past experience has been. The classroom culture that they have been socialized into during their school years is directly at odds with our teacher expectations. At the elementary school level, lots of noise and individual antics are allowed, but as Japanese children reach the junior and senior high level, the school culture forces students to be more adult-like. They have to face the discipline of studying for important tests, and they learn that more self-control is demanded. The goal is to get 'correct answers,' and compared to individual opinions or guesses, correct answers are limited (there is usually only one). Students certainly do not want to make mistakes in front of everyone, so often the best tactic is to choose silence. Seen from their point of view, maybe we can say they are being practical—even wise.[1]

Yet if you see your quiet students outside of the classroom with their friends, chances are they are talkative and full of energy—you may not even be able to recognize them! Our challenge, then, is to create and then cultivate our own classroom culture where students can be their more natural selves. Where mistakes are accepted as a natural part of everyone's learning. Where speaking is made easy, and where it is valued. Where guessing is encouraged. Where trying to excel is the norm. Keep in mind, though, that changing ingrained behavior is extremely difficult (some would say impossible). However, remember too that as teachers it is incumbent on us to refuse to give up in the face of these long odds. It takes time to build up that classroom culture. We must keep chipping away.

Believe me I've tried all kinds of things. I want my students to just communicate! I've tried games that are fun, games that are competitive, activities that require movement, real-life tasks, silly riddles, humorous quizzes—you name it.

It's commendable that we are trying to be creative, but one note of caution is that our students do not see those types of activities as being serious enough. It's been drilled into them that English is very, very important, so it cannot possibly be fun. In their previous classes, English was the *object* of study, NOT the means of communication. English study meant rote memorization, translating isolated sentences, focusing on targeted grammar points, and speaking in class only when called upon. The problem is that what we are trying to teach and what our students have experienced are two mutually exclusive endeavors, yet *both* are called English. To be completely fair, then, can we really blame our students for not making the giant leap from their past English classes to our "creative" activities where active participation is expected? It may be our responsibility, then, to help our students navigate this giant gap between English-to-use and English-to-pass-tests.

Also, when introducing something new, it is important to prepare the class very well beforehand. Some of my best ideas faltered because I didn't spell out step by step exactly what the students were supposed to do. Upon reflection, I realized that my students were not used to non-routines, and they got confused easily. From my viewpoint, giving very detailed steps is virtually the same as too much hand-holding. I now realize that this "hand-holding" represents *my* bias. If my students need this extra help for the activity to be successful, then I have to admit that I have to provide it. If it takes too much time, I will have to decide if the benefits of the activity will outweigh the time needed. Perhaps I need to reconsider and see that hand-holding is an important introductory step to a new activity.

In front of the class, I feel I'm like a 'performer.' In order to get the class going, I practically have to stand on my head! My teacher education courses didn't prepare me for that!

True, many of us have been there. When we think about it, it is logical that we would end up performing. I think we are doing several things at once: we are trying to get the whole group's attention, and then keep each student's attention in order to carry out our lesson. We are oftentimes playing to different levels among the students—some can understand much of what we are saying, while others may understand practically nothing, so they are carefully watching our body language to try to understand us. Getting every student's attention is all-important to carry out a lesson.

On the whole, students *like* this type of arrangement. The focus is on the teacher and not on *them*. It also seems that they enjoy these teacher performances and reward us by looking interested (even though they may not always laugh at our jokes!). If we're not careful, we can get too used to performing on the stage as it may be easier than 'teaching'. . . it can be addicting.

I don't want to sound judgmental, but I actually know teachers who really don't 'teach.' Some perform, but others aren't even entertaining—they just do ALL the talking, even in what are supposed to be discussion classes. Frankly, it bothers me because here I am working so hard, and these others get away with this time after time.

It's true. There are all kinds of teachers and, unfortunately, unless we are in a more powerful position, we don't have much influence as far as who gets hired. Universities and colleges are required to have student evaluations, so perhaps students can have some influence. Well, on second thought, those evaluations are rarely used by administrators for quality control—they are mostly a required ritual and peripherally directed to teachers to show them how they compare to the other teaching staff. When applying for new work, however, some employers will ask to see a few years' worth of a teacher's student evaluations, so like them or not, it is important to hold on to them if you are considering changing jobs. These evaluations can also be particularly important for part-time and adjunct teachers in being re-contracted.[2]

Why do many students assume that having a foreign teacher is better for English classes than a Japanese teacher?

It's not just students. It is administrators and other teachers. This stereotyping is especially unfortunate for well-qualified Japanese teachers of English. Their pay is sometimes lower; they are not always assigned to the classes where they can be the most effective; and their expertise is not considered. Having had to learn English just like their students, they often have good insight into the difficulties that students face and how to surmount them. They are typecast by simply being Japanese! This is an issue that is completely invisible here in Japan to the detriment of us all.[3]

As is well known here, the stereotypical idealized foreigner (*gaikokujin*) is blond and blue-eyed, while the reality is that the non-Japanese teachers who are currently teaching are a widely diverse group. Take my personal experience. As a Japanese–American born and raised in the U.S. and trained in language teaching, I have learned (retrospectively) that for almost every English teaching job that I have been interviewed for, the issue has come up in the search committee as to whether my ethnicity would be an issue for the students or the school. For the school, PR brochures with photos of the idealized teachers are a high priority, and it is important to make their school look 'international.' This is rarely expressed directly, but decisions are made tacitly and under the usual radar.

Many years ago, I was told by a friend that I was turned down for a position even though the school needed to fill the position and I was well qualified. She said she was shocked that despite the fact that she had highly recommended me, the man in charge selected someone who did not actually have proper credentials. These kinds of stories of how appearance outweighs qualifications are sadly all too numerous. It was not only appearance, however. Apparently in the interview I came across as too self-assured and too direct (I was told later). I did not fit the proper norm of "a Japanese woman" even though I wasn't one. So it seems that not only appearance, but also behavior can make a difference.

With regard to students, some have actually registered disappointment when they saw that I was going to be their English teacher. I tried not to hold this against them as I knew this simply reveals that they have had little experience meeting different kinds of *gaijin* teachers. On a happy note, these students accepted and liked the fact that I was their teacher after I shared a bit of my biography and after a number of lessons. However, to illustrate the persistence of their belief system, they still asked me if I was *haafu* ('half' or someone of biracial, mixed heritage), even though they had been told I was *nikkei sansei*, a third-generation Japanese American. As is often the case, appearance overpowers the facts.

Why do students (and institutions) want a native speaker of English for their English teacher?

As mentioned before, this kind of thinking reflects a biased and a stereotypical view. In truth, it is based on a fallacy—"the native speaker fallacy."[4] Just because a person's mother tongue is English does not automatically mean she or he will be a good teacher. What is important is credentials and good teacher education. Many non-native teachers are as qualified as the trained native English-speaking teacher, and quite a number of them are even more qualified because in order to be accepted as a professional, they know they have to work several times harder. Kramsch points out that the native speaker has been idealized, and no one speaks an idealized standardized English.[5] As we become more aware of the multi-cultural diversity of teachers, we can see that it is not a simple dichotomy. Teachers around the world are raising (and finding) their voices to challenge the existing system[6] and to acknowledge the rich variety of world Englishes. Unfortunately, it may take some time for this shift in thinking to be fully accepted here in Japan.

Turning back to our students and our frustrations—why are there are so many absences for club activities, job hunting, and other extracurricular activities? Why does the school administration seem to allow this? How should we handle this?

The reality is that this situation is not just a pedagogical issue, but also a political and economic one. According to McVeigh, higher education in Japan has been greatly influenced by rapid modernization and the needs of the state and its corporations. He claims that "the boundary between education/schooling and employment/economics is blurred."[7] It is well known that companies do not place a high priority on what their new workers have achieved at the university because through the initial company training process, the new employees will be socialized into the company's work culture. This is another reason why our students in their last year of study may be absent numerous times—because of their new employer's schedule. And students, who have still not landed a job officially but who need to take the long view of their future, will naturally prioritize job interviews and *"setsumeikai"* (company explanatory briefings) over class attendance.

University administrations handle this situation differently. Generally, though, there is no written rule telling teachers to excuse these absences and, when asked, the administration often says that it is up to the teacher how to deal with this. However, it becomes quite clear when at the end of the term, there might be a call from the office asking about a student's failing grade and requesting an additional report or a test. Numerous English teachers have been either explicitly or implicitly encouraged to pass a student despite their poor record. Teachers complain that this goes against their 'principles,' and this causes frustration when they feel that they have been forced to trample on their idea of fairness. It seems, though, that those who remain in the system eventually succumb to the more powerful cultural force of *shikata ga nai*, "It can't be helped."

Some students have tried to explain away their poor performance in pairs or groups due to the fact that they didn't know their partners. To me this is totally unrelated and NOT a legitimate excuse.

Actually, there is a possible cultural explanation. Though it is a generalization, there is some truth to the idea that Japanese culture rates high on the uncertainty avoidance index,[8] where people feel threatened or uncomfortable in unknown or ambiguous situations. The tendency is to stay with the known and to depend on familiar structure. A corollary to this is risk avoidance, which also explains why students suffer from "excessive self monitoring [which] inhibits academic ability," as anthropologist Brian McVeigh notes.[9] While being aware of student beliefs, I try to prove them wrong, and to that end, many students have thanked me for having made new friends. They should congratulate themselves and not thank me!

I like teaching, but to be honest, there are days when I feel like I am really not doing a good job. I'm just a highly paid babysitter. Also, other people I know have way too many students and so many different duties that they have given up on even trying to do their best.

The duties of English teachers vary greatly. Those who are tenured or have full-time contract positions often have faculty meetings, committee work, advisees, and other duties in addition to their teaching load. Part-time teachers are usually only responsible for their teaching hours; however, in order to make a living, many of them have to work at several schools and must spend a great deal of time commuting. They usually do not have benefits, such as research funds, university-sponsored health insurance, salary bonuses, and so on, and they cannot count on a secure schedule every year. Worry and burnout are common complaints from many teachers.

Get involved and stay engaged

As in any job, there are ways to deal with these strains, but I think English teachers in Japan are fortunate because there are positive ways to cope. Compared to several decades ago when English teachers were rather isolated, now there are many organizations that offer workshops, lectures, conferences and, most importantly, the opportunity to interact with other teachers. Getting involved is easy because there is a huge array of different interests to choose from, such as academic and research work, practical teaching approaches, further education, social justice, personal development, and even finding the next job. (See some suggestions in Appendix 1.) I highly recommend joining professional organizations because getting involved will provide different and often unexpected perspectives, which can change the entire way that we look at and experience our teaching. Yes, informal talks with friends are extremely useful (like those over a cup of coffee or during lunch), yet getting involved in an organization offers a richer form of professional development. This not only helps the individual teacher, but also the profession as a whole.

Notes

1 In this *Handbook*, Chapter 14, "Nails that still don't stick up: revisiting the enigma of the Japanese college classroom," and Chapter 15, "Creating engagement and motivation in the Japanese university language classroom," explore in detail the classroom culture and teaching styles that Japanese university students have experienced during primary and secondary education, and how these have influenced the communication styles and learning attitudes they have in college.
2 See Chapter 3 in this *Handbook*, "The *ronin* teacher: making a living as a full-time part-timer at Japanese universities."
3 See Chapter 19 in this *Handbook*, "The Japanese university teacher of English," to learn more about their experiences.
4 See Robert Phillipson's *Linguistic Imperialism* (Oxford University Press 1992) for the origin of the native-speaker fallacy.
5 See Claire Kramsch's "The Privilege of the Non-native Speaker." *PMLA*, 112, 359–369, 1997.
6 In particular, see George Braine's *Non-native Educators in English Language Teaching* (Lawrence Erlbaum 1999), as well as Chapter 20 in this *Handbook*, "Beyond the native speaker fallacy: internationalizing English-language teaching at Japanese universities."
7 McVeigh, B. *Japanese Higher Education as Myth* (M.E. Sharpe Inc 2002), p. 10.
8 See Geert Hofstede's *Cultures and Organizations: Software of the Mind* (McGraw-Hill 1991).
9 See Brian J. McVeigh's provocative book *Japanese Higher Education as Myth* (M.E. Sharpe Inc 2002), p. 23.

17 English language policy in Japan and the Ministry of Education (MEXT)

Emphasis, trends, and changes that affect higher education

Paul R. Underwood and
Gregory Paul Glasgow

Standing in front of neat rows of students in a freshman English class, instructors can anticipate two things: one, despite having studied English in junior and senior high school for a minimum of around 500 class hours over the past six years,[1] communicating in English will be a challenge for students; and two, although some will be able to speak English, they'll likely be reluctant to actually speak out in class—"nails that don't want to stick up" as some educators have observed. We can all, of course, recall a freshman class that has pleasantly surprised us, but for the majority of university language instructors, the scenario described here has been the longstanding reality.[2]

Educational policy in Japan, however, has been far from static. The skill and motivation levels that we can expect of freshman students today exceed—in curricular comparisons at least—what could have been expected fewer than ten years ago. And Japan's MEXT (Ministry of Education, Culture, Sports, Science and Technology) intends to raise the bar for English education even higher in forthcoming revisions to the national curriculum. This chapter aims to orient both new and more seasoned university instructors to where their students have come from in the past, where they might be heading in the near future, and the obstacles that remain in their path.

Schooling in Japan and the national curriculum for English

The school system

Compulsory education in Japan begins with elementary school (Grades 1 to 6) from the age of six and continues through to junior high school (Grades 7 to 9), ending at the age of 15. Senior high school (Grades 10 to 12) is not compulsory but almost all students attend. At present, approximately half of all senior high school graduates continue to a four-year university.

Most senior high schools are either vocational, offering specialized courses such as industry and commerce, or academic, providing general courses in preparation for university education. Approximately three quarters of schools are publicly funded by municipalities and prefectures, and one quarter are financed by a combination of private funds and government subsidies.

Funding is one way to account for the differences in English abilities that university instructors encounter in their classes. Given their sources of independent funding, private primary and secondary schools have greater curricular freedom. They often devote substantially more hours to English, some with English-intensive departments and even study-abroad experiences. An additional explanation for uneven English preparation and proficiency is the after-hours tutoring some students receive. One recent study found that after their normal school day ends, about 53% of the public junior high and about 20% of public senior high students reported studying intensively at *juku* (college preparatory and cram schools).[3]

The national curriculum and MEXT policy

All elementary, junior, and senior high schools in Japan provide compulsory English in MEXT's national curriculum, the "Course of Study" (*Gakushuu shidou youryou*). With input from a range of experts in the academic community and in consultation with the public, the curriculum is revised approximately every ten years and then phased in, starting with elementary schools.

English instruction in Japanese elementary schools has a very short history, unlike South Korea where it has been compulsory since 1997 and China where it was mandated starting in 2001. Under Japan's Course of Study 2009, "foreign language activities"—which basically means English speaking and listening activities—became compulsory for Grades 5 and 6 from 2011. Under the revisions, English is a mandatory school subject for these grades, and foreign language activities are compulsory for Grades 3 and 4.

English classes became required in senior high schools only in 1989 and in junior high schools from 1999 (though most schools had some form of foreign language education, mostly English). Through integrated-skills courses, the situational, notional–functional syllabus aims to develop communicative ability, a positive attitude toward foreign languages, and a deeper understanding of culture. The Japan Exchange and Teaching (JET) program employs native-English-speaking teachers (Assistant Language Teachers or "ALTs") in most public high schools to help with this curriculum. While junior and senior high school courses both focus on interpersonal communicative abilities, senior high electives emphasize English for academic purposes, including "presentation" and "debate." Here, students are expected to draw on the critical thinking skills developed through other curriculum subjects. Another important emphasis is that teachers should not focus on explaining grammar. Instead, grammar teaching should support activities in which students actually communicate. In this way, MEXT is attempting to steer teachers away from "traditional" grammar-translation methodology (*yakudoku*), which has had a prominent—though not exclusive—place in English instruction since the Meiji Era. Since 2013, senior high school English teachers have also been expected, in principle, to teach courses largely in and through English, which extends to junior high schools under new revisions. In a recent national survey by MEXT, an increasing number of public senior high school teachers reported speaking in English for more than half of their class.[4]

Recognizing the importance of English in a rapidly globalizing society, in 2014 MEXT announced its *English Education Reform Plan Corresponding to Globalization*. In the same year, it launched a five-year Super Global High School Program for 56 schools in 32 prefectures across Japan.[5] In partnership with corporations, international organizations, NPOs, and domestic universities, the mandate for these schools is to develop and implement curricula that hone students' communicative and problem-solving abilities, with the ultimate goal of producing leaders who can succeed on various "international stages." Yet, with this program focused on only approximately 1% of Japan's senior high schools, it is reasonable to be skeptical of its broader influence.

Those who see their glass of *sake* as half empty would also refer to Japan's consistently poor track record on the TOEFL iBT.[6] In 2016, Japan was considerably outperformed by North Korea; of 31 Asian countries, it ranked bottom in the speaking section of the exam (South Korea ranked 7th and China 12th overall.) The optimistic among us would point to MEXT's 2016 CAN-DO survey. This reports a substantial increase over the last four years in public senior high school students' perceived ability to use English. Moreover, their actual performance on the four-skill *Eiken* Pre-2nd Grade Test shows steady, albeit slow, improvement during this period. Such surveys and tests are often used by the Japanese government as a measure of curricular and policy achievement. Clearly, though, it is premature for MEXT to be toasting its achievements in raising the level of English skill, and significant obstacles remain to English language competence.

The high-stakes nature of schooling

Of the present 781 four-year universities in Japan, 86 are national, 92 public, and 603 private. Admission procedures for many universities have diversified over the last 20 years. *Juken jigoku* is the "entrance examination hell" senior high school students go through to make it to university. Currently, the admissions process begins in January with the first-stage national Center Test, widely known as the *Senta Shiken*, which contains 30 tests in six subjects. The English test includes a reading and a listening section. At present, approximately 89% of four-year universities use the *Senta* as a requirement of admission,[7] although there are other exams universities can use either instead of or in addition to the *Senta*. In late January or February, for example, a second-stage examination is normally administered by individual institutions, called the *ippan nyuushi*. The content, construction, and administration of second-stage examinations are entirely under the control of individual institutions, and as universities charge students to take their own tests, these have become important moneymakers for cash-strapped schools. The number of individual second-stage examinations administered yearly is certainly in excess of 1,000, as many faculties or departments even within a single university offer separate examinations, and students must take these to apply to different faculties (humanities versus law) within the same university.

A smaller number of students are often accepted through a "recommendation" system called *suisen*, in which a university saves a certain number of seats for, in principle, the top students of particular high schools. The *suisen* allows a select number of students to be accepted to universities without having to take their regular entrance exams, although *suisen* usually involves other types of assessments, such as interviews, essays, or both.

To better their chances of passing the examinations of top universities, most high school students attend rigorous after-school tutoring in private college preparatory institutes called *juku*. And despite communicative curriculum mandates to the contrary, during the day their high school teachers continue to "teach" to these examinations, with grammar translation being the primary tool of the trade.

Challenges and change

This contradiction between national curricular directives and teaching practice is ironic given that high school English teachers actually view communicative approaches positively. Yet, when it comes to classroom implementation, there are numerous challenges facing teachers. A major one is lack of training. Prospective English teachers in Japan complete a stringent pre-service education program, including a highly competitive examination and a teaching practicum. The content and quality of teacher training varies and does not ensure that prospective teachers gain the pedagogical skill to teach the curriculum (i.e., teaching English through English, managing pair and group work, and integrating grammar teaching with communicative tasks). Once on the job, in-service training to guide teachers is sporadic, which means they often end up fending for themselves.

Teachers also face difficulties with large class sizes, student passivity, low student motivation, low English language proficiency—their students' and their own—poor critical thinking skills, difficult-to-use ministry-approved textbooks, and unsupportive colleagues. It should be noted that Japanese teachers work substantially more hours than those in any other OECD country, reporting the heavy load of administrative and extracurricular duties as an impediment to lesson planning. Such duties are especially onerous for English teachers, who have a significantly higher workload due to the centrality of English in entrance examinations. In academic senior high schools where the de facto goal is preparing students to succeed on examinations that emphasize reading skills, school administrators prioritize resources, including teachers' time, to this end.

MEXT has been making several concrete efforts to overcome these shortcomings. One is the introduction of a teacher license renewal system in 2009, which requires 30 hours of professional development every ten years. The establishment of the National Center for Teachers' Development in 2015 provides school-management training and promotes problem-solving and collaboration among teachers.

Changes to the university examination system are also in the works and may have a significant impact on English-language learning and language testing. In 2023, the

English component of the Center Test will be discontinued. In its place, universities will be encouraged to accept scores from four-skill certification examinations (such as the TEAP, Eiken, TOEFL iBT, and IELTS) as part of a wider range of admission procedures. Japan's 86 national universities have already decided to adopt this system from 2020. A new focus on these kinds of examinations will certainly provide a much-needed incentive for high schools to redirect their resources towards promoting the productive skills of speaking and writing, in addition to the current focus on grammar, listening, and reading.

However, one obstacle to MEXT's Masterplan remains. Approximately 77% of Japan's universities are privately run and receive substantial revenue from creating and administering their own second-stage entrance examinations—exams that largely emphasize reading and grammar. Although the examinations of many of the top schools are changing and more universities are starting to use certification examinations for admission, it's highly unlikely the vast majority will take up this practice anytime soon. So a disconnect will likely persist between the English objectives of the national curriculum and actual teaching in high schools oriented towards entrance exams.

Policy initiatives in Japanese higher education

There is no formal continuity between high school and university curricula stipulated by MEXT, so university instruction does not begin where high school courses end. In general, freshman students are required to take 90 hours of English in total to graduate (equivalent to two 90-minute classes a week for two semesters of 15 weeks each), though many universities require English study during sophomore year, too, and offer further electives for juniors and seniors.[8]

Faced with external pressure to improve the standing of Japanese universities on the world stage, the Top Global University Project was initiated in 2014. The 37 universities selected make up two principal groups. The first is the *Type A* "Top Type"—13 universities seen as having the potential to rank in the top 100 global universities, meaning that an emphasis should be placed on research output (mainly in the "hard" sciences). The second *Type B* "Global Traction Type" consists of 24 universities that are expected to make their institutions more internationally appealing by increasing content courses in English, attracting international students, and increasing foreign faculty positions. The *Type B* universities also make greater use of four-skill certification examinations in the admissions process.

Challenges to an era of "internationalization"

In spite of the policy rhetoric surrounding the "internationalization" of higher education in Japan, the 37 institutions selected for the Top Global University Project represent less than 5% of the nation's universities overall, so the broader impact of the project's initiatives on higher education across Japan may seem at first glance to be minimal. However, the selected universities tend to already be the top "movers and shakers" of Japanese higher education, and, as has always been the case, other universities are expected to emulate the changes they make. Yet key questions remain at the classroom level. The challenges facing MEXT in implementing its high school curriculum are leaving students at a disadvantage when it comes to their English proficiency upon entry to university, especially in terms of the productive skills. For instance, given the focus of students' language study in high school, they and their university teachers face significant challenges in engaging in discussion and writing activities that in addition integrate critical thinking skills. What's more, the English-medium programs in Japanese universities vary widely from *ad hoc* courses to entire undergraduate degrees offered in English, making it difficult to design high school curricula that can prepare students for the various types of English programs they are likely to encounter at university.[9]

The challenges Japanese learners face are not limited to language proficiency problems alone. In one particular Global Traction Type university, where one of the authors teaches an "Intercultural Exchange" course, Japanese sophomores who major in Intercultural Communication prepare themselves for a mandatory trip to study abroad by taking classes alongside international students. Some of these Japanese students struggle to get their ideas across, but many of them also find it difficult to overcome "the wall of silence" between themselves and foreign students because of their cultural inhibitions to speak up in classroom settings. Students taking content courses in English may not only suffer from poor language abilities but also a lack of intercultural awareness. If universities want such courses to work, they must "walk the talk," face up to this reality, and come up with curriculum plans that "internationalize" not only through rhetoric but also through action. For example, they could supplement the curriculum with intercultural communication seminars, courses that focus on college life planning, or encourage third- or fourth-year students who have already studied abroad to give talks, sharing their experiences with first-year students and advising them on what to expect.

Castles built on . . . ?

Certainly, the gaps between policy and practice at the high school level are significant and far from being reconciled. So, do the more progressive trends highlighted here merely represent castles built on sand? For now, yes. The wheels of change turn slowly in Japan, yet the policy efforts we have described in this chapter are driving institutions and teachers at all levels of education out of their comfort zones and into uncharted territory. The global competition Japanese businesses face—largely in an English-language environment—is also pushing policy. Ultimately, English-education in Japan has been found wanting, and so "education as usual" can no longer be an option.

Notes

1 In junior high schools, English is a four-skill course with 420 class hours across three years. In senior high schools, the required four-skill course, English Communication I, is three credits and amounts to approximately 87 hours. Schools are allowed to exercise flexibility in awarding fewer or more credits/hours for English Communication I. Most senior high schools also offer many more additional elective courses.
2 See Chapter 14, "Nails that still don't stick up: revisiting the enigma of the Japanese college classroom," in this *Handbook* for an in-depth discussion of the interaction patterns and cultural dynamics underlying the pragmatics of the university classroom.
3 For further details see 青少年の体験活動等に関する実態調査(平成26年度調査) by the National Institution for Youth Education (2016), p. 133, Q11–13.
4 平成28年度英語教育実施状況調査(高等学校)の結果 (MEXT 2016).
5 MEXT has invested heavily in this program with annual budgets amounting to 2 billion yen.
6 The validity of ranking countries according to their TOEFL iBT scores does not stand up to empirical scrutiny, but given the economic resources at Japan's disposal, some comparisons can be permitted. One reason that Japanese students as a whole score so low on the test is that a far larger portion of the population takes the test (in contrast to North Korea and even China), and their average score suffers a regression to the mean. In other measures such as the EF English Proficiency Index, Japan also ranks low, but here, too, issues with unrepresentative sampling have been reported.
7 "平成30年度大学入試センター試験参加大学・短期大学数について" (独立行政法人大学入試センター December 2017).
8 Information on credit requirements for English courses in Japanese universities is difficult to track down. Hajime Terauchi provides some details in his chapter in Eun Sung Park and Bernard Spolsky's (Eds) *English Education at the Tertiary Level in Asia: From Policy to Practice* (Routledge 2017), pp. 65–84.
9 See Howard Brown & Bethany Iyobe's (2014) "The Growth of English Medium Instruction in Japan" in Sonda & Krause (Eds) *JALT2013 Conference Proceedings* for further information on issues regarding English as a medium of instruction in the Japanese university context.

Part 4
The workplace

18 "He said, she said"
Female and male dynamics in Japanese universities

Diane Hawley Nagatomo and Melodie Cook

Background: a striking imbalance

In 2015, only 23.2% of the 182,723 full-time and 29.8% of the 196,623 part-time positions in Japanese universities were held by women. Non-Japanese teachers[1] comprised 5.4% of all university teachers and 32% of these were foreign women.[2] One common explanation for this 3 to 1 gender imbalance is that there are more western men than western women in Japan, particularly those married to Japanese nationals, who become university English teachers. However, there are in fact many western women, also with Japanese spouses, who wish to forge careers in Japanese higher education.[3]

The overriding questions guiding this chapter are, how do the experiences of foreign female and male university English teachers in Japan differ and how do these differences shape their careers? To answer these questions, we draw on data from a recent survey of 171 non-Japanese university teachers (83 men and 88 women) and our discussion extrapolates from five of the survey's optional open-ended questions on harassment, career development, and difficulties in balancing professional and family life.[4]

Harassment

After the first successful academic harassment lawsuit in Japan in 1998, others followed. Complaints included being denied first authorship on papers, withholding of research funds, and being gossiped about in a sexually inappropriate manner.[5] In 1999, sexual harassment (unwanted sexual behavior disadvantaging an employee) and hostile environment sexual harassment (an intimidating or offensive work environment) were added to the Equal Opportunity Law.[6]

In the survey, many respondents blurred the line between sexual and academic harassment, and so these two issues will be discussed together in this section. Harassment wasn't experienced or witnessed by everyone. For example, a recent arrival said he was "too new to notice." Long-termers, however, particularly those with insider perspectives as tenured faculty, had numerous stories to tell. Back in what some called the "old days," sexual harassment was openly tolerated. One woman had heard stories from students "about a [now retired] certain full-time professor," and despite attempts to report him, nothing was ever done. One man described a similar situation where early in his career "male teachers made laughing references to [one professor's] apparently notorious conduct."

Sexual harassment reported by the survey participants was mainly verbal, although two men said they had been stalked by female colleagues. One of the stalkers later publicly dismissed the importance of the man's work, his career, and his qualifications. For the most part, however, sexual harassment involved offensive language and inappropriate questions from students and colleagues. Examples included "belittling younger female foreign colleagues," "being treated dismissively," "being portrayed as emotional," "verbal comments on stereotypes of women as jokes by male colleagues," and "comments about appearance." One woman labeled such behavior as merely annoying, but another endured harassment that was systematic and persistent. She wrote,

> In my previous workplace I was the only female teacher in a shared office with five full time teachers and a handful of part time teachers. I routinely had to listen to comments about my hobby (yoga) being sexual and how seeing a woman doing yoga made them feel. One or two of my male colleagues would also routinely give me lewd looks and tell me I looked sexy. This made me feel uncomfortable, but since there was no physical contact there was nothing I could do about it. (F)

She was not alone in feeling powerless. Women who filed complaints about harassment reported being ridiculed for taking what some male colleagues believed to be "inappropriate and unproductive" actions.[7] Even the head of a language institute in a prominent Tokyo university was unable to stop the "pervasive sexism by a minority of [foreign male instructors] which had reached the level of misogyny."[8] Fiona Creasor, a harassment specialist, maintains that universities are aware that harassment exists but hesitate to establish policies because they are afraid of being "inundated with complaints." Yet even when harassment policies are established, unless they are enforced, people often "suffer in silence," like the woman above.

The survey suggests the situation may be improving, however. As one woman wrote, sexual harassment incidents were taken seriously in her university, and teachers had been fired "for text stalking a female student" and "for repeated touching of female students." Another colleague had been "reprimanded for inappropriate touching of a female colleague."

Power harassment, according to a working group established by the Japanese Ministry of Health, Labor, and Welfare in 2011, includes issues such as physical assault, intimidation, isolation, forcing employees to perform menial tasks, and invasion of privacy.[9] The survey respondents also complained of similar issues, such as being excluded from workplace information, being required to work outside the scope of employment contracts, not being given teaching autonomy by those in power, and being caught in the middle of workplace political factions.

It included bullying, hurling insults, denigrating or appropriating someone else's ideas, shouting, and making subtle and not-so-subtle threats about contract renewal. In fact, one man left a tenured position after suffering from such actions.

Harassment was also seen as "subtle racism," particularly by the men. One wrote, "In my early years, the chair of the department would often get drunk and confess to me that he detested white people . . . even in the midst of hiring white teachers." Non-Japanese teachers, regardless of their national culture or origin, were lumped together and segregated from Japanese staff. This, he argued, contributed to an overall negative atmosphere. Another reported being forced to rehearse a university-sponsored workshop before an administrator multiple times, but no Japanese teacher had been asked to do so. And yet another complained of being held to different standards than Japanese colleagues, and this delayed his promotion.

Among the harassers cited in the survey were Japanese colleagues, male colleagues, older female professors, tenured and full-time staff (including women), and administrators. Interestingly, men seemed to accept harassment as "institutionalized bullying in Japan" which was "a normal part of Japanese systems." As one man wrote, "It would be hard to imagine a Japanese workplace where power harassment isn't happening on some level, conscious or unconscious."

Career development

Some women respondents to the survey believed their gender made "no difference" and that they had been "incredibly lucky" with "good opportunities." As one woman wrote, "My being female had nothing to do with it as far as I'm concerned." However, the majority of women who responded to the questionnaire felt that their professional experiences differed significantly from men's. When it came to job hunting and career advancement, they believed that men were often given priority. One said she had been "passed over for a full-time job in favor of a man, who was less committed to the job" than she was. Many women felt they had to work harder than their male counterparts but received less respect from colleagues and administrators.

Some women felt that men were taken seriously as "breadwinners," but they were perceived as working merely for "pocket money."[10] One woman's married brother, for instance, "only had a BA but no publications or teaching qualifications," yet his take-home salary was higher. And while he was provided with housing, she was not. In other words, marriage for men is seen to enhance their careers, but marriage for women appears to do the opposite. One woman complained that people assumed she didn't work hard because she was a mother, and yet she had never missed a day of work.

Both men and women agreed that such attitudes helped men but held women back. They also stated that these attitudes were rooted in Japanese culture where traditionally gender roles are firmly divided and strictly enforced. The men knew that they were perceived as being likely to put work before family. They agreed that this wasn't fair, but they accepted the benefits this brought them without too much fuss. As one man explained, his colleagues in "an overwhelmingly male department," had "no interest in gender balance."

The men also felt they were more likable. The following comment, where one wryly accepts his gendered advantage, succinctly sums up what many of the men and women observed. He wrote, "I am relatively young, I'm certainly not ugly, I have blue eyes and I'm a bloke. To deny that all these things have helped me in this country would be remarkably short-sighted."

However, both the survey results and recent hiring trends suggest that times are changing and men are not given automatic priority over women in Japanese universities anymore. Institutions are actively recruiting more women. While such moves were generally viewed positively, some women reported feeling like tokens gathered to correct the gender imbalance, as illustrated in the following: "I feel like I'm there sometimes to make up the numbers and not really taken seriously." While many of the men supported these measures, some had mixed feelings, calling it "bias" or "reverse discrimination." For example, one man said he lost job opportunities because "a woman was preferred to fill the position." Another said such measures, which he believed disadvantaged more qualified job applicants, were simply unfair. He wrote,

> I know of many jobs looking for women and turning down men of higher qualifications. I don't disagree as we need more women teachers for role models, but still being turned down for a job based solely on your sex does rub me the wrong way.

Balancing family and work

The final issue we wish to address is differences in how men and women balance their personal and professional lives, in reality and as suggested by the survey. All those with families said they had difficulties, but for different reasons. Most of the women were married to Japanese salaried workers. Unlike their male counterparts who often have "supportive Japanese wives," they shouldered the bulk of household and family responsibilities. One woman stated that her professional and personal life "blur into each other so I feel I never have a day off." The following comment by a different woman was fairly representative of others:

> During the semester, I am barely keeping up with laundry, housework and shopping. My husband has to help out more, but he is barely at home. Still, most of the responsibilities of childcare, after-school lessons, family finances, shopping, cooking, etc. falls to me no matter what is going on with my career.

Many women felt overwhelmed in trying to balance work and family, and this led to feelings of guilt. One felt she was "shortchanging" her career by giving presentations instead of publishing papers in order to have more time with her children. She felt guilty for not being fully present for her children *and* for leaving work early to pick them up from daycare or missing work when they were ill. Many women said they had put their careers on hold, finding the freedom to pursue doctorates or engage in research only after children were older.

The men believed they made sacrifices, too. But they also admitted having good support systems at home. A few workplaces were supportive of the men as they tried to balance their personal and professional life. One man's university relieved him of administrative duties when his children were small and another professor occasionally brought his children to work with him. Another said he didn't teach the last period of the day because he needed to rush home to take care of children since his working Japanese wife came home later than he did.

However, the majority of the men considered themselves breadwinners in the traditional sense, and they felt compelled (or were compelled) to follow the Japanese male work ethic. For instance, one man said he had no choice but to "come in on weekends and stay late for meetings [because] family concerns are never a priority [for the university]." Another wrote, "Our university expects us to be workaholics while paying lip service to the need to maintain a proper work-life balance. We were admonished to work considerably longer. Apparently nine hours is too lax."

Many such men regret putting teaching, studying, researching, and attending conferences ahead of their families. As one professor observed,

> The writing of academic papers is very intensive, keeps me away from my family, as does doing the PhD (going back to UK often for tutorials etc.) and attending conferences. Furthermore, I work night classes for extra money. Often my boy is in bed when I get back. I have tried to be more mindful of this and I am around as much as I can be.

Perhaps the most striking difference between the lives of working mothers and fathers is found in the following comment. Unlike many of the women, who reported daily struggles juggling their work and family, this man felt he had a "rough" time caused by *one* stolen afternoon with his son:

> It's always a challenge, especially when facing deadlines for research projects or other school duties. I try my best to keep things separated, but that's not always possible. Things bottle up sometimes, and I have to spend evenings and weekends focused on work. My kids are young and growing fast, so I'm mindful of the importance of not overdoing it with work. Just the other day I had a pile of things to do, so instead I took the afternoon off and went to see a movie with my son on his last day of spring vacation. We had a great time, and although I had a rough day yesterday catching up, I didn't mind because I knew I had made the correct decision.

Conclusion

While there is still a long way to go to correct the gender imbalance among teachers in Japanese higher education, we feel the outlook is positive. Both men and women face challenging issues. Many universities are instituting anti-harassment policies, taking affirmative action steps, and offering parental leave. Perhaps in the future, more women will find satisfying employment in universities where they will feel safe, valued, and supported, and both men and women will be able to comfortably take on professional roles as university English teachers and personal roles as parents.

Notes

1. Although there was no breakdown of individual academic areas, we assume that the majority of foreigners teaching in Japanese universities are engaged in English-related teaching.
2. MEXT (2016). *MEXT Statistics Manual*. mext.go.jp/b_menu/toukei/002/002b/1368900.htm
3. For a thorough discussion, see Diane Nagatomo's *Identity, Gender and Teaching English in Japan* (Multilingual Matters 2016).
4. It goes beyond the scope of this chapter to correlate the responses with the length of Japan residency and/or with the type of employment held, but these issues may have strongly influenced the participants' answers.
5. See Normile, D. "Women Faculty Battle Japan's *Koza* System" in *Science* [electronic version, February 2001]. Retrievable from sciencemag.org/content/291/5505/817
6. Creasor, F. "Harassment Prevention Policies at a Japanese University" in *The Journal and Proceedings of the Gender Awareness in Language Education (GALE) Special Interest Group of the Japan Association for Language Teaching* 5 (2013), pp. 22–36.
7. Appleby, R. *Men and Masculinities in Global English Language Teaching* (Palgrave Macmillan 2014), pp. 144–145.
8. Harshbarger, B. "A Faulty Ivory Tower: Reflections on Directing the ELP from 2006–2012." *Language Research Bulletin 27*. ICU: Tokyo. (2012: 9).
9. Naito, S. "Workplace Bullying in Japan," JILPT REPORT No. 12." *The Japan Institute for Labour Policy and Training* (2013).
10. For more discussion on gendered attitudes toward female teachers' income, see Diane Nagatomo's "In the Ivory Tower and out of the Loop: Racialized and Gendered Identities of University EFL Teachers in Japan" in Cheung, Y.L., Said, S.B., and Park, K. (Eds) *Advances and Current Trends in Language Teacher Identity Research* (Routledge 2014), pp. 102–115.

19 The Japanese university teacher of English

Asako Takaesu and Mikiko Sudo

Introduction by Paul Wadden

In the thousands of university departments across Japan in which English courses are offered—required or elective—mild-mannered professors toil in obscurity. Their scholarly focus might be the role of prepositions in phrase structure in Chomsky's generative grammar or the biographical origins of female characters in the short fiction of Henry James. The more obscure and specialized the topic, the better. Traditionally, the thinking goes, anyone can be a generalist and gain knowledge about broad topics, but a scholar should probe subjects that few others understand. Polite, self-effacing, and far more erudite than they let on, these Japanese professors of English are the unsung human infrastructure behind most universities' language programs and English course offerings. This is because in addition to teaching courses and pursuing their own research, they chair committees, draw up teaching schedules, and coordinate curricula. They work long hours behind closed office doors, rotating from the entrance exam committee to the personnel committee to coordinator of foreign teachers to department chair. When something goes wrong—students complain, a senior fails, a non-Japanese doesn't show up for work, a part-timer abruptly quits—they take responsibility.

Like the archetype of Joseph Campbell's *A Hero with a Thousand Faces*, the Japanese professor of English metamorphoses into many different human forms and eludes a single stereotype. But when you meet them in the hallway, greet them with respect. They are typically learned and dedicated, and the department you teach in would not function without them. Compared to the past, they are now more apt to be fluent in spoken English, on top of having mastered grammar, vocabulary, and the scholarly prose in their area of expertise. They may ask you to proofread an article they have written, for they typically take their research commitment seriously, regularly contribute to university journals, and courageously write in their second language. They also likely participate in—beyond your purview—*kenkyukai* and *gakkai* research groups of like-minded scholars. If they are younger, they may have spent several years doing graduate work abroad and come back to Japan as "higher-ed returnees" acquainted with contemporary TESOL practices and applied linguistics theory.

The best means for understanding these important colleagues and how they function is found in Chapter 4 of this *Handbook*, "The chrysanthemum maze: understanding your colleagues in the Japanese university." There, Curtis Kelly and Nobuhiro Adachi analyze how Japanese universities work and how they shape faculty relations and personal character, identifying the demands institutions make upon Japanese professors and the values that guide their actions. Among these are a careful attention to form (doing things properly), a feeling that one's group or oneself should faithfully uphold assigned responsibilities (*sekinin*), a commitment to consensus and the welfare of the group over the desires of the individual, a willingness therefore to accept appearances (convenient falsehoods) over what may actually be the case (inconvenient truths that can cause disruptive change or discomfort), and often, even to a fault, personal humility and self-deprecation.[1]

In recent years, this institutional landscape has become more complex for these professors because many universities no longer grant tenure to Japanese faculty upon hiring. Like their non-Japanese counterparts, many now undergo trial years in a tenure-track position. Especially at universities with international curricula and English-language programs, more are also being employed on fixed-term contracts. These particular teachers have their own unique yet common challenges, for despite their fixed-term, full-time status, they often have more responsibility than their non-Japanese counterparts while teaching courses parallel to them in the curriculum. Following are two of their many voices speaking to the difficulties they face as Japanese teachers of English and reflecting on what they and their colleagues offer their students and institutions.

Japanese teachers of English: who are they?

Like our students, Japanese teachers of English fall into three broad categories: some like *me* (Mikiko) learned English entirely in Japan and have never lived or studied abroad; others like *me* (Asako) were primarily educated in Japan but also spent several post-graduate years studying or working in an English-speaking country before returning; still others, fewer in number and ethnically Japanese, grew up or lived for many years abroad and are largely native English speakers although they also speak Japanese. Despite the fact that these various Japanese teachers of English have diverse backgrounds and differing perspectives on language teaching, they tend to be assigned common teaching roles and administrative responsibilities. In what follows, we first speak from Mikiko's perspective as a *jun japa* who learned English almost wholly within the Japanese educational system, and then from Asako's *higher-ed returnee* vantage point as one who completed her undergraduate study in Japan and then did graduate study and worked overseas before coming back a few years later. We describe courses we teach, administrative and coordinating duties we're often assigned, the expectations of students, and the difficulties we face. Although many Japanese English teachers teach in departments largely staffed by Japanese faculty, our experience is mainly in programs which have internationalized and include significant numbers of foreign English teachers. By recounting our challenges and presenting our perspectives, we hope to offer insight into the roles, teaching practices, and viewpoints of Japanese teachers of English.[2]

Challenges of the *jun japa* journey (Mikiko)

For 20 years I've been teaching English as a *jun japa*—a playful term meaning a "pure Japanese" with no study abroad experience. In the era of globalization, *jun japa* teachers like me are declining in number but still diligently doing their best for students. Some of us are no doubt your colleagues.

My first job teaching English was offering a content course in a university program founded and supervised by TESOL professors. All teaching staff were native English speakers except for two of us. The other teacher was a Japanese who had taught in middle schools in America for many years. She was a strong and dignified woman who spoke English fluently without hesitation or an accent. From my *jun japa* viewpoint, she was the third type of teacher mentioned above, a virtual native speaker. I felt I had little in common with her, though we were both viewed as "Japanese staff" and often tasked with interpreting and translating duties.

During my first few years, I was concerned about my shaky situation as a relatively inexperienced Japanese university teacher responsible for a variety of 90-minute English content courses related to global issues. I had never taught global issues, with topics ranging from international politics to environmental issues, in English. The economics readings, in particular, included vocabulary whose general meaning I knew but were specialized terms in that field. These were words such as "depression," "liberalization," and "protectionism" whose roots students might recognize but which had different denotations and connotations in general English, in related Japanese loan words, and in economics. In addition, the readings contained mathematical formulas and I did not know the proper pronunciation of half of them (it is surprisingly difficult to figure out the pronunciation of mathematical symbols, and 20 years ago electronic dictionaries had no audio function!).

I was desperate and I frequently bothered my colleagues, most of whom I barely knew, to ask, "I am terribly sorry, but do you have a minute? Could you please tell me how to pronounce this mathematical symbol?" For me, that was face-threatening. I wanted to pretend that "of course, I know everything and I'm totally OK with English," just like that other Japanese teacher who lived in America and taught middle school. At night, I thought that the university must regret it had hired such an ignorant Japanese English teacher and I worried that maybe this would be my last semester before they fired me.

Looking back, however, I feel I was fortunate. Even though the university administrators and my colleagues knew I had limited knowledge of economics and mathematics, and native-speaker gaps in my English knowledge of idioms and specialized vocabulary, the university didn't fire me, and my colleagues always replied pleasantly to my elementary questions. But at the end of one day, when I asked a native English-speaking teacher a specific question about usage, she told me, "You should just stop being a nervous wreck all the time. You worry too much about such small things!" It was a powerful blow. I just gazed at her, speechless. Looking back now, I know exactly what I should have said in response. Something like, "There is nothing wrong with being concerned with details! That's how I became fluent in English. I have never lived in an English-speaking country, and I have to work twice as hard to make up for that!" How could she know, also, that in Japan a teacher of English is considered by students to be "an expert" who knows what they don't know? But at that time, I had nothing to say. In one instant, I could see that all of my hard work to master the language and be a worthy teacher for my students was seen as pointless "busyness" to a native speaker.

Not being native

It is a matter of course that native English teachers have advantages over Japanese English teachers in their intuitive knowledge of their mother tongue. They don't have to imagine facing challenges from students throughout the entire semester, like we do. Native speakers can insist, "It's OK to make mistakes. They are precious learning experiences, so you don't have to be ashamed. Look, even a native speaker of English like me makes mistakes!" This is what they openly say to their students in classrooms when they misspell words on the whiteboard or they offer an "unconventional" (e.g., completely wrong) explanation of the past perfect progressive tense and excuse themselves by concluding it's not important because, "Well, people don't really use it anyway." Students are unquestioning of their expertise as native speakers and satisfied with these kinds of responses. I, on the other hand, would not receive such a generous reception when providing mistaken information or misleading explanations. The thought of making mistakes in front of students used to—and still does to some extent—keep me awake at night. In many respects, whether real or imagined, the Japanese teacher of English is held to an impossibly high standard by her students. One reason is that the principle of mastery is deeply embedded in the Confucian ethic that underlies Japanese culture: a teacher knows subject matter and students do not know. That is the basis of their relationship. It took many years (and continued mastery) for me to finally become a teacher who could laugh with students about her little mistakes.

Another more contemporary belief also complicates the relationship between Japanese university students and Japanese teachers of English. Many students innocently expect to be taught by native English-speaking teachers in university. Their reasoning is, "We already learned the basics of English from Japanese teachers of English in middle school and high school. Now we want to learn from 'real teachers' who have correct pronunciation and native understanding of the language." Therefore, students tend to perceive Japanese teachers of English as less qualified than native speakers, even when their academic degrees and teaching credentials are more extensive. This is a hard reality. If taken negatively, this reality can push us into the abyss and make us feel we have wasted our professional lives as English teachers. But if taken positively, this is a powerful "push" given only to non-native teachers of English. To compete with native-speaking teachers, we should have "something special" that distinguishes us—both individually and collectively.

The "higher-ed" returnee teacher of English (Asako)

One important role that Japanese English teachers play involves filling language gaps and bridging cultural differences. Many students entering universities are unprepared—or at least feel unprepared—for classes conducted solely in English. While the JET (Japan Exchange and Teaching) program over the past two decades has given many more Japanese junior and senior high school students exposure to native speakers, their overall contact hours with native-speaking teachers are minimal. Moreover, the tasks that the students are expected to do in English are largely receptive rather than productive: comprehend reading texts, understand listening passages, and answer multiple-choice questions about both. These are the main tasks expected of them, for instance, on university entrance exams.[3]

Despite their limited exposure to English, for more than 20 years I have challenged my students by conducting my English classes entirely in English. This gives them direct input, allows them to actively engage the language, and teaches them the pragmatics of the English classroom. Since I have never worked in a department made up mainly of Japanese faculty, what follows may not be representative of the majority of Japanese English teachers, but it may shed some light on the often unnoticed work we do, and the something special, to use Mikiko's words above, that we offer in university English education.

First, with our practical bi-cultural knowledge, Japanese English teachers often act as "liaisons" between cultures and demonstrate effective ways to deal with differences. One example is the differing pragmatic expectations for students in classrooms in Japan and in the West.[4] As readers of this *Handbook* might be well aware, Japanese students new to "English only" classrooms seldom ask questions or speak their minds for fear of being "nails that stick out," whereas in the West, students are expected to openly express their opinions and take initiative in classroom discussions. Coming from the same cultural milieu as our students, Japanese teachers can generally share and understand our students' feelings and fears. We can thus be less intimidating in the students' eyes, even as we conduct our classes in English. We can, for example, explicitly compare cultural values and classroom activities, explaining to students the different expectations in each context. We can also build students' confidence by providing scaffolding activities to gradually acclimate them to behaviors aligned with what is expected in English-speaking countries. In my courses, for example, I transition students from asking questions within small groups, to having a group leader pose the group's questions to the class, to having students participate individually themselves in a whole-class discussion. Foregrounding for students the differences between Socratic and Confucian educational styles also gives them a valuable meta-understanding of communicative differences between classrooms and cultures. This knowledge serves them well when studying abroad or interacting with "foreigners" later in their careers.

Furthermore, as Japanese teachers, we are perceived as understanding and appreciating the struggle that motivated students go through as they embark on the arduous journey of studying abroad. When we teach advanced courses, we are able to bridge the students' past educational experiences with what will be expected of them when they arrive in their host countries. For example, at the university where I presently work, I teach academic writing to a select group of students in the international program, as well as a CLIL course in global issues for honors students. My experience in the Japanese educational system combined with my understanding of comparative culture from my life in Michigan during my master's study, and my grasp of cross-cultural rhetoric from subsequent work in journalism for newspapers based in Chicago and Tokyo, give me the basis to explain contrastive rhetoric. When teaching essay writing and research writing, I am able to juxtapose organizational styles and writing conventions students learned during their first 12 years of schooling with those they will have to learn to write competently during their academic study overseas. This sort of understanding of cultural difference and contrastive rhetoric equips many Japanese teachers of English to be particularly effective in teacher education, training students for careers as English teachers in high schools and universities where they in turn can better educate their own students about these same differences.

Despite my experience and so-called expertise, I still struggle from day to day, like Mikiko, as a non-native speaker, probably because it takes much longer for me to do a job comparable to native English speakers. I used to think it was simply due to my perfectionist nature. However, it dawned on me that it was more likely because I am thinking, writing, and working in a foreign language. From reading documents to making lesson plans to creating teaching materials to writing comments on students' essays to writing my own papers, it takes me an inordinately long time. No wonder we Japanese teachers of English are generally the last ones to leave the office!

The rewards of being a Japanese teacher of English

In addition to the difficulties of working in a second language, there are also some rewards. It is exciting for me to create a classroom environment where critical thinking is fostered among students who are not particularly familiar with the concept. Yet they get it and find it meaningful. I can see their minds opening. This is particularly evident in academic writing courses when they begin to substantiate their arguments with evidence and logical reasoning. Another example is in the media literacy component of my CLIL course when students begin to perceive the diversity of opinions on any given issue, and no longer cling to one particular view, nor take what they read from one source as indisputable truth. When students returning from a study abroad program tell me that they were able to complete their composition and content courses overseas because they understood how to organize an essay and support their arguments with good reasons and evidence, I feel that teaching English is deeply rewarding.

Less visible roles Japanese English teachers play (Asako)

If students expect to have native-speaker English teachers and if Japanese universities claim they are trying to "globalize" their curricula, why do they continue to hire *jun japa* and higher-ed returnee teachers like us? One reason is we ourselves have successfully acquired a second language—in fact, the very language we are asking our students to learn. We know the linguistic challenges of this process—from the complexity of grammar to the polysemous nature of vocabulary to the elision of words in idiomatic speech—and we have used learning strategies to succeed at it. We are direct role models for the students. Our presence and our previous success can potentially inspire them in ways other than native English teachers can. In other words, whether as *jun japa* or higher-ed returnees, we are living proof that they can do it, too. We are also proof that motivated students with determination and perseverance can pursue their studies in English-speaking countries and even excel in western educational institutions.

Another more mundane role that we Japanese teachers of English play is in the day-to-day functioning of the department. Out of public view, we write course descriptions in Japanese for the college catalog, talk one-to-one with students experiencing difficulties (most cannot adequately express their personal problems in English), translate documents, and serve on committees that meet over and over throughout the year. The writing, proofreading, and proctoring of entrance exams also requires many hours outside the classroom.

Yet another role we often must play, like it or not, is acting as intermediaries between the Japanese administration and foreign faculty. Sometimes this means translating relevant documents from Japanese to English or vice versa (few universities have professional translators on their staff). More challenging than literal translation is the subtle interpretation of policies for the non-Japanese faculty—the "true intent" and "unstated context" of many university communications is hard to grasp and challenging to explain. How we interpret such policies and regulations is delicate and can even put us at risk, for when we are asked to clarify or advise on a policy (how grades should be allocated, whether a course can be cancelled for a particular reason, what a foreign teacher "should do" in a particular situation), it also implies our endorsement. Although such tasks are rarely included in our list of official duties, we are obliged to perform them. In fact, it's almost impossible for us to say no. This undoubtedly saves the administration from having to hire extra personnel to deal with foreign teachers bewildered by an array of official policies and tacit practices, not to mention the constant stream of perplexing emails and announcements they receive each week. Yet often, we, too, are bewildered and perplexed by them!

Separate but equal, yet rather impractical (Mikiko)

One way universities try to justify employing different classes of language teachers—especially the dichotomy of native speakers and Japanese teachers of English —is to set up what we call "habitat segregations" in their departments. There, non-Japanese typically teach speaking skills, academic writing, and presentation courses, whereas Japanese handle reading, grammar, and test-skills classes. In our view, such segregation is harmful. For one thing, it functions as a kind of *sakoku*—an ad hoc protection of Japanese teachers of English from the rest of the world; for another, this separation serves to isolate them. One result of such separate but *allegedly* equal divisions of curriculum is that, unsurprisingly, factions begin to form along racial and ethnic lines, and it isn't long before conflict and distrust emerge in a department or program. Both "sides" want to protect what is theirs, including the allocation of faculty positions, and a divided curriculum in turn results in a racial–cultural divide. The irony, of course, for both Japanese and non-Japanese university teachers, is that it could *ALL* be theirs, if they were willing to share. In today's higher education environment, faculty are more qualified than ever before to teach a variety of courses. To limit ourselves to our own "habitat"—such as reading and grammar on the one side and oral skills and writing on the other—deprives us of the chance to develop as teachers, to meaningfully collaborate with each other as professionals, and to connect with students in richer ways.

Final thoughts

At the end of my first semester teaching English, I, Mikiko, received students' evaluations. One comment predictably said, "She should improve her English pronunciation." I remember feeling crushed at the time. I showed this comment to the program director and asked for his advice. He laughed and said, "Don't worry about it. We never would have hired you if we thought so." A part of my self-loathing as a *jun japa* English teacher melted away. And while there are still moments of self-doubt, I can finally say that I no longer sweat the small stuff, like I did all those years ago. There are many moments I can be proud of myself, as an experienced English teacher with skills, knowledge, and in particular, sensitivity to see and predict where and why students struggle in the process of learning English. I know I deserve to be where I am now. But I still care about details and errors, and you will have to pry my electronic pronunciation dictionary out of my cold, dead hands.

I, Asako, could say that my overall role as a Japanese teacher of English is to pass on the knowledge and skills I have garnered, through my own long and arduous journey, to another generation of students. Learning languages expands our world, helps us become more willing to accept diversity, deepens our critical faculties, and increases our future options. Thus, despite my struggles, it makes me feel content and proud to have been able to contribute to the meaningful growth of my students.

Notes

1 I once spent nearly a year exchanging pleasantries with a senior professor on the elevator and occasionally sharing lunch with him in the college cafeteria before I learned from another faculty member that he was one of the most distinguished linguists in Japan.
2 Please also see Chapter 20 of this *Handbook* "Beyond the native speaker fallacy: internationalizing English-language teaching at Japanese universities," for explanation of the Native Speaker Fallacy, the Native Speaker Learner Fallacy, and many other issues related to our work as Japanese teachers of English and which we mostly avoid replicating here but which are equally relevant to our teaching context.
3 Sometimes they also must translate brief portions of text from English into their native Japanese. Tests of English speaking and writing are extremely rare.
4 Although "the West" is an imprecise and overly broad term, I use it here to refer to cultures with strong Greco–Roman and Judeo–Christian roots, particularly in English-speaking countries such as Britain, Ireland, the United States, Canada, Australia, and New Zealand.

20 Beyond the native speaker fallacy
Internationalizing English-language teaching at Japanese universities

Tiina Matikainen

Introduction

A billion and a half people speak English worldwide but only 375 million are native speakers, which means about 75 percent are non-native speakers.[1] Most of them use "English as a Lingua Franca" (ELF), defined as "use of English among speakers of different first languages for whom English is the communicative medium of choice."[2] Who then taught them English? About 80 percent of the English teachers in the world are non-native English speaking teachers (NNETs).[3]

The misconception that native speakers make the best English teachers remains prominent in TESOL even though the field itself has been moving away from what Robert Phillipson insightfully called the "native speaker fallacy."[4] Influenced by Critical Applied Linguistics, World Englishes, and ELF movements, the English-language teaching field has started to embrace teachers who transcend the mold of the idealized native speaker. Ahmar Mahboob explains the basis for this change and its significance: "The [Non-Native English Teacher's] lens. . . . is a lens of multilingualism, multinationalism, and multiculturalism. It takes diversity as a starting point in TESOL and applied linguistics practice and research and questions the monolingual bias in the field."[5]

Although progress has been slower in Japan compared to some countries, many Japanese universities and their English departments are now diversifying their faculty to include NNETs. Part of the lag has been due to traditional language-teaching discourse and its deeply ingrained native speaker and non-native speaker dichotomy. This convention is still conspicuously present, for example, in position announcements in which a stated requirement is being a native speaker or having "near native speaker fluency." Other advertisements for university English-teaching positions conversely require native or near native Japanese ability. This dual "native speaker" focus obscures an important third group of language teachers, non-native non-Japanese English teachers (NNNJETs) like myself.

Fortunately, many universities and departments are now recognizing how such teachers diversify their faculty, provide students with enriched language-teaching pedagogies, and contribute to the advancement of the ELT field in Japan. For example, Tamagawa University in Tokyo has established the Center for English as a Lingua Franca to provide a campus-wide ELF program to its students. The university actively recruits teachers who are expert users of English but not necessarily native speakers, and many such teachers are represented in their ELF faculty. Other universities, often less visibly, are following their lead. In this chapter, I will first outline some of the challenges NNNJETs face in attempting to legitimize themselves in the face of a native-like model of the successful English learner in Japan. Next, I will discuss the strengths of NNNJETs and their potential to advance ELT in Japanese higher education. Finally, I will suggest some ways to help enable this transformation.

An unrealistic learning model

The Japanese model for a proficient language user is—strange as it seems when held up to scrutiny—the native speaker. Students have a deeply rooted belief that they should speak like a native speaker in order to be considered a competent English user. Students themselves perceive a "good language student" to be one with high oral fluency in the language and fail to acknowledge the value of their ability in the important skills of reading, writing, and listening. Also, a student who works hard, is motivated, and is making steady progress in learning the language, no matter how slow this progress is, but lacks this oral fluency, is also not necessarily viewed as being a good language learner. Given these views of language proficiency, it is hardly surprising that students are *not* willing to use the language because they intuitively feel they will never achieve this goal of speaking English like a native speaker. This can be called the *native speaker learner fallacy*. Granted, the field of TESOL has not helped this false ideal by positing concepts such as interlanguage and fossilization which implicitly suggest that it is impossible for a learner to achieve native-like fluency. Rather than the near impossible task of creating foreign-born native speakers, the goal of English teaching in Japanese higher education should be for learners to develop a communicative working knowledge of the language as well as intercultural awareness. The Japanese students in our classrooms today will be the country's business leaders, journalists, diplomats, and educators of tomorrow. In a globalized society using ELF and a variety of World Englishes, communication and cultural skills are the key to participation and even prosperity. In fact, it is inherently disabling to motivated, intelligent Japanese students to be taught English with the aim of making them more proximate to American, British, or Australian speakers. English today, as mentioned at the outset, is a global language of 1.5 billion speakers with far more non-native speakers than native speakers; it is therefore a language we should cherish for its varieties and whose speakers should be respected for their imperfect but admirable communicative and functional language skills. In Japan, it is imperative that this paradigmatic shift in thinking takes place amongst educators, administrators, and students themselves. Without this shift in thinking, Japanese students will continue to strive for an unrealistic ideal of the English-language user and continue to fall prey to the demotivating native speaker learner fallacy.

One obvious way to engender this shift is to improve the language user models for students. For this purpose, Japanese universities should consider having more NNNJETs.

The power of non-native non-Japanese English teachers

To date, NNNJETs who have been able to gain positions in universities face unique challenges in their professional lives while their transformative power is underutilized and undervalued. Among their assumed weaknesses are imperfect pronunciation, less knowledge of the target language, less familiarity with the native culture, less desirability by students, and lower professional credibility. Very little research has confirmed these weaknesses and their impact upon language instruction; some has even debunked them. Among the significant strengths of this group of teachers, on the other hand, are serving as role models to students, effectively presenting professionally informed and personally used language-learning strategies, greater empathy for students' problems, more sensitivity to their needs, and often a profound explicit knowledge of the language. These have been well documented in research.

Personally, one of the greatest strengths I have as a NNNJET is being able to communicate to my students that I understand how they feel and that their teacher truly knows how difficult and frustrating learning English can be at times. I can say, "I have been there." As a non-native speaker of English, I may not be able to expose them to perfect "native-level pronunciation," but I can be a model of how to speak English intelligibly and proficiently; I can exemplify language use in a way that is more realistic and more desirable for them. Having had to carefully and consciously learn the conventions of English, I know the rules and even where usage diverges from the rules. With my personal experience and my teaching background, I am capable of explaining conventions and usage in a comprehensible way. More importantly, through my own experience and life story, I help my students see and experience how English can enrich one's life journey.

For many students, this stirs their deepest motivations for learning English: the possibilities of new relationships, the acquisition of new knowledge, the adventures of foreign cultures, the dream of new worlds.

Many of the students that I have taught in Japan have cherished and appreciated me as their English-language teacher, not despite my non-native status, but often *because* of it. At the end of many of my courses, I ask students to reflect on their learning journey with me, and many echo the following comments: "You encourage me to study English because you are not a native English speaker. You motivated us not only for this class but for other courses and even our future lives," and "When I think of you, I am motivated to study English even though I am not a native English speaker. Your advice and example always cheered me up." As these comments show, having a language user model that is not the perfect native speaker can be enormously motivating. Having exposure to capable English teachers from non-English-speaking countries can empower students to actually envision themselves as potentially able to use English regardless of the country of their birth. This insight can play a crucial role in Japan, breaking the native speaker learner fallacy, spurring motivation, and enabling language learning.

The passion for English that teachers like myself have should also not be overlooked. For many of us, this is the most important reason we became English teachers. I care about the language at a deeply personal level because learning it has opened up doors for me and guided the direction of my life not only professionally but also personally. In academia, in business, in relationships, and in my personal life, English has opened new worlds to me. Students themselves dream about these possibilities.

Expert language users as English teachers

In reality, the language background of a teacher is not the most important quality that Japanese students value. Pedagogical and personal qualities combined with experience and qualifications are far more important than "nativeness." These are reflected by the teachers' personal qualities, the relationships they develop with their students, and the quality of their teaching. Several studies have confirmed this. One study[6] conducted with my students found that the most important characteristics for a good language teacher in their opinions were, in the following order: the ability to motivate students, the teaching of practical English, the creation of a communicative classroom, sense of humor, the qualities of kindness and patience and passion, the use of a variety of engaging materials, and being a good user of the language. Being a native speaker of the language was hardly cited. In fact, native-like pronunciation and native-level knowledge of the language were considered as some of the least important characteristics of a good language teacher. Still, it is important to acknowledge despite these results that, depending upon their perceived race, other non-native non-Japanese teachers may not have had such an overwhelmingly positive experience with their students. The connection between race and the idealized native English teacher being Caucasian is well documented in Japan; it is possible that white non-native speakers also enjoy a Caucasian halo effect. The confounding of racial stereotype, quality of teaching, and character of the teacher is unfortunately a topic too complex to explore here but one that deserves further professional research and discussion.

Regardless of race, establishing professional credibility with colleagues and administrators can at times be challenging for NNNJETs due to the deep-rooted beliefs about native speakers being the ideal foreign language teachers. Just categorizing language teachers into native, non-native, or Japanese teachers is fraught with difficulty. One "progressive" university where I worked devised a chart for English teacher hiring purposes. Lecturers were divided into four categories: category A at the top comprised western native speaker teachers from English-speaking countries, and category D at the bottom comprised non-native English speakers from countries other than Japan. (They had a hard time deciding where to place someone from Singapore.) Categories B and C included Japanese teachers of English divided into two groups based on whether they had lived abroad for an extensive period of time or not. Despite this university's attempt to accommodate more prototypes of language teachers, they ended up creating a hierarchy of value with native teachers at the top (As) and non-native non-Japanese teachers at the bottom (Ds), inadvertently and unconsciously reproducing the very cultural prejudice they were attempting to move beyond. As this example shows, more thought needs to be put into how we conceive of language teachers to keep the focus on their expertise, professionalism, character, skill, and ability to motivate students, and how their identities and backgrounds will contribute to the university.

Ethically, it can be argued that the labels of "native" and "non-native" themselves marginalize quality teachers and mar the TESOL field as a whole. Practically, the labels prevent many NNNJETs in Japan from establishing a respected and legitimate position in the ELT field. Ultimately, this is a disservice to Japanese students themselves, considering the powerful role these teachers can play in their language learning and in their lives. One partial solution is to adopt the concept of an *expert English speaker* or an *expert English user* as the ideal language teacher, regardless of language background or race. This encourages Japanese learners to emulate and become proficient users of English. It also offers inclusion to institutions that would benefit from more diversity.

Conclusion

In his ground-breaking book *World Englishes: Implications for International Communication and English Language Teaching,* Andy Kirkpatrick surmises,

> In the contexts of World Englishes, the real problem is caused by many people believing that native speakers are necessarily better at speaking English than non-native speakers, and that native speakers are necessarily better at teaching English than non-native speakers [i.e. the NS myth]."[7]

The antidote to this problem is to recognize that this group of teachers—the NNNJETs—can be an asset to diversify the ELT field and to strengthen the status of ELF in Japan. This recognition will help dissolve the arbitrary native/non-native dichotomy that promotes false standards and sets unrealistic learning goals for students. What the English-language teaching field in general and Japan in particular need are *expert English users* who have the experience and the qualifications to inspire students to reach their language-learning goals and achieve their full potential. The transformative power that NNNJETs bring into the classroom, therefore, should be celebrated and appreciated.

I hope Japan continues to cherish the changing landscape of English and appreciate those who teach it to future generations of its citizens. I hope administrators hire the best teachers—meaning the most skilled, the most experienced, the most committed, the best models of learning for their students, the ones who can most connect with their classes. I hope NNNJETs will become more common in Japanese classrooms because they have the power to inspire Japanese English learners.

Notes

1 From *Statista*, 2017. statista.com/statistics/266808/the-most-spoken-languages-worldwide/
2 From Seidlhofer, B. *Understanding English as a Lingua Franca: A Complete Introduction to the Theoretical Nature and Practical Implication of English Used as a Lingua Franca* (Oxford University Press 2011).
3 From Canagarajah, A.S. (Ed.) *Reclaiming the Local in Language Policy and Practice* (Lawrence Erlbaum 2005).
4 From Phillipson, R. *Linguistic Imperialism* (Oxford University Press 1992).
5 From Mahboob, A. *The NNEST Lens: Non Native English Speakers in TESOL* (Cambridge Scholars Publishing 2010). This book offers an insightful collection of teachers', researchers', and teacher educators' views on how TESOL can develop if we use the multilingual, multicultural, and multinational perspectives of NNESTs to re-examine the field.
6 Full discussion of this study can be found in a chapter by me titled "Cultures of Learning in Japanese EFL Classrooms: Student and Teacher Expectations" in the book *Foreign Language Education in Japan: Exploring Qualitative Approaches,* edited by Horiguchi, S., Imoto, Y., & Poole, G. (Sense Publishers 2015).
7 Kirkpatrick, A. *World Englishes: Implications for International Communication and English Language Teaching* (Cambridge University Press 2007), p. 8.

21 Walk a mile in the shoes of the non-Japanese administrator

Stephen M. Ryan and Peter McCagg

Although nearly unthinkable in years past, non-Japanese faculty are now sometimes finding themselves in senior administrative positions within Japanese universities. In this chapter, we draw on our own experiences as Vice President for Academic Affairs (VPAA) in Peter's case and University President in Stephen's case, to offer a sense of life on the inside, and explain why as a foreign administrator—in a world based on consensus and compromise—you may not always get what you want, but if you try somehow (and in the right ways), you just might find, you get what you need.

Getting the nod

Why would universities appoint a non-Japanese to an administrative post? While an outsider, by virtue of administrative acumen, academic achievements, ability to articulate pathways to greater harmony and institutional success, power of personality, and popular acclamation may reach the triumphant top (or the churning center) of a Japanese university, a foreigner may also be appointed simply because it looks good in publicity materials. Or the appointment may respond to the desires of non-Japanese teaching staff, or two opposing faculty factions may have battled to a standstill on their preferred Japanese candidates. Yet having an "outside" view represented at the table when decisions are made about admissions policies, curricular reforms, personnel matters, or any of the many other issues that management teams must deal with can increase the breadth of opinions drawn on and enhance the sense that the university is acting on an international, rather than purely local, stage. On the other hand, when it comes to a non-Japanese being appointed as an administrator, it may also just be the foreign professor's "turn": many administrative jobs, especially the heads of lower level committees and minor university units, are staffed largely on a rotational basis, the prevailing assumptions being that (a) we each bring the same levels of competence and dedication to the tasks involved and (b) we each have an equal amount of unwillingness to do the job. In short, you're in the post because it seems fair to take turns (see Figure 21.1).

This might suggest that competence and ability are consistently trumped by factors such as random chance or, sometimes, nationality. While this can often be

> ❏ I am an easygoing person unlikely to cause much harm (. . . or innovate very much)
> ❏ It was "my turn" to do this job. (Oh, well.)
> ❏ Everyone else refused to do this job. (Purchase flak jacket; gird loins.)
> ❏ Our university badly needs to "up its profile" and my foreign face on the pamphlets will make it look more international and help PR. (Work on your smile.)
> ❏ I have come to know the institution rather well. It may just be possible that I have good ideas about how to improve things and a manner that enables me to build consensus around them. (Have another glass of beer and *gambatte kudasai*.)

Figure 21.1 I was likely appointed to a leadership role based on (check all that apply):

the case for lower level appointments, there is a common understanding that one way to avoid more onerous responsibilities is to mess up the administrative and committee duties you initially have as a faculty member, either by underperforming or by excessive stubbornness in fighting for your corner. As a result, those appointed to higher level administrative positions tend to be distinguished by their conscientiousness (unwillingness to mess up) and ability to adjust (consider competing viewpoints), if not necessarily by their competence and suitability for the job. Faculty who underperform outside the classroom tend to be passed over without comment for higher administrative roles and at some universities are not even considered for promotion to the full professor academic rank that would then make them eligible for higher level administrative duties.

Re-learning the ropes

Once appointed to an administrative position, the first experience of the new administrator is interaction with a widening circle of people. For a new head of an academic department (*gakka-cho*), this usually means working on committees with people from other departments. For heads of other university units (Admissions, International Center, etc.) it also means much more interaction with non-teaching staff. The teaching/non-teaching distinction is an important one as the two different spheres exist within every university, with largely separate hierarchies, in which non-teaching staff ultimately report to the Head of Office (*jimukyoku-cho*) and teaching staff to the President. For non-teaching staff whose work barely impacts the educational mission of the university (Accounting, Physical Plant, Personnel) the separation is almost complete, but for departments with a direct educational impact (Library, Admissions), it is common for the department to be headed by a member of the faculty who has voting rights at the Faculty Meeting, which generally has overall responsibility for the educational and research activities of the institution.

Interactions with both teaching and non-teaching staff at this level of the university are strongly influenced by the assumption that just about everybody involved is tenured or permanently employed. While there are increasing numbers of non-tenured employees on Japanese campuses (and especially among the non-Japanese teachers), management practices at many universities are still based on the tradition of hiring staff with tenure from the outset. "Contract," part-time or temporary employees, will know that they have very little say in the way the university is run. It is the permanent employees who count, and they are constantly aware, in their dealings with each other, that they are likely to be working together for a long time. Naturally, this leads to a reluctance to rock the boat in terms of personal relations and sometimes results in a determined drive for consensus, which can inhibit innovation and agility in decision-making. Decisions on which there is no consensus can be repeatedly kicked into the long grass, in theory until a consensus can be formed, but in practice sometimes forever. For better or worse, non-tenured faculty who have little compunction about making waves—or who often are not even really aware they are causing conflict—are unlikely to be around long enough to benefit from the desired harmony. In fact, one of the worst mistakes new faculty members—or new administrators—can make is to propose improvements to existing structures, procedures, or courses before they have carefully observed over time how things work and who is working them.[1] In Japan, our experience is that a new administrator learns more by listening than speaking.

Making sense of the inner workings of the university

You might expect that non-teaching office staff (*shokuin*) will defer to the teaching staff (*kyouin*) in matters that impact teaching and research. At odds with this assumption is the fact the office staff often have a great deal more experience in the actual running of a university than do the faculty. Indeed, the office staff know and are expected to enforce the rules. Failure on the part of a teacher to recognize this can lead to resentment from the staff, who may already feel discriminated against due to the superior working conditions enjoyed by faculty members (private offices, days free of teaching each week, long breaks between terms, travel to conferences in exotic locales, etc.). Failure to recognize this can also lead to frustration on the part of the faculty who may feel thwarted in seemingly simple things—say reimbursement for taxi receipts on a research trip—by zealously inflexible bureaucrats. To the extent possible, it is advisable to read and understand the fine print (where it exists) or to discreetly consult with a senior colleague before assuming that doing something—say rearranging your class hours to accommodate a field trip—is just "common sense."

On a larger scale, the common sense assumption that in Japanese universities teachers teach, staff staff, and administrators administer may lead the unwary astray. Sooner or later, most teachers are asked to deal with issues that are not directly related to their teaching. This may involve accepting a committee assignment, or giving a demo lesson at a weekend promotional event, or serving as an entrance exam writer or an applicant interviewer. Faculty in Japan are notorious for arguing that unwelcome administrative duties make it impossible for them to do adequate research or (less frequently) to teach well. In general, though, it is assumed that over the course of a career a faculty member will spend one third of his or her time teaching, one third doing research, and one third performing administrative tasks. The balance at any given time, however, may be quite different. Keeping non-teaching responsibilities under control and meetings short and relevant is a constant battle for administrators who feel pressure to consult widely and comprehensively on proposed changes of policy before seeking their approval.[2]

Decision-making: extreme democracy?

Historically, any decision with educational impact has required approval by the Faculty Meeting. While much of the official power may be shifting away from the Faculty Meeting into the President's hands, in a land known for consensus decision-making, this gathering remains a centrally important cultural event at most institutions. To avoid overly long and taxing gatherings of the whole faculty, detailed consideration is delegated to university committees (Academic Affairs, Student Affairs, Admissions, etc.), usually consisting of a representative from each section of the university with a role in the area covered by the committee. Committees debate and determine the fate of proposals, and members report back to the sections of the university they represent to keep everyone in the loop. By the time a proposal reaches the Faculty Meeting, it should have been discussed, usually more than once, within committees and in departments. In fact, if a matter comes to the Faculty Meeting that the key players have not been previously aware of, something has gone wrong—or something more nefarious may be afoot. As a result, by the time a proposal comes up for decision, ideally, all the controversy has been removed from it. As a result, Faculty Meetings can be uninteresting in the extreme. Indeed, they are designed to be that way.

Chairing a meeting, then, at any level, can be taxing. Not only do potential sources of dissent need to be identified and dealt with ahead of time, but also the appearance must be given that everyone has had a chance to speak on the matter. At the same time, the short attention span of faculty members asked to consider non-teaching issues needs to be allowed for. There are various mechanisms for dealing with these tensions, including extensive private discussions with likely dissenters before the meeting (a process known as *nemawashi*), scheduling controversial issues towards the end of an agenda so that fatigue and the desire to finish the meeting will curtail discussion, and repeatedly postponing decisions until issues arising from them have been resolved in advance.

In a context where communication tends to be more nuanced, oblique, implicit, hedged, and tentative than many non-Japanese are used to, where silence rarely means consent, where financial constraints and poorly matched cultural values can add further layers of complexity to meetings and make genuine mutual understanding elusive, finding a comfortable place to contribute positively requires a great deal of patience. Also helpful are a healthy willingness to listen (often over and over to repeated arguments as each interested party has a say), a good sense of timing, that is, knowing when to speak (last is usually best), believing that others at the table are well-intentioned (even when they might seem not to be), and having the confidence that one's own contributions are taken seriously. The proof of this last case is when an administrative policy, curricular initiative, or personnel proposal one supports is ultimately implemented.

Governance, oversight and the Ministry of Education (MEXT)

Above the Faculty Meeting, often completely outside the awareness of non-administrators, is the Board of Governors (*riji-kai*), advised by the Board of Trustees (*hyougi-kai*). Collectively they work with the Chairman of the Board (*riji-cho*) to chart the operations of the school as a business. The President sits on the Board, often together with other senior academic administrators. While the Faculty Meeting, chaired by the President, traditionally has ultimate responsibility for educational decisions, responsibility for the administration of the school as a business rests with the Chairman of the Board. The Board considers educational matters only insofar as they impact the school as a business, reserving their main attention for balance sheets, personnel matters, and long-range planning. The President straddles both worlds, often speaking for educational matters at the Board and for business matters at the Faculty Meeting. As alluded to above, there are moves afoot, both at the ministerial level and within certain universities, to reduce the role of the Faculty Meeting in decision-making and leave most decisions in the hands of the President or Chairman of the Board. In some cases, the President is also the Chairman of the Board (a so-called "one-man" university), essentially giving the President enormous decision-making powers. To get ahead, though, you need to know where you fit in. And no single individual in Japan can successfully climb, claw, or cling to the fore without having a great deal of personal and institutional support. The wise leader engages in extensive rounds of consultation prior to making any major decisions that may affect the nature of the institution.

And then there is MEXT, the ministry responsible for higher education in Japan. Its involvement in the administration of universities is often misrepresented, partly because it is easy to blame its staff for unpopular decisions and policies. In theory, the involvement of MEXT in the affairs of private universities extends only to overseeing the setting up of new universities or departments within them and to seeing that these new entities are run in the way that was intended when they were proposed. In practice, since universities are constantly reconfiguring themselves and adding new departments, MEXT has almost constant scrutiny of ongoing and proposed operations. On any given issue, MEXT will usually defer to the judgment of the President or Chairman of the Board, but if a university is found to have strayed from the principles on which it was established, or a program to have diverged from the purposes for which it was approved, administrative sanctions (usually the blocking of new activities) can be applied. Through this mechanism, the ministry tends, over the years, to run a series of campaigns throughout the whole higher education sector. In recent years, campaigns have included requiring that a 15-week semester has 15 teaching weeks, encouraging curricula and courses that enhance the employability of students, and, most recently, initiatives that internationalize the university experience.

Embrace the new normal

Finally, faculty members who play administrative roles tend to have a number of ceremonial duties. These can include serving as MC at school ceremonies, announcing the names of students at the Graduation Ceremony, pep talks to entering freshmen, and meet-and-greets with leaders of the local community. These roles can be challenging for non-Japanese administrators as they involve not only language but also important elements of Japanese etiquette that we seldom have a chance to observe or practice. Unlike, say, chairing a Faculty Meeting, which we have many years to observe before being asked to do it, making a speech on the retirement of a long-serving member of the cleaning crew is a one-off event, with no apprenticeship available. If you have to do one of these, consult with one of your predecessors or colleagues.

In Japanese institutions where there is a significant multicultural flavor to the faculty, it can be very useful to recognize that—in a society which operates on the fiction that everyone is the same and therefore people are basically interchangeable—effective ways of collaborating with one's Japanese colleagues may differ significantly from working with one's non-Japanese colleagues. It is of course dangerous to generalize about either of these categories of colleague, but we have found that making a public appeal for volunteers to be early adopters, say to experiment with a desired curricular initiative, can be enough incentive to spark welcome action among western faculty, whereas Japanese colleagues rarely volunteer for a new assignment based on an open appeal. If they are approached privately, though, and given a personal explanation about why you need them to step up and play some leadership role, the desired result is more often accomplished (see Figure 21.2).

Ultimately, being a successful administrator in Japan (and anywhere, we suspect) involves knowing how you fit in and the direction you want to go; understanding the aspirations, interests, and concerns of the various people you are privileged to work with; and being able to articulate a common vision to pursue together. Creating a healthy and successful workplace involves having the resources to attract, secure, and reward good people; nurturing an inclusive and collegial atmosphere; and defining a clear common purpose, where people are committed to the mission and learning goals of the institution. With this

> Checklist
>
> ❏ The proposal I am making is likely to be supported by….
>
> ❏ I personally talked to everyone in the department and beyond about this change.
>
> ❏ The higher-ups (deans, vice president) not only appear to support my change publicly (*tatemae*) but are indeed sincerely committed to it (*honne*).
>
> ❏ There are several people who will tell me the truth about the proposals I am making or the real reasons for difficulties I am having (such as one or two Japanese colleagues late at night after becoming very drunk). They tell me this will fly….
>
> ❏ I have positive relations with the people under me.
>
> ❏ I have liaised with all non-teaching staff to be affected.

Figure 21.2 "Instruction manual for non-Japanese administrator initiating change" (break glass in event of emergency)

much shared, allowing room for individual choice, creativity, expression, and maintaining a healthy degree of cultural humility can make the work of an administrator in Japan—non-Japanese or otherwise—a rewarding experience. You may even manage to get some good work done and make a difference.

Notes

1. See Chapter 23 in this *Handbook*, "Navigating the chrysanthemum maze: off-hand advice on how to tiptoe through the minefield of the Japanese university," for discussion of the challenge of when and how to propose change.
2. See Chapter 4 in this *Handbook*, "The chrysanthemum maze: understanding your colleagues in the Japanese university," for more on this point.

22 Conflicts, contracts, rights, and solidarity

The Japanese university workplace from a labor perspective

Gerome Rothman

You are an educator, and when you picked up this *Handbook*, you expected advice from experienced colleagues about how to ply your craft in Japan. This chapter will be a little different. Think of it as a "teach-in" class by activists. It examines the problems educators experience *as workers* and presents means at their disposal to confront them. It begins by explaining types of labor contracts, then identifies pressing problems like the so-called "five-year rule," then examines various grievance resolution mechanisms for dealing with common issues such as harassment. It outlines a number of government offices particularly helpful in clarifying your employment situation. The conclusion explains your rights in Japan—particularly your constitutional right to form a trade union—and urges you to build solidarity with your colleagues.

Preconceived notions

To begin, when considering the university as a workplace, stop thinking of your profession as one that is special. You are just like any other person who works in exchange for a wage—a person with a labor contract and work rules to follow who can be promoted and fired. You have a boss. Your employer may break the law or fail to enforce the law. Across universities in Japan, unfortunately, this often happens. Professionals must face these facts head on with accurate understanding using appropriate language.

Next, let go of preconceived notions about the rules governing labor contracts. Those from the United States might be accustomed to having few legal protections from unfair dismissal and their workplace rights largely defined by their particular state of residence. Europeans might be used to robust protections from the central government. Both groups—and non-Japanese workers in general—incorrectly imagine Japan as a country with few workplace protections.

Japan's Labor Standards Law defines your rights to a 40-hour workweek, overtime pay, regular breaks, paid annual leave, and other protections. The social insurance scheme, when employers follow the law, is comprehensive and generous. Your right to form a union, bargain collectively with management, and take industrial action is guaranteed in the Constitution. Knowing your rights is critical to protecting yourself, your colleagues, your employment status, and ultimately your profession.

These rights and labor protections do not mean Japan is a worker's paradise. Women routinely face sexual harassment or gender discrimination and the discourse on LGBT rights has just begun. Employers, particularly universities, often ignore and even flout labor contract law. It is this abuse that creates the overarching challenge to improving working conditions.

One particular challenge is the employment term itself. As you likely know, universities infrequently hire language teachers into tenured or tenure-track positions. A search on JREC-IN or JACET websites confirms the paucity of full-time, *permanent* employment. Term-limited contracts for language teachers can be as short as a year, their renewals are never guaranteed, and universities often limit the number of renewals and impose a maximum term of employment. Such insecurity influences your working conditions and your options for bettering them.

Your labor contract

Fired on day one: the term-limited contract

Although specific labor contracts can differ, there are two main categories of employment contracts: term-limited (*yuki koyou*) and permanent (*muki koyou*). Term-limited means your contract has an end date. The employer is not legally allowed to terminate the contract before its term ends without meeting strict legal requirements. Once the contract term expires, however, the employer is under no obligation to renew it. There are some exceptions. For example, management must follow consistent renewal procedures and it cannot non-renew employees in an effort to discriminate against union members. Courts have ruled that if there is a history of management signing renewal contracts late, employees may be deemed permanent. There are also cases where non-renewals have been overturned because there was an expectation of renewal. But these are exceptional cases.[1]

The bottom line is that term-limited employees have no guarantee of renewal, even if your work performance is exemplary and everyone at the university loves you. Non-renewals in these cases are not only common but also perfectly legal. Permanent employment, by contrast, means an employer must have rational and compelling reasons to dismiss an employee and must exhaust all options before doing so. There must have been several warnings, re-trainings, and a well-documented record of no improvement. Strict rules also govern dismissal for economic reasons. Dismissing a permanent employee is extremely hard. It is a job for life.

One should not confuse the full-time/part-time distinction with the permanent/term-limited distinction. While it is true that almost all academic part-time positions are also term-limited, there are exceptions. In some rare cases, a long-time part-time employee may achieve permanent status. However, the vast majority of university language teachers are on term-limited contracts; that is, they hold non-tenured positions. Note that the word "tenure" itself also creates confusion. In Japanese, a similar word for permanently employed teachers is *sennin*, or for non-teachers *seishain*. From the standpoint of the labor contract, the only difference between a tenured instructor and a non-tenured instructor is that a tenured instructor is a permanent employee who cannot be dismissed for arbitrary reasons. It is misleading to consider tenure to be some sort of academic achievement granted to a select few accomplished professionals.

At its core, a tenured position is simply one with a permanent employment contract identical to most Japanese employees. That does not stop universities from exploiting the idea of a tenured position by making them rare, attaching administrative responsibilities, or making them appear to be managerial. Traditionally, in Japan, tenure was actually granted to faculty members upon hiring. Currently, the granting of tenure is increasingly contingent upon completing years-long probationary periods. The tenure process often lacks transparency or due process and subjects applicants to arduous research and publication requirements. The reward at the end is permanent employment, financial security, and the right not to be treated arbitrarily.

The "five-year rule"

In April 2013, the Japanese government enacted a far-reaching change to labor contract law known as the five-year rule. It stipulates that employers must make term-limited employees permanent if they work longer than five consecutive years with the same employer (five years + at least one day). Employees must request in writing permanent status at any point during the contract term that crosses the five-year mark. The employer must agree, and you become officially permanent after five years and one day.

There are many problems with this policy. Though touted as a means of regularizing term-limited employees to make them permanent, what it really did was paint a target on their backs. Beginning in April 2013, universities across Japan instead began setting a five-year maximum for employment. The law's many loopholes caused further problems. For example, the clock does not begin until the start date of the employee's first contract *following April 2013*. That means for many teachers their five-year clock did not start until months or even years after April 2013, regardless of how long they had already worked at the university. Also, university teachers lose credit for time on the calendar not covered by their labor contract. This is because some contracts cover only months that university classes are in session, not breaks. Therefore, the law might only count the year you spent teaching at a university as nine months. If you believe that your current contract crosses the five-year line or your employment now exceeds five years, you should take your contract to a labor consultation center (see page 233) to ascertain your status before requesting permanent employment.

The universities' "ten-year rule" gambit

Yet another problem involves a law which took effect in December 2013. Universities lobbied for the five-year rule to stipulate a sector-wide educational exception allowing universities to employ *kyoin* (educational researchers and quasi-faculty members) on term-limited contracts for ten years. The universities argued that they employ *kyoin* as researchers on special projects that last more than five years. For purposes of this exception, a *kyoin* is a university professional who meets at least *one* of the following criteria:

1 Conducts "cutting-edge interdisciplinary research"
2 Is an assistant professor
3 Conducts educational research with a term stipulated by the university or the specific research plan the university is participating in.[2]

If you are reading this *Handbook*, you are likely not the *kyoin* described above. You are a teacher who may do research, but you are not hired to conduct one specific cutting-edge research project as is common in engineering or medicine. Many universities have even attempted to redefine *kyoin* to mean all teachers, including even part-time teachers on term-limited contracts (*hijokin koushi*). This would allow them to keep teachers for a longer period before terminating them (or making them permanent). While it has led some universities to extend their five-year caps in favor of ten-year caps, this exception for *kyoin* has created confusion unlikely to be resolved until it reaches court or is clarified in a further revision to the law.

It is unclear specifically how the five-year/ten-year rule will play out, but we do generally know that universities are committed to maintaining a temporary workforce of instructors on a permanent basis. This flexibility in discharging employees makes trying to improve your working conditions seem scary, but also more imperative and worth the effort. It is important to be informed and to have courage. There are resources and strategies you individually, and you and your co-workers together, can employ to improve your security and protect your rights in the university workplace.

University grievance processes and government resources

If you believe your rights are being violated or your working conditions violate labor law, what should you do?

First, you will want to gather information to better confirm your suspicions. Rumor and misinterpretations are rampant in universities. Discreetly speak with several trusted Japanese and non-Japanese colleagues to get their understanding of common practices at the university. Are you in fact teaching an overload or being excessively assigned duties? Are you actually being denied benefits? Are other teachers experiencing the same workplace issues you are? Have any filed complaints? You may want to talk to your department chair if you have a good relationship. Universities vary, but many have human rights committees and some have human rights officers. Do not assume they are effective. Try to find out if they have taken any action on previous complaints. Sometimes they can provide helpful mediation or counseling, but often their purpose is to make it merely appear as if the university is meeting its obligations to seriously consider workplace abuses and harassment complaints.

Government agencies and offices can be a more reliable source of information and assistance. They were created to help workers in Japan (including you), and their staff often take their jobs seriously. Following are some of the most important.

A **Labor Consultation and Information Center** (*rodo sodan joho senta*) is stop one for objective and useful information about what the law says and what your options are for redressing grievances. Staff offer advice and mediation services, though it is important to note that they have no power to enforce laws. They are experts with experience at government agencies such as the **Labor Relations Commission (Labor Commission)** and the **Labor Standards Office (LSO)**. Usually, translation services are available. The Tokyo center publishes a book called the *Foreign Workers Handbook*, though it is actually a handbook about the rights of all workers in Japan, not merely non-Japanese.[3]

Hello Work is the agency responsible for enforcing unemployment insurance enrollment and distributing benefits. Its staff also determines eligibility for maternity and paternity leave. **The Pension Office** (*nenkin jimusho*) is responsible for enforcing the pension law. If your employer has not enrolled you in the *shakai hoken* system (Japan's national employees' health insurance and pension system), they can investigate to see if you are eligible for enrollment.

Your employer will be notified of any investigation from any of these agencies, so one limitation to initiating investigations is that it could expose you to retaliation. This is illegal, but can be difficult to prove. Using the courts to redress illegal retaliation can take years, and if the retaliation was in the form of termination, being term-limited only increases your vulnerability. Of course, permanent employees and tenured faculty cannot be discharged as arbitrarily as term-limited teachers whose contracts can simply be non-renewed. You are much safer asking government agencies to investigate complaints if you are permanent; this is yet another reason why universities prefer to maintain term-limited contracts.

Harassment

Certain workplace problems have become so commonplace that employers are legally required to implement systems addressing them. **Sexual harassment** (*sekuhara*) is a broad category of harassment that includes being unwillingly exposed to words and deeds of a sexual nature at the workplace or being discriminated against for not assenting to participation in sexual activity. **Power harassment** (*pawahara*) occurs when a person with formal or informal authority over the victim uses that authority to emotionally manipulate or elicit personal favors from the victim. This may include verbal abuse, a disproportionately heavier workload, or a reduction in classes (and salary).

Employers are required to designate a person who is responsible (*tantosha*) to take reports of harassment, investigate accusations, and resolve problems; unfortunately, this position is usually just filled by someone from the personnel office. There are many well-intentioned human resources professionals out there, but remember, they are there to protect the university, not you. If you are experiencing sexual or power harassment, seeking the advice of a third party such as the consultation center mentioned above is recommended *before* considering the in-house option.

Regardless of which approach you take to address harassment, abuse, unfair treatment, or workplace violations—through government organizations or university committees, or both—you must carefully document what has been said or done to you and retain all correspondence and contracts. If you meet with a representative of a human rights committee, you may wish to tape record your discussion. Take careful notes of what government officials advise you. Keep a detailed personal record (a diary or series of personal memos) and share it with a few trusted colleagues as the experiences occur so that you can document them in time. A tangible record is important regardless of the redress you seek or the avenue you take to obtain it.

Solidarity is the way forward

So far, most of the remedies discussed in this chapter imply action on the part of the individual. But in Japan, far more than in western countries, the individual is weak and the group is strong. Here, even heroes come in groups—the seven samurai, the multitude of Power Rangers, Sailor Moon with four fellow guardians and her additional sailor soldiers—in contrast to the individualistic western protagonists such as Batman or Wonder Woman who rely on their own strength to right wrongs and see that good triumphs over evil. In the university workplace, if a complaint is filed or a grievance is made, it carries far more weight when it comes from the Power Rangers than from Batman. In Japan, group action is respected. And group action, in solidarity, is far more effective than an individual response.

Yet another important reason for solidarity is the quality of employment for university teachers in Japan appears to be gradually declining. Chapter 2, "Making a career of university teaching in Japan: getting (and keeping) a full-time job," and Chapter 3, "The *ronin* teacher: making a living as a full-time part-timer at Japanese universities," suggest that course loads are rising, salaries are falling (or stagnating), fixed-term contract and part-time positions are proliferating, and secure working conditions are becoming rarer. The projected decline in Japan's college-age population over the next two decades will further impact employment for university faculty and result in more universities adopting a permanent temp workforce. One of the ways that university language teachers as a profession can maintain or improve their employment is by sticking together.

Labor rights in Japan

The root of labor problems in the academic workplace is the same as everywhere: management is strong and workers are weak. Management implements systems benefiting from competition among workers and casual forms of employment. Government regulations and their enforcing agencies are a counterweight to employers' enormous power, as is the Japanese Constitution. But in themselves, they are not enough, especially when one or more individual teachers face off against a large organization with a full-time staff, professional administrators, legal expertise, and financial resources.

The Constitution gives all workers in Japan the right to form unions, including immigrant, term-limited, and part-time employees. Only civil servants have abrogated trade union rights; however, this does not apply to university teachers or Assistant Language Teachers (ALTs). The right to solidarity (*danketsuken*) means that management does not have the right to divide the workforce by interfering with union activity, including recruitment and dues collection. Management cannot legally discourage union activity in any way, nor are they allowed to infringe on the right to collective bargaining (*dantaikoshoken*). Management does not have to agree to union demands, but they must bargain in good faith. If management and the union cannot reach agreement, workers have the right to take collective action (*danntaikoudouken*) such as strikes and protests. If management violates any of the above it is called an Unfair Labor Practice (*futoroudoukoui*) and unions can sue for redress with the Labor Commission.

Labor unions in Japan have a long history and protect workers' rights and employment conditions. Unions are not help centers like the consultation center referred to on page 191, but democratic organizations that work to improve the employment conditions of their members. Their members are responsible for their operation and meet frequently to distribute responsibilities and strategize. Unions are an influential force in Japanese society, and about 18% of workers are union members.[4]

Yet organizing a union is not easy. A labor union is not a business. It offers no product. Members are not customers. Organizers give advice, but the hardest and most important work is done by the members themselves. Even though being a member of a union gives its members protection against retaliation from administrators (retaliation is illegal), attempted reprisals are possible so members might have to stand firm to assert their rights. If you are considering joining or forming a union, first consult the contacts on pages 194 and 195 of this chapter, but—*do not* speak with management or human resources about union activity until after consulting with a union organizer. There is no protection for you as a *potential* union member prior to formal declaration. Once you form a union, negotiations could go well, but protracted impasses are also possible. Such conflicts may strain relationships or even become labor disputes. Is it worth it? It depends.

What a union can do

To workers seeking a fast solution to workplace problems, no such solution exists. Many people contact unions too late, after experiencing something bad, for example, non-renewal or sexual harassment, or after their appeals to human rights committees have failed. Depending on last-minute (*kakekomi*) case policies, unions can negotiate on your behalf, and they have organizers and attorneys who know the law. These sorts of negotiations may result in financial settlements but usually waste everyone's time. Unions are supposed to be *proactive*, to borrow a corporate word. Teachers should consider organizing only if they want to remain at their current university workplace, even if on a term-limited contract. The union can include recognition of permanent employment status in its demands. While it is difficult to succeed, with enough numbers and solidarity (i.e. the collective effort of you and your colleagues), *it is possible*.

You may also be able to leave the legacy of a better workplace at your university for others in your field.

At present, it is more economical for universities to marginalize language-teaching faculty and keep them compliant by having them compete for part-time and fixed-term appointments. The promise of a wage that can support a family, not to mention regular raises and promotions, disappears when teachers must constantly change jobs. Administrators can also manipulate teachers into taking on extra responsibility since it is hard to say no to that university committee, extra course, or university promotional work if you feel renewal hinges upon it. Nothing tells educators that their dedication and experience do not matter like being fired on day one. This harms your students, too, since turnover means that institutional knowledge is continually lost, teachers have little reason to collaborate, and their freedom of speech and thought are sharply curtailed since disagreeing with superiors is too risky.

Cooperation, not competition

Language educators in Japan prize cooperation, as evidenced by the professional organizations, conferences, and informal networks to assist them when seeking employment. In such a collaborative environment, it is stunning that university teachers accept constant competition with one another for their livelihoods in short-term employment and an ever-shrinking number of tenure-track jobs. Part of the reason is that educators tend to think of their job as a calling rather than a profession. They risk forgetting that they are still workers with basic human needs: stability to plan their lives, enough money to support their families, a manageable workload, and a respectful administration.

University language educators will not save their profession from these problems by competing with each other or by only looking out for themselves. Struggling alone likely means more of the same—insecure employment and powerlessness. The only way forward is solidarity, which means more hard work. Forming unions requires sacrifice, shared risk, and regular meetings. The task is daunting, but the precedent for cooperation is apparent in both academic professional organizations and the university unions already in existence. The tools and resources exist; use them. The only way to win a fight is to show up for it. The choice is yours. What is it going to be?

Whom to Contact

Zenkoku Ippan Tokyo General Union
294 Yamabukicho, Shinjuku-ku, Tokyo-to, Kokubo Bldg 3B
tokyogeneralunion.org

NUGW Tokyo Nambu
5-17-7-2F, Shimbashi Minato-ku, Tokyo-to 105-0004
Tel: 03-3434-0669   Fax: 03-3433-0334

General Union

Osaka office
530-0043, Osaka, Kita-ku Temma 1-6-8 Rokko Temma Building 201
Tel: 06 6352 9619   Fax: 06 6352 9630   union@generalunion.org

Tokai office
450-0003 Nagoya-shi Nakamura-ku Meieki Minami 2-11-43 Nissho Bldg 2F NPO Station
Tel/Fax: (052) 561-8555   nagoyaoffice@generalunion.org

Fukuoka General Union
4A Komori Building, 3-6-1 Hakataekimae, Hakata-ku, Fukuoka-shi 812-0011 JAPAN
Tel/Fax: 092-473-1222   Mobile: 090-8396-7268   fukuoka-general-union@nifty.com

Notes

1 This happened in the Toshiba-Yanagimachi Factory Case. For more details, see Hifumi Okunuki's "No Legal Cure-all for Fixed-term Job Insecurity" in *The Japan Times* (2014, April 24).
2 For more information on this change and what it could mean, see Louis Carlet's "Are University Teachers in Japan Covered by the 'Five-year Rule'?" in *The Japan Times* (2017, July 30) and Hifumi Okunuki's "'Five-year Rule' Triggers 'Tohoku College Massacre' of Jobs" in *The Japan Times* (2016, November 27).
3 The handbook provides a concise overview of your rights under labor standards law, trade union law, and labor contract law. You should download a copy and share it with your colleagues and friends. Someone you know will need it: hataraku.metro.tokyo.jp/sodan/siryo/foreign-e/index.html
4 For more information, see the OECD statistics from 2017 on trade union density worldwide: stats.oecd.org/Index.aspx?DataSetCode=UN_DEN

23 Navigating the chrysanthemum maze

Off-hand advice on how to tiptoe through the minefield of the Japanese university

A dialog with Curtis Kelly and Charles Browne

On trying to implement change . . .

CURTIS KELLY: Okay, Charlie. You've worked for years to get your PhD, developed a stellar record of publications, given sweat, blood and tears to learn Japanese, landed a job as a tenured professor, and you are rarin' to make a real difference at your school. Clear sailing from here on, right?

CHARLES BROWNE: Clear sailing, Curtis? Yeah, right into the eye of the storm. That bit in the book in Chapter 4, "The chrysanthemum maze," about Ben making a proposal that fell flat is my story, too. Over and over.

CK: And mine. In fact, I made a rule for myself. For the first year, don't make any proposals, even in committees. Just listen. Learn the system. Get accepted. For speaking up at a *kyoujukai* (faculty meeting), wait ten years.

CB: Oh, yeah. And feel out your colleagues for where they stand. Of course, your Japanese colleagues might not always give you a straight answer—being able to read between the lines is truly a survival skill at a Japanese university.

CK: LOL. How about an example? Read between these lines from Nike: "Just do it!"

CB: I read trouble. So don't "just do it." Take time. Measure the situation. Ask for advice, and watch out for false bottoms.

CK: False bottoms?

CB: Uh-huh. In one of the first faculty meetings I attended, someone specifically asked me for ideas or suggestions on how to improve the English language program.

CK: Uh-oh. I can hear that trap door opening. So Charlie, you answered right? But not in the tempered way you were supposed to.

CB: Yeah. I unfortunately made the mistake of answering their question with concrete ideas and suggestions. Not a single one was accepted or implemented. For a while, I took the failure personally.

CK: Ouch.

CB: But time passed and I learned more about the history of our department and about "the system." Previous proposals like that had also failed. You really have to prepare well before you answer, and that includes taking all the stakeholders into account and doing some *nemawashi*, as discussed in "The Chrysanthemum Maze" and "Walk a Mile in the Shoes of the Non-Japanese Administrator" chapters. On the plus side, one reason change is so challenging is because Japanese universities are in some sense radical democracies—more so than their European and North American counterparts. Permanent faculty and staff have a strong say on what happens and it can be exasperating. However, once you find a like-minded Japanese colleague and the right committee to work with, you can do amazing things.

CK: You are absolutely right, Charlie. I guess I was a bit too negative in the Maze chapter. Both of us have been involved in doing important things for our schools, innovative things, and those have been some of the most meaningful experiences of our careers.

What about emails? If proposing something directly at a faculty meeting is risky, don't you think the next best thing would be to write a carefully worded email to explain your plan with reasons for why it could work out better?

CB: Actually, you need to be pretty careful with emails as well. Even in departments of English, where most of your colleagues are supposed to be fluent in that language, many will struggle with emails that are longer than a few lines. In fact, a Japanese friend of mine who is a tenured professor at a different university sometimes shares stories about his foreign colleague's many lengthy emails to him and the rest of the department members, usually to try to convince them to do something differently. Sadly, most of the emails go largely unread and ignored by the faculty and have unfortunately hurt her reputation at the school, adding to the image of her as someone who doesn't really understand Japanese university culture and expectations.

CK: How about short emails?

CB: Honestly, I only send emails to my colleagues when absolutely necessary and even then, only about matters where I am agreeing, helping or supporting them, not when I want to make a change or need a favor.

On attending everything . . .

CK: You know, Charlie, part of that satisfaction comes from our tendency to see our impact as a measure of success. We always want to fix things.

CB: Yes. My wife hates that.

CK: But for many Japanese it is not really like that, is it? Just being a member and offering support is valued. Just being there is important. In fact, that reminds me of something. I ran into Martin Pauly recently, a guy who worked in a Japanese university for 23 years. He said that I gave him a valuable piece of advice way back in 1984. Apparently, I told him, "Attend everything." He took it to heart. "The number of events/meetings I missed could be counted on one hand," he said.

CB: Curtis, I like that. "Attend everything." That shows your sincerity. In fact, in my 20+ years as a tenured faculty member, the most common complaint I have heard about foreign faculty is that some of them miss meetings. Granted, the meetings might be inefficient. And you might be useless in them. You might not even understand what they are saying. But just being there wins hearts. It shows you appreciate all the work everyone else is doing. Not being there makes you look lazy, selfish, and unappreciative.

CK: In fact, dare I say it? Not attending is an art in itself. It draws upon some deep cultural mores: the Japanese intricacies of *wagamama* and *tatemae*. For example, it is acceptable to miss an event for medical or academic reasons, but not for *wagamama*, personal, reasons. It can be difficult figuring out where the line is drawn. It might be somewhat okay to miss a *kyoujukai* to attend the birth of your baby . . .

[Curtis means the husband, not the wife . . .]

. . . but maybe not okay if you miss monitoring a *senta shiken* (entrance examination) for that reason. It's tricky. But sometimes missing something you don't really need to attend can be achieved through *tatemae*. Your superior knows you are taking a quick trip abroad to visit your parents, something personal, but he or she understands its importance. That superior might emphasize something that makes your absence more acceptable, such as your parents' infirmity, thereby using *tatemae* on your behalf. I suggest, though, don't even think about using these tools on your own.

On the perils of asking . . .

CK: So, Charlie, you have mentioned many times that it is good to check things out with Japanese colleagues. I agree, but . . .

CB: Absolutely. You can get into big trouble doing something you shouldn't. Part of this is because information flows differently in Japanese organizations. Many foreign teachers believe they have "a right to know" and that "somebody should have told me." But universities don't openly distribute information that way: It takes a long time to figure out what questions to ask, and then what further questions to ask.

And it is not always clear what is taboo. I know a part-time teacher who got fired for trying to sell a homestay tour in one of his classes. He thought he was helping his students go abroad. The administration thought he was endangering the school by offering a non-school tour that parents might think is a school tour, because it was being promoted by a teacher of that school.

CK: You don't want to cross any lines, right? So you might ask, "Is it okay if I take my students to a movie?" "Would it be all right if someone else handled one of my classes on the day I have to meet the Emperor?" But questions like these are problematic, too.

CB: I think I see where you are going with this. It has to do with responsibility, right?

CK: Exactly. As soon as you ask someone else if **your** doing such and such is **all right** or not, and that person says, "Yes," you are transferring the responsibility of the action to that person. If someone complains later . . .

CB: And there are lots of complainers in faculties.

CK: If someone complains later, it will be the person you asked who gets in trouble. After all, "yes" is a kind of "permission." Asking if you can take your students to a movie is really asking if that person is willing to take the heat if anyone complains about your taking students to a movie. (Or if something happens to one of them before, during, or after the movie.) No wonder so many questions like that get a "no." It is better to ask what would happen if someone in general took their students to a movie.

On not asking . . .

CB: In short, not wanting to take risks, admin offices usually say "no" if asked anything not predefined by the rules. I remember being stymied by the administration time and time again when I tried to create a path for my students to do international volunteer work. Yet I eventually found a way to do it.

CK: Okay, Charlie. Now I see where you are going. You stopped asking, right?

CB: Exactly. I simply stopped asking for permission ahead of time. Of course, what I was doing had to fit the university's framework. I also had to make sure all the students were on board. Yet I was able to make "a student circle for international volunteer work" that is still in existence today, more than ten years after I left that school.

CK: Brilliant! Sometimes not asking, not making things public, allows administrators to "avert their eyes," so to speak. Eventually, they might even change the rule that was causing the snafu. At the same time, wouldn't you say that as much as possible it's best to follow university policies and protocols to the T?

CB: Absolutely. Get known as the teacher who humbly teaches any course you are asked to teach, faithfully completes all paperwork, irrepressibly meets deadlines, and humbly hands in grades on time. Build up some social and political capital for when you might need it . . . wait . . . scratch the "might."

On dealing with criticism . . .

CB: And I am sorry to say that once you are accepted as one of the faculty, you are likely to encounter someone who criticizes you and you will need it. You know, Curtis, no matter how carefully you place your feet, you are bound to step on a hidden landmine at least once. Oddly, the more you try to justify or defend yourself, the more attention you draw to yourself, and thereby more potential criticism.

CK: And it is not always just crossing a line. Departments all over the world tend to have some, well, difficult faculty in them. I suspect they didn't have many friends when they were kids so they spent time reading books instead.

CB: Or maybe it comes from always being listened to and revered as a teacher. I find myself being especially careful when hanging out with you for example . . .

CK: Hey! But the point is, you are bound to step on one of those landmines. (One of my Japanese colleagues says he doesn't have any legs left.) And it is really upsetting when you get criticized.

CB: Even just figuring out what is happening is hard. Your first reaction is to assume that person is trying to hurt you, especially if their language is assertive or curt . . .

CK: Did you just say "curt"?

CB: It feels like that person is attacking you, but they might just be passing on a tacit understanding everyone else has on how things are done. I can't tell you how many foreign faculty newbies I've met who mistakenly think they are being persecuted, but in most cases, the Japanese faculty is really just informing them of a norm. For example, at one school I worked at, it first felt like criticism when I was told to pass a student I thought should fail, but I later found out that the reason for this was that the school had an unofficial (but widely followed) policy to support students who were attending the school on sports scholarships.

CK: Something like that happened to me, too, even though I had already been a full-timer for 30 years. I was told that my emails to a committee I was on were too chatty. That confused me. Was it a reprimand or suggestion? Just one person's preference or a hidden policy? I later found out it was the latter. Committee emails tend to be like kyoujukai announcements, objective and fact-oriented once the opening greeting is over. As we discussed a couple pages ago, writing opinions on how things should be done should be avoided or handled with care.

CB: I'm always trying to figure out whether a comment is just that person's opinion or representing the bigger system.

CK: Indeed, Charlie, just figuring out what is going on has always been hard for me. Is that critic crossing a line, or have I? That difference is crucial because it determines your response. Do you meekly apologize? Defend yourself? Or raise the stakes and get angry back. I do not recommend the latter, and I am not good at it, but I have seen Japanese colleagues use anger splendidly to defend themselves and delineate their territory.

In the end, and I think you feel this way, too, that no matter how absurd the criticism seems, you are better off being quiet and apologetic until you hear a Japanese person's view of the situation. And maybe even after that, too. Always remember that if the fight is in Japanese, you can't win.

CB: Curtis, I agree that fighting back almost never works in your favor. Choosing to be quiet and apologetic can also be a successful strategy because it is a kind of Japanese virtue to "grin and bear" a criticism with a *"Hai, Wakarimashita"* (Yes, I understand). My advice is to not react directly to the criticisms, continue to do your best, and let the many positive fruits of your labor be your response. Also, any long-term positive relationships you have built with your colleagues—especially the earliest and longest—will quietly come to your aid during times of difficulty. The importance of maintaining good will with other faculty, through thick and thin, can't be emphasized enough!

CK: I agree. For one long-term problem, I was advised to ignore it. I was told that by being a good teacher, a sincere hard-working colleague, and someone who does not cause trouble, I would get the respect of the rest of the faculty. That would be even better than engaging in a fight and winning.

On giving the staff love . . .

CB: I really liked the part of the Chrysanthemum Maze chapter that emphasized showing appreciation and respect to staff. And I think it's really true. A university is a bureaucracy and staff have a heavy workload and even more rules to follow than we do. If you need regular help from them, it's a good idea to spread it around and not burden the same staff member with all your requests. The same is true with faculty—avoid relying on a single colleague, or mentor, or administrator because eventually they'll move on or retire. It's best to cultivate relations throughout the department, administration, and staff. Taking a few extra minutes, for example, to courteously interact or give thanks, especially to staff, is really appreciated.

CK: And you might make a friend who will work behind the scenes to help you get things done.

CB: Yes. And of course, the reverse is also true. I once worked with an American colleague who had excellent Japanese skills combined with a very sharp temper and tendency to berate others. His way of interacting not only got him in trouble with the students and faculty, but also led many of the staff to avoid him and drag their feet on his requests and demands. A word of advice here is that you should always try to be positive and polite, even when things don't go your way. So, if you get angry at something because it seems rude or unfair, maybe 99 percent of the time, it is because you have misread the situation.

CK: I completely agree. If a Japanese colleague says, "It's difficult," or "I'll think about it," it probably really means "No way."

CB: It's been a pleasure talking with you, Curtis. Let's end on a positive note.

CK: I agree, Charlie, and I have just the thing. In regard to all the scary stories we are told, I think there is one more aspect we need to add. If you are sincere in trying to do things the right way, almost everyone will forgive your trespasses. It is one of the things about Japan I love. It is just about impossible for us not to step on one of those landmines and do something unacceptable, rude, or selfish by Japanese standards, but they get it. They have traversed that minefield, too.

CB: Yes. Yes. We portray human relations in Japanese universities as tricky, and they are, but the fact that Japanese are so good at picking up on when people are acting with genuinely good intentions and motives is also one of the the best parts of working here. I wouldn't trade it for the world.

Appendix 1
Resources for university educators in Japan

Glen Hill

Since links change over years, please google the organizations, associations, books, journals, and other resources below to find out more about them.

Professional organizations

The Japan Association for Language Teaching (JALT) is dedicated to the improvement of language teaching and language learning at all educational levels in Japan. JALT has nearly 3,000 members, a large proportion non-Japanese, in 32 regional chapters from the tip of Hokkaido to the bottom of Kyushu (and also in Okinawa). These local chapters sponsor activities ranging from symposia to teacher-training workshops. JALT's additional Special Interest Groups (SIGs) similarly sponsor events and many publish their own journals or newsletters, including those shown in Figure A1.1.

The Japan Association of College English Teachers (JACET) focuses specifically on language teaching and language education research at the university level. JACET also has nearly 3,000 members and sponsors conferences, conducts

• Bilingualism (BIL)	• Literature in Language Teaching (LiLT)
• Business Communication (BizCom)	• Materials Writers (MW)
• College and University Educators (CUE)	• Mind, Brain, and Education (BRAIN)
• Computer Assisted Language Learning (CALL)	• Other Language Educators (OLE)
	• Pragmatics (PRAG)
• Critical Thinking (CT)	• School Owners (SO)
• Extensive Reading (ER)	• Speech, Drama, & Debate (SD&D)
• Framework and Language Portfolio (FLP)	• Study Abroad (SA)
• Gender Awareness in Language Education (GALE)	• Task-Based Learning (TBL)
	• Teacher Development (TD)
• Global Issues in Language Education (GILE)	• Teachers Helping Teachers (THT)
	• Teaching Younger Learners (TYL)
• Japanese as a Second Language (JSL)	• Testing and Evaluation (TEVAL)
• Learner Development (LD)	• Vocabulary (VOCAB)
• Lifelong Language Learning (LLL)	

Figure A1.1 JALT SIGs

workshops, and publishes research. The JACET organization is comprised of a headquarters unit and seven chapters covering all of Japan: Hokkaido, Tohoku, Kanto, Chubu, Kansai, Chugoku-Shikoku, and Kyushu-Okinawa. JACET has a high concentration of Japanese university English teachers as members. Its additional Study Groups, organized mainly by interest area but in some instances also by region, are the following (see Figure A1.2):

• Academic & Teaching Portfolio • Applied Cognitive Linguistics • Applied English Grammar Based on Latest Linguistic Theories • Autonomous Learning • Bilingualism and Bilingual Education • CALL (Computer Assisted Language Learning) Hokkaido • CEFR (Common European Framework of Reference) • Classroom-Centered Research • Critical Thinking • Developmental Education (Kanto) • Developmental Education Chubu Chapter • Developmental Education Kansai Chapter • Discourse Analysis Circle of Hokkaido (DACH) • Discourse Pragmatics SIG • English as a Lingua Franca • English Education • English for Academic Purposes • English for Japanese Scientists • English Lexicography • English Vocabulary Research • ESP Chubu Chapter • ESP Hokkaido Chapter • ESP Kanto Chapter • ESP Kansai Chapter	• ESP Kyushu-Okinawa Chapter • Foreign Language Education Abroad • Global Education/Education for International Understanding • JACET Materials Development Group • Japanese and English Usage • Language Contact • Language Policy • Language Teacher Cognition • Learner Development • Literature in Language Education • Listening • Multicultural Coexistence and English Education • Oral Communication Study Group • Oral Presentation & Performance • Pedagogical English Grammar • Politeness Research Group • Special Interest Group on Reading • SLA (Kanto) • Teaching Materials • Testing • The Study Group for English Education in East Asia • The Writing Research Group • The Writing Research Group, the JACET Kansai Chapter • World Englishes and Cross-Cultural Understanding

Figure A1.2 JACET study groups

Other Japan-based academic associations and study groups (language teaching, linguistics, literature, communication, translation)

A multitude of academic organizations (*gakkai*) and study groups (*kenkyukai*) exists for nearly every academic field in Japan, from economics to environmental biology and physics to physiology. If you are teaching subject-specific or EMI (English-medium instruction) courses in these fields, ask your colleagues about them. For example, there are currently 1,274 Japanese academic societies in medicine and related fields listed on the website of the University Hospital

Medical Information Network (UMIN) Center. You can research societies and publications in even more fields in the humanities, social sciences, and sciences through J-Stage (Japan Science and Technology Information Aggregator), the Japanese Association of Higher Education Research, and the Science Council of Japan (SCJ is an academic community that, contrary to its name, includes the humanities, social sciences, and engineering as well as the life sciences, earth sciences, and natural sciences). Among the associations related to language teaching, linguistics, literature, education, communication, and translation are the following:

American Literature Society

Association for Japanese Literary Studies

Association for Modern Japanese Literary Studies

e-Learning *Kyouiku Gakkai* (WELL)

English Literary Society of Japan (ELSJ)

English Teachers in Japan (ETJ)

IEEE Professional Communication Society, Japan Chapter (PCSJ)

Japan Association for Asian Englishes (JAFAE)

Japan Association for Developmental Education (JADE)

Japan Association for English Corpus Studies (JAECS)

Japan Association for Interpretation Studies

Japan Association for Interpreting and Translation Studies (JAITS)

Japan Association for Language Education & Technology (LET)

Japan Association of Conference Interpreters (JACI)

Japan Association of Higher Education Research

Japan Association of Self Access Learning (JASAL)

Japan Association of Translators (JAT)

Japan Business Communication Association (JBCA)

Japan CLIL Pedagogy Association (J-CLIL)

Japan Comparative Education Society (JCES)

Japan Education Research Association (JERA)

Japan Foundation

Japan Second Language Association (J-SLA)

Japan Society of Stylistics

Japanese Association for American Studies

Japanese Association for Asian Englishes (JAFAE)

Japanese Association for Semiotic Studies (JASS)

Japanese Association for Social Research

Japanese Association for Studies in English Communication (JASEC)

Japanese Association of Sociolinguistics Science

Japanese Society for Language Sciences (JSLS)

JSET (Japan Society for Educational Technology)

Linguapax Asia

Linguistic Society of Japan (LSJ)

Mathematical Linguistic Society of Japan

Moodle Association of Japan (MAJ)

National Institute for Japanese Language and Linguistics (NINJAL)

National Institute of Japanese Literature

Phonetic Society of Japan

Society for Intercultural Education, Training and Research (SIETAR Japan)

Society for Intercultural Education, Training and Research (SIETAR Kansai)

Society for Writers, Editors, and Translators (SWET)

Variation Theory Forum of Japan

Women Educators and Language Learners (WELL)

Additional journals related to language teaching and linguistics

Most of the JALT and JACET SIGs on pp. 202 and 203 publish their own journals. Google the groups to find their publications and submissions guidelines. In addition, do not overlook the universities you already teach at—part-time or full-time—because most university departments have their own in-house journals called *kiyou* which exist for the purpose of publishing the less stringently reviewed research papers of their faculty. Following are some additional journals related to language teaching and linguistics, and an important database for finding journals in all fields:

Accents Asia (Journal of the Teachers College Columbia University Japan Alumni Association)

Asian English Studies (publication of The Japan Association for Asian Englishes)

JACET Journal

JALT Journal

Japan Journal of Multilingualism and Multiculturalism

Journal of Intercultural Communication (SIETAR Japan)

J-Stage (a database curated by the Japan Science and Technology Agency [JST] consisting of thousands of Japan-based academic journals and *kiyou*, covering all disciplines. Searchable in English and Japanese: jstage.jst.go.jp)

The Language Teacher

PanSIG Proceedings

Post-Conference Publication (JALT)

Second Language (research journal of the Japan Second Language Association)

Studies in Language Sciences (Journal of the Japan Society for Language Sciences)

Books related to language learning and university teaching in Japan

Apple, M., Da Silva, D., & Fellner, T. (2014). *Language learning motivation in Japan*. Bristol, UK: Multilingual Matters.

Appleby, R. (2014). *Men and masculinities in global English language teaching*. Houndmills, New York: Palgrave Macmillan.

Barker, D. (2008). *An A-Z of common English errors for Japanese learners*. BTB Press.

Bradford, A., & Brown, H. (Eds) (2017). *English-medium instruction in Japanese higher education: Policy, challenges and outcomes*. Bristol, UK: Multilingual Matters.

Eades, J. S., Goodman, R., & Yada, Y. (Eds) (2005). *The 'Big Bang' in Japanese higher education*. Melbourne, Australia: Trans Pacific Press.

Gordon, J. A., Fujita, H., Kariya, T., & LeTendre, G. (2007). *Challenges to Japanese education: Economics, reform, and human rights*. New York, Yokohama: Teachers College Press and Seori-Shobo.

Gottlieb, N. (2005). *Language and society in Japan*. Cambridge, UK: Cambridge University Press.

Hall, H. T. (1998). *Cartels of the mind: Japan's intellectual closed shop*. New York: W.W. Norton & Company.

Houghton, S., & Rivers, D. (Eds) (2013). *Native speakerism in Japan—Intergroup dynamics in foreign language education*. Bristol, UK: Multilingual Matters.

Jung, I., Nishimura, M., & Sasao, T. (2016). *Liberal arts education and colleges in East Asia*. Singapore: Springer.

Kanno, Y. (2003). *Negotiating bilingual and bicultural identities: Japanese returnees betwixt two worlds*. Mahwah, New Jersey: Lawrence Erlbaum.

Kanno, Y. (2008). *Language and education in Japan: Unequal access to bilingualism*. Basingstoke, UK: Palgrave.

Kikuchi, K. (2015). *Demotivation in second language acquisition: Insights from Japan*. Bristol, UK: Multilingual Matters.

Kobayashi, Y. (2018). *The evolution of English language learners in Japan: Crossing Japan, the West, and South East Asia*. New York: Routledge Research in Language Education.

Koike, I., Matsuyama, M., Igarashi, Y., & Suzuki K. (Eds) (1978). *The teaching of English in Japan*. Tokyo: Eichosa Publishing.

Maher, J., & Yashiro, K. (Eds) (1995). *Multilingual Japan*. Bristol, UK: Multilingual Matters.

Makarova, V., & Rodgers, T. (Eds) (2004). *English language teaching: The case of Japan*. Munchen, Germany: LINCOM.

McVeigh, B. J. (2002). *Japanese higher education as myth*. New York: Routledge.

Myskow, G., Underwood., P., & Hattori, T. (2012). *EFL writing in Japan: Theory, policy and practice*. Tokyo: Media Island.

Nagatomo, D. (2012). *Exploring Japanese university English teachers' professional identity*. Bristol, UK: Multilingual Matters.

Nagatomo, D. (2016). *Gender, identity and teaching English in Japan*. Bristol, UK: Multilingual Matters.

Nakanishi, C. (2006). *A teaching approach to Japanese college students' EFL writing*. Tokyo: Keio University Press.

Poole, G. (2010). *The Japanese professor*. Rotterdam: Sense Publishers.

Seargeant, P. (2009). *The idea of English in Japan: Ideology and the evolution of a global language*. Bristol, UK: Multilingual Matters.

Seargeant, P. (Ed.) (2011). *English in Japan in the era of globalization*. Basingstoke, UK: Palgrave Macmillan.

Simon-Maeda, A. (2011). *Being and becoming a speaker of Japanese: An autoethnographic account*. Bristol, UK: Multilingual Matters.

Stanlaw, J. (2005). *Japanese English: Language and culture contact*. Hong Kong: Hong Kong University Press.

Swan, M. (2016). *Practical English usage* (4th ed.). UK: Oxford University Press.

Tsuchimochi, G. H. (1993). *Education reform in postwar Japan: The 1946 US education mission*. Tokyo: University of Tokyo Press.

Underwood., P., Myskow, G., & Hattori, T. (2012). *EFL reading in Japan: Theory, policy and practice*. Tokyo: Media Island.

Wadden, P. (Ed.) (1993). *A handbook for teaching English at Japanese colleges and universities*. New York: Oxford University Press.

Yoshihara, R. (2017). *The socially responsible feminist EFL classroom: A Japanese perspective on identities, beliefs and practices*. Bristol, UK: Multilingual Matters.

Government agencies and language testing organizations

EIKEN eiken.or.jp/eiken/en/

JLPT (Japanese Language Proficiency Test) jlpt.jp/e/

JSPS (Japan Society for the Promotion of Science) websites below are for grants (*kakenhi*)

    jsps.go.jp/english/e-grants/

    kaken.nii.ac.jp/en/

MEXT (Japanese Ministry of Education, Culture, Sports, Science, and Technology)

    mext.go.jp/en/

English language practice sites

    breakingnewsenglish.com

    duolingo.com

    eapfoundation.com

    elllo.org

    englishcentral.com/videos

    englishforuniversity.com

    engvid.com

    er-central.com

    grammarly.com

    learningenglish.voanews.com

    quizlet.com

    sulantra.com

Jobs and careers

    jrecin.jst.go.jp/seek/SeekTop

    jacet.org/job-openings

    jalt-publications.org/tlt/departments/career-development-corner/jobs

    careercross.com/en

    jalt-publications.org/archive/proceedings/2008/E074.pdf

    careers.tesol.org

Labor consultation, pension, and union offices

Labor Consultation and Information Center (*roudou soudan jouhou senta*). Provides objective information on labor law and redressing grievances. Staff also offer mediation services. Centers exist in all prefectures, and English support is available through Tokyo offices: hataraku.metro.tokyo.jp/sodan/sodan/foreign.html

Hello Work. Agency responsible for enforcing unemployment insurance enrollment and distributing benefits; staff also can determine eligibility for maternity and paternity leave. Offices are located nationwide: hellowork.go.jp/

The Pension Office (*nenkin jimusho*). Office responsible for enforcing pension law; if your employer has not enrolled you in the *shakai hoken* system (Japan's national employees' health insurance and pension system), staff can investigate your eligibility. Several offices exist in each prefecture. nenkin.go.jp/files/about_jps_operation.pdf

Union offices

Zenkoku Ippan Tokyo General Union. 294 Yamabukicho, Shinjuku-ku, Tokyo-to, Kokubo Bldg 3B info@tokyogeneralunion.org

National Union of General Workers (NUGW) Tokyo Nambu, 5-17-7-2F, Shimbashi Minato-ku, Tokyo-to 105-0004 Tel: 03-3434-0669 nugwnambu.org/

General Union, Osaka office: Osaka, Kita-ku, Temma 1-6-8, Rokko Temma Building, 201 530-0043 Tel: 06 6352 9619 union@generalunion.org

Tokai office: Nagoya-shi, Nakamura-ku, Meieki Minami 2-11-43, Nissho Bldg 2F, NPO Station 450-0003 Tel/Fax: (052) 561-8555 nagoyaoffice@generalunion.org

Fukuoka General Union, 4A Komori Building, 3-6-1 Hakataekimae, Hakata-ku, Fukuoka-shi 812-0011 JAPAN Tel/Fax: 092-473-1222 Mobile: 090-8396-7268 fukuoka.generalunion.org/

Appendix 2
Types of universities in Japan

Chris Carl Hale and Paul Wadden

A complete list of universities in Japan, organized by prefecture, is currently available in English on Wikipedia, and a simple click on the university's name will bring you to its Wikipedia page with further links, typically, to the school's own English website and its self-descriptions of its history, faculty, and student make-up. These webpages are excellent beginning points for job searches in your own geographical area as well as for finding out more about the university at which you currently teach. There has never been so much information about Japanese universities so readily available. This appendix therefore focuses on types of universities—National, Public and Private—with brief explanations of each and some selective rankings.

National universities (*kokuritsu daigaku*) are the historical descendants of the Imperial Colleges established during the Meiji Period. They are funded and overseen by the national government, although in recent years they have been granted more self-governance. Because of their relatively low tuition and high status, they are sought after by students and their parents. Nine of the top ten universities in Japan, according to one international ranking, are national universities (for these and other rankings in this appendix, see "The Times Higher Education World University Rankings 2018").[1] There are 86 four-year national universities in Japan, with at least one in each of Japan's 47 prefectures. Among the most prestigious of the general national universities are:

Tokyo University
Kyoto University
Nagoya University
Osaka University
Hokkaido University
Tohoku University
Kyushu University

National universities also include more specialized schools devoted to a particular area of study such as science and technology, foreign languages, education, and medicine. Among the most highly regarded are:

Tokyo Institute of Technology
Nagaoka Institute of Technology
Tokyo University of Foreign Studies (foreign languages)
Kyoto University of Foreign Studies (foreign languages)
University of Tsukuba (education and research)
Hitotsubashi University (commerce, law, social sciences)
Ochanomizu University (women's university)
Nara Women's University (women's university)

Public universities (*kouritsu daigaku*) are overseen by prefectural and municipal governments. Like national universities, their tuition is more economical due to government funding. In general, they are considered less prestigious than national universities and top-tier private universities, though there are exceptions, such as Akita International University, which in the Times ranking is 12th among all Japanese universities. There are currently 92 public four-year universities. Among the most notable are:

Akita International University
The University of Aizu
Tokyo Metropolitan University
Osaka City University
Akita Prefectural University
The University of Kitakyushu
Nagoya City University
Osaka Prefecture University

Private universities (*shiritsu*) are far more numerous than either national or public universities, and their quality and prestige varies widely. Keio University, for instance, is considered the oldest university in Japan and among the most highly regarded. Over the last 25 years, most of the growth in higher education has come from this sector. Private universities receive some government support on a per student basis, though they are far more expensive than their more fully funded government counterparts. Among the most highly regarded 781 four-year private universities are:

Waseda University
Keio University
International Christian University
Sophia University
Ritsumeikan University
Ritsumeikan Pacific University
Meiji University
Doshisha University

Two-year junior, vocational, and technical colleges (*tandai*)

The three categories above—national, public, and private—historically applied to two-year junior, vocational, and technical colleges as well; however, starting around 2005, these schools began closing at a steady pace, and there are currently no public junior colleges left. The reasons for the closures and consolidation of two-year colleges is due to the shifting educational dynamics—more students are opting for four-year colleges, partly because they are easier to get into at present, but also because many four-year schools now offer the vocational programs that were once the purview of the two-year colleges. Most of the contraction in higher education over the last few decades has come in this sub-sector (see Chapter 1, "The landscape of Japanese higher education" for a discussion of student demographics and institutional growth rates related to these trends). In 1993, there were nearly 600 two-year colleges in Japan. Today there are 337 and many of these focus on childcare, pre-school, and kindergarten teacher certification. Traditionally, some of the better known two-year colleges were affiliated with major universities, such as Rikkyo University and Meiji University. However, many of these kinds of two-year institutions have now closed or been absorbed into four-year university programs.

Top-ranked four-year Japanese universities

Since 2010, partly as a result of educational policy initiatives under Prime Minister Shinzo Abe, efforts have been made to raise the international profile of Japanese universities by emphasizing internationalization of curricula and research output of faculty. The Ministry of Education, in particular, has awarded hundreds of millions of dollars in grants to universities adopting its international educational aims and meeting its globalization metrics. These efforts have had an impact as some Japanese universities have risen in both the global and more local (Asia-based) rankings (see Figures A2.1 and A2.2).

Rank	University name	Prefecture	Type
=1	University of Tokyo	Tokyo	National
=1	Kyoto University	Kyoto	National
3	Tohoku University	Miyagi	National
4	Tokyo Institute of Technology	Tokyo	National
5	Kyushu University	Fukuoka	National
6	Hokkaido University	Hokkaido	National
7	Nagoya University	Aichi	National
8	Osaka University	Osaka	National
9	University of Tsukuba	Ibaraki	National
10	Keio University	Tokyo	Private
11	Waseda University	Tokyo	Private
12	Akita International University	Akita	Public
13	Hiroshima University	Hiroshima	National
14	Hitotsubashi University	Tokyo	National
15	Sophia University	Tokyo	Private
16	International Christian University	Tokyo	Private
17	Tokyo University of Foreign Studies	Tokyo	National
18	Kobe University	Hyogo	National
19	Chiba University	Chiba	National
20	Kanazawa University	Ishikawa	National

Figure A2.1 Japanese university rankings

Rank	University name	Prefecture	Type
8	University of Tokyo	Tokyo	National
11	Kyoto University	Kyoto	National
28	Osaka University	Osaka	National
30	Tohoku University	Miyagi	National
33	Tokyo Institute of Technology	Tokyo	National
35	Nagoya University	Aichi	National
48	Kyushu University	Fukuoka	National
55	Hokkaido University	Hokkaido	National
60	Tokyo Medical and Dental University	Tokyo	National
63	University of Tsukuba	Ibaraki	National
83	Fujita Health University	Aichi	Private

Figure A2.2 Ranking in Asia according to the *Times Higher Education* 2018 rankings

Note

1 The *Times Higher Education* World University Rankings 2018, available online.

Appendix 3
Academic admin hierarchy chart

Academic/Teaching-related Administrators *kyouin* (教員)	
Chairman of the Board	*riji-cho* (理事長)
President	*gaku-cho* (学長)
Vice President VP for Academic Affairs VP for Financial Affairs	*fuku-gaku-cho* (副学長) *gakumu-fuku-gaku-cho* (学務副学長) *aimu-fuku-gaku-cho* (財務副学長)
Dean of College/School/Faculty	*gaku-bu-cho* (学部長)
Academic Department Chair	*gakka-cho* (学科長)
Academic Program Head/Director	*daihyo/shunin/koosu-cho* (代表/主任/コース長)

Figure A3.1 Academic administration hierarchy

Non-teaching staff *shokuin* (職員)	
Head of General/Office Staff (Learn this person's birthday and names of children)	*jimukyoku-cho* (事務局長)

Educational Affairs	*kyomu* (教務)
Student Affairs	*gakusei* (学生)
Library	*toshokan* (図書館)
Research	*kenkyu* (研究)
Entrance Testing	*nyushi* (入試)
Marketing	*koho* (広報)
General Affairs	*somu* (総務)
Finances	*zaimu* (財務)
Personnel	*jinji* (人事)
Physical Plant	*kanri* (管理)

Figure A3.2 Names and titles of non-teaching staff and offices

Teaching staff *kyouin* (教員)	
Professor emeritus	*meiyo kyōju* (名誉教授)
Professor	*kyōju* (教授)
Associate professor	*jun-kyōju* (准教授)
Lecturer / Instructor	*kōshi* (講師)
Assistant professor / Research Associate	*jokyō* (助教)
Full-time, tenured	*sennin* (専任)
Contract (term-limited)	*shokutaku* (職託) / *tokunin* (特任) / *joukin* (常勤)
Dispatched (from a dispatching company)	*haken* (派遣)
Visiting	*kyakuin* (客員)
Part-time	*hijoukin* (非常勤)

Figure A3.3 Teaching staff titles and ranks

Index

A+ strategy 51
academic associations 14, 203–205
academic performance 104–105, 141
Academic Word List (AWL) 84, 85, 90
acculturation 134
activation 43, 44, 52
active learning 44, 114
activity frames 48–49
Adachi, Nobuhiro 9, 32–40, 166
administrators 8, 33, 180–186, 194
advanced learners 93
Akita International University 7, 10n4
ALTs *see* assistant language teachers
Anderson, Fred E. 125–136
Anki 113
appearance 147
applied linguistics 8, 19, 20, 174; Japanese teachers of English 165; master's degrees 13; part-time work 27; vocabulary 85, 87
apps 87, 110, 111, 113, 121
argumentative writing 71, 72–73
assessment: EMI classes 107, 108; entrance exams 6, 96n4, 137, 152–154, 169, 171; Extensive Reading 60; homework 116, 118, 120–121; language proficiency tests 104–105, 107; listening 75; speaking 44, 53; supporting competence 140–141; vocabulary 85, 86, 90, 91, 92; writing 72–73
assistant language teachers (ALTs) 11, 13, 26, 78, 127, 151, 193
attendance 121
audiences 100, 101
audio 113
authenticity 78–79, 82
autonomy 138, 139–140
AWL *see* Academic Word List

Barnlund, Dean C. 35
Beatty, Ken 111
benchmarks 107
"blending in" 133
Blommaert, Jan 136n15
Board of Governors 184
body-related presentation techniques 98, 99–100
bottom-up processing 76–77
Bourdieu, Pierre 134
Bradford, Annette 103–108
brainstorming 81
bring-your-own-device 110
Britton, Joseph 100
Brown, Howard 103–108
Browne, Charles 55, 84–96, 107, 196–201
BSL *see* Business Service List
Buehner, Carl W. 102
bullying 161
bureaucratic structure 33–34
burnout 149
business English 91–92
Business Service List (BSL) 55, 92, 96n14
Butler, Chrystabel 25–31
"buy-in" 45, 50, 52–53

CALICO Journal 111
CALL *see* computer-assisted language laboratories
Campbell, Joseph 165
career development 161–162
Castellano, Joachim 109–114
CEFR *see* Common European Framework for Languages
ceremonial duties 185
Chairman of the Board 184, 185, 216
challenge 138, 139
Chamberlain, Basil Hall 9

change 32–33, 36, 186, 196–197
Chapelle, Carol 111
class meetings 126
classroom community 141–142
classroom dynamics 125–136
CLIL *see* Content and Language Integrated Learning
coercion 116, 133
coherence 59
collaboration 119, 141, 142, 194
collective action 129
collective bargaining 187
Colored Connections activity 59
committees 35, 36, 165, 171, 183
Common European Framework for Languages (CEFR) 104–105
communication: autonomy-supportive teaching 140; classroom dynamics and communication styles 125–136, 169–170; meetings 184
community, building a classroom 141–142
commuting 29, 149
competence 138, 140–141
competition 133–134, 141, 194
complaints 190, 198
completion rates 6
comprehension: listening 76–77, 78–79, 80, 82, 133; reading 56, 57, 58, 169
computer-assisted language laboratories (CALL) 110–112, 114
confidence 140, 141, 142, 169
conformity 38, 129; *see also* group-mindedness
connected speech 78–79, 80, 81, 82
consensus 35, 125–126, 130, 166, 182; consensus-checking 126, 129, 134
Constitution 187, 192–193
contacts 14, 21
Content and Language Integrated Learning (CLIL) 65, 69, 93, 103–108
context 95
contracts: contract terms 13; full-time 23n2, 26, 28; legal protections 187; limited term 18, 28, 166, 188–190, 191, 192; part-time 28; permanent 23n3, 188, 189, 191
contrastive rhetoric 170
controlled language practice 69–70
conversations 50–51, 119
Cook, Haruko Minegishi 131
Cook, Melodie 159–164
Cook, Vivian 78, 83n7
cooperation 133–134, 194
copying 118–119; *see also* plagiarism

Creasor, Fiona 160
credibility 177
critical thinking 151, 153, 155, 170
criticism, dealing with 199–200
Culligan, Brent 96n4, 107
culture 32, 39; classroom 144–145; communication styles and classroom dynamics 125–136, 169–170; cultural assumptions of textbooks 108; cultural norms 17; gender roles 161–162; language relationship 135, 136n15; of listening 130–131; mastery 168; uncertainty avoidance 148; Western/Japanese dichotomy 128, 169
curriculum 7; controlled 30; curricular revisions 127, 150, 152; listening 75; national curriculum 151–152, 154
CVs 22, 27, 38

decision-making 35–36, 125–126, 130, 182, 183–184
deductive instructional techniques 67
deliberate learning 93, 94, 95
demographic changes 3
dialogues 47–48
digital flashcards 113
discrimination 39, 162, 188, 191
discussions 49–50, 81, 155
disengagement 137, 138
dismissal 187, 188
Doi, Takeo 38
drills 45–47, 64, 69, 119

e-resources 110
EAP *see* English for Academic Purposes
EFL *see* English as a foreign language
EIKEN 104, 154, 208
ELF *see* English as a Lingua Franca
ELLT *see* Essential Language Learning Tech
emails 39, 197, 200
EMI *see* English Medium Instruction
emotion 100
employers 148
engagement 137, 138–139, 142
English as a foreign language (EFL) 12, 13, 15–16, 18, 19
English as a Lingua Franca (ELF) 134, 174–175
English as an international language 134–135
English for Academic Purposes (EAP) 30, 55, 105, 107, 151

English for Specific Purposes (ESP) 65
English-language universities 7
English Medium Instruction (EMI) 19, 75, 103–108; academic associations 203; vocabulary 85, 93–94
enrollments 3, 6, 10n1, 26, 34
entrance exams 6, 96n4, 137, 152–154, 169, 171
ER *see* Extensive Reading
Ericsson, Anders 53n7
errors 70–71; *see also* mistakes
ESP *see* English for Specific Purposes
essay samples 66
Essential Language Learning Tech (ELLT) 112–113
exchange students 104
expectations 17, 51, 72, 169; classroom dynamics 133; homework 121; listening 76; publishing 12, 37
experience: students 45; teachers 13, 21, 27
expert English users 178
Extensive Reading (ER) 60–62, 90–91
extracurricular activities 147–148
eye contact 98, 99

faculty 6–7, 25–26; bureaucratic structure 33; CLIL classes 105; EMI classes 105–106; General Faculty Meetings 33, 35–36, 40n7, 130, 182, 183–184, 196; "habitat segregations" 172; intermediaries 171; Japanese teachers of English 165–173; non-Japanese administrators 180–186; non-native non-Japanese English speaking teachers 174–178; relationship building 30, 200–201; staff titles and rank 217; support from 34; *see also* tenure
failure 116, 121
false beginners 43–44, 45, 47, 52
family-work balance 162–163
Fanselow, John 9
feedback: engagement and motivation 138, 139; peer 71–72, 119; purposeful speaking practice 52; supporting competence 140; teacher-directed 70–71; technology 114; vocabulary 91
Ferreira, Dan 109–114
Ferris, Dana 71
Field, John 78, 82n5, 83n8
"five-year rule" 13, 23n3, 189

fixed term contracts 18, 23n3, 28, 166, 188–190, 191, 192
flashcards 86–87, 90, 92, 93, 113
flipped classrooms 52, 113
flow theory 138–139
fluency: oral 175; reading 56–57, 60; speaking 48–49; vocabulary 87, 90, 94
form, attention to 38–39, 130, 166
form-focused instruction 64
friendships 33–34
Fujimoto, Donna 144–149
full-time work 7–8, 12, 23n2, 25, 26, 188; additional duties 37, 148–149; experiences with contract jobs 16; labor laws 18; limited term contracts 28; qualifications for 21
funding 23, 34, 151; *see also* research budgets

gakkyukai 126
gakubatsu 33
Gallo, Carmine 100
games 133–134, 145
gender issues 159–164
General Faculty Meetings 33, 35–36, 40n7, 130, 182, 183–184, 196
genre analysis 66–69
gestures 98, 99
Glasgow, Gregory Paul 150–156
Global 30 Project 104
globalization 7, 213; *see also* internationalization
Go Global Japan Project 104
goals: CLIL/EMI classes 108; engagement and motivation 138, 139; social 65; technology 114; vocabulary 84, 91, 92, 95
good intentions 201
Google 110, 113
graded material 78, 82, 83n11
grades 116, 118, 120, 121, 141; *see also* assessment
grammar: discussions 50; entrance exams 153, 154; error codes 71; false beginners 45; flipped classrooms 52; focus on 137, 145, 151; listening 80; peer feedback 72; reading 56, 58, 61; teacher training 153; translation methodology 54; writing 64
grants 7
grievances 190–191
group-mindedness 125–126, 128, 129, 166, 192; *see also* conformity

group work 51, 133–134; discussions 49–50, 81; presentations 100; small group study 126; student engagement 142; teacher training 153; uncertainty avoidance 148; vocabulary 93
Guess the Fib activity 69

"habitat segregations" 172
habitus 134, 135, 136n14
Hale, Chris Carl 3–10, 75–83, 211–215
Halliday, M.A.K. 59
"hand-holding" 145
hand position 99
hangakushu 126
hansei 38
happyo 126, 134
harassment 159–161, 164, 188, 190, 191–192, 193
Hasan, Ruqaiya 59
Hearn, Lafcadio 9
Helgesen, Marc 43–53
Hello Work 191, 209
homework: EMI students 105; repeated listening 80; videos 113
honne 38, 121
honorific language 130
human relations 9, 201
humility 38, 166
Hyperlink activity 55–56

ICLHE *see* Integrating Content and Language in Higher Education
IELTS 75, 91, 104, 107, 154
inductive instructional techniques 67
industrial action 187, 193
informal professional development 144
institutions: bureaucratic structure 33–34; culture 32; decision-making 35–36; EMI classes 103–104, 105–106, 107; entrance exams 152–154; gender issues 159–164; hierarchies of teachers 177–178; Japanese teachers of English 166; non-Japanese administrators 180–186; number of 3, 5; policy initiatives 154–155; responsibility 36–37; technology resources 109–110, 112; types of 7, 211–215; values 37–39
Integrating Content and Language in Higher Education (ICLHE) 108
"interactional umbrella" 130
Intercultural Exchange courses 155
international students 3–6, 104, 155

internationalization 104, 154, 185; *see also* globalization
Internet 112, 120
interrogations 50–51
interviews 11, 14, 22, 147

J-CLIL *see* Japan CLIL Pedagogy Association
JACET *see* Japan Association of College English Teachers
JACET 8000 list 85, 96n3
JALT *see* Japan Association for Language Teachers
Japan Association for Language Teachers (JALT) 13–14, 21, 108, 202; *CALL Journal* 111; job postings 12, 27; journals 205, 206
Japan Association of College English Teachers (JACET) 14, 188, 202–203; JACET 8000 list 85, 96n3; job postings 27; journals 205, 206
Japan CLIL Pedagogy Association (J-CLIL) 108
Japan Exchange and Teaching (JET) program 11, 13, 78, 127, 151, 169
Japan Society for the Promotion of Science (JSPS) 208
Japanese: students' use of 51; teacher's proficiency in 13, 19, 21
Japanese Language Proficiency Test (JLPT) 208
Japanese teachers of English 105–106, 165–173; *see also* non-native English speaking teachers
JET *see* Japan Exchange and Teaching program
JLPT *see* Japanese Language Proficiency Test
job interviews 11, 14, 22, 147
job security 28
journals 21, 205–206
JREC-IN 12, 21, 27, 188
JSPS *see* Japan Society for the Promotion of Science
junior colleges 213

Kagan, Spencer 69
kaizen 38
Kelly, Curtis 9, 32–40, 97–108, 166, 196–201
King, Jim 131
Kirkpatrick, Andy 178
Kitakyushu University 11
Klassen, Kimberly 90–91

koma 16, 28, 29–30
Kramsch, Claire 147
Kurita, Tomoko 82n4
kyoin 189–190
kyoujukai (General Faculty Meetings) 33, 35–36, 40n7, 130, 182, 183–184, 196

Labor Consultation and Information Centers 191, 209
Labor Relations Commission 191, 193
labor rights 187–188, 190, 192–193
Labor Standards Law 187
Labor Standards Office (LSO) 191
language-focused learning 94
language proficiency tests 104–105, 107
language skills 19
Larson-Hall, Jenifer 11–24
learning: active 44, 114; EMI classes 105; technology 110–111, 114
Learning Management Systems (LMSs) 80, 87, 111–112, 113
lectures 75, 84
lecturing style 133
Leech, Geoffrey 95
legal protections 187–188
limited term contracts 18, 23n3, 28, 166, 188–190, 191, 192
Linguist List 12
listening 44, 75–83, 127, 175; activities 80–82; authentic materials 78–79, 82; bottom-up 76–77; business English 91–92; challenges of the Japanese learner 77–78; entrance exams 152; flipped classrooms 52; homework 118; integrated 77; lecturing 133; meaning-focused input 94; receptive tasks 169; repeated 80; role of the listener 130–131; short clips 79–80; textbooks 82; top-down 76, 77; vocabulary 87–90
LMSs *see* Learning Management Systems
LSO *see* Labor Standards Office

Mahboob, Ahmar 174, 179n5
master's degrees 13, 19, 27
mastery 168
Matikainen, Tiina 174–179
maturity 38
McCagg, Peter 180–186
McVeigh, Brian 148
meaning-focused input 94, 95
meaning-focused output 94, 95
meetings 165, 183; attending 197–198; class meetings 126; General Faculty Meetings 33, 35–36, 40n7, 130, 182, 183–184, 196
memorization: presentations 97, 98, 101; rote 95, 145
memory cards 98
metacognitive skills 71, 77, 81
Microsoft 110
Ministry of Education, Culture, Sports, Science and Technology (MEXT) 34, 78, 208; curricular revisions 127, 150, 152; English Medium Instruction 19; globalization initiatives 7, 213; homework 120; involvement in university administration 184–185; policy initiatives 154–155; professional development 153
mistakes 70–71, 145, 168
Miyamoto, Masao 40n4
model assignments 117
Monbukagakusho 34
Moore-Howard, Rebecca 68
motivation 79, 137–143; homework 115–116; non-native non-Japanese English speaking teachers 176–177; vocabulary 91
Mreader.org 90
Myskow, Gordon 54–63, 64–74

Nagamoto, Diane Hawley 159–164
Nation, Paul 56, 84–96
national curriculum 151–152, 154
national universities 211–212
native English speakers 168, 169, 174, 175, 177–178
"native speaker fallacy" 8, 147, 174, 177, 178
"native speaker learner fallacy" 8, 175
NAWL *see* New Academic Word List
NAWL Builder 87
NAWLT *see* New Academic Word List Test
nemawashi 37, 196
networking 30
New Academic Word List (NAWL) 55, 84, 85, 86–87, 90, 107
New Academic Word List Test (NAWLT) 85, 86, 96n5
New General Service List (NGSL) 55, 85, 86–87, 88, 92
New General Service List-Spoken (NGSL-S) 95
New General Service List Test (NGSLT) 85, 86, 87, 92, 96n5
newgeneralservicelist.org 55
NGSL *see* New General Service List

NGSL Builder 87, 89, 92
NGSL-S *see* New General Service List-Spoken
NGSLT *see* New General Service List Test
Nishida, Kitarō 136n14
NNETs *see* non-native English speaking teachers
NNNJETs *see* non-native non-Japanese English speaking teachers
non-Japanese administrators 8, 180–186
non-native English speaking teachers (NNETs) 174; *see also* Japanese teachers of English
non-native non-Japanese English speaking teachers (NNNJETs) 174–178
non-teaching staff 181–182, 217
Noro, Takuji 82n3
numbers 102

Ochs, Elinor 136n9
office staff 182, 217
online study sites 120
opinions: A+ strategy 51; giving 38, 200; opinion-gap work 47
outsourcing 28
overseas study 91
oversupply of teachers 26

pair work 133–134; reading 56–57; speaking 45–47, 48–49, 51; student engagement 142; teacher training 153; uncertainty avoidance 148
para-tence activity 57–58
paragraph writing 65–66
part-time work 8, 25–31, 32, 149, 182, 188, 192
pauses 101
pedagogies 6–7
peer feedback 71–72, 119
peer pressure 116, 118–119
Pension Office 191, 209
performing, teaching as 145–146
permanent contracts 23n3, 188, 189, 191
permission, asking for 198, 199
personalization 45, 47, 113
PHaVE List 55
PhDs 17, 18, 19, 21
Phillips, J. 107
Phillipson, Robert 174
phonology 77
photos 112
phrasing 101

plagiarism 66, 68–69
podcasts 113
policy 150–156
Poole, Gregory 33, 38, 40n7
Pop-up activity 56–57
portfolios 116
posture 98, 99
power harassment 160–161, 191–192
power relations 33, 34
PowerPoint 101–102, 112
preparation 50, 97
presentations 97–108; body-related techniques 98, 99–100; making the audience care 100; PowerPoint 101–102; question-answer strategies 102; small techniques 98–99; speaking words 101
Presidents 33, 180, 183, 184, 185, 216
privacy 38
private schools 151
private universities 154, 212–213; bureaucratic structure 34; enrollment quotas 10n1; experiences with contract jobs 15–16; salaries 12
problem-solving tasks 138–139
professional development 144, 149, 153
professional organizations 13–14, 21, 149, 202–203
proficiency tests 104
profiling tools 55
promotions 20, 37, 161–162
pronunciation 76, 77, 78–79, 82; Japanese teachers of English 172; non-native non-Japanese English speaking teachers 176, 177; vocabulary learning 91
"proposal gestation" 36
proposals 35–36, 37, 183, 186, 196
public universities 212
publishing 14, 17, 21, 23, 27, 37
Puentedura, Ruben 111
"pulling the nails up" 133

qualifications 6, 20, 21; master's degrees 13, 19, 27; "native speaker fallacy" 147; part-time work 27; PhDs 17, 18, 19, 21
question-answer (Q-A) strategies 102
questions 129, 140, 198
Quiz Master activity 55
Quizlet.com 86–87, 88, 90, 92, 113

racism 161
rapport 44

Rayson, Paul 95
reading 54–63, 175; business English 91–92; entrance exams 152, 153, 154; Extensive Reading 60–62, 90–91; fluency 56–57; high-frequency vocabulary 55; homework 118; intensive 58–59, 94; meaning-focused input 94; receptive tasks 169; skills 57–58; word recognition 55–56
recommendations 27
relatedness 138, 141–142
relationship building 30–31, 200–201
relevance of homework 117
renewal of contracts 13, 188
repetition with change 47, 48, 49, 53
rereading 56, 80
research budgets 12, 16, 20–23
residence 28–29
resources: technology 109–110, 112, 113–114; vocabulary 94–95
responsibility 36–37, 142, 165, 166, 194, 198
Reynolds, Garth 101
Richards, Jack C. 82n6, 83n9
rights 187–188, 190, 192–193
Risager, Karen 136n15
risk avoidance 36, 148, 199
Ritsumeikan Asia Pacific University 7, 10n4
ritualized speechmaking 130
Robb, Thomas N. 115–121
role models 171, 176
ronin teachers 25–31
rote memorization 95, 145
Rothman, Gerome 9, 187–195
rubrics 72–73, 141
Running Dictation activity 69
rural colleges 15
Ryan, Stephen M. 180–186

salaries 12–13, 22, 192; part-time work 26, 28, 29; tenure 20
samples 66
satisfaction surveys 31
scaffolding 60, 78, 106, 108, 169
schedules 106, 165
schema 81
Schieffelin, Bambi B. 136n9
schools 150–153, 156n1
Scollon, Ron and Suzie 134, 136n14
sekinin 37, 166
self-deprecation 38, 166
self-determination theory 138, 139–142
self-management 142

sentences 57–58, 101
sentencing 64, 65, 69
sexual harassment 159–160, 188, 191–192, 193
Showdown activity 69
SIGs *see* special interest groups
silence 125, 127, 128, 131–132, 144, 145, 184
skills: EMI students 107; flow theory 138; metacognitive 71, 77, 81; presentations 98–99; reading 57–58; teacher's language skills 19; vocabulary 94
slides 101–102, 112
small group study 126
smartphones 87, 90, 91, 110
Smith, Larry 135
Snyder, Bill 137–143
social insurance 187
socialization 129, 131, 134, 135n4, 136n9, 144
sociolinguistic culture 133, 136n15
solidarity 192, 193, 194
speaking 43–53; activation and active learning 44; activities 45–51; assessment 141; encouraging the use of English 51; flipped classrooms 52; homework 118; impact of Extensive Reading 61; meaning-focused output 94; presentations 101; purposeful speaking practice 52–53; ritualized 130; textbook choice 51–52
special interest groups (SIGs) 14, 202, 205
speech rate 76, 80
speeches *see* presentations
Spot the Difference activity 58–59
SSR *see* Sustained Silent Reading
standardized tests 75
standards 6, 27, 34
stereotypes 128, 137, 146, 160, 177
Stewart, Jeffrey 11–24
stories 101
students 8, 144–149; activation 43, 44, 52; attitudes towards Japanese teachers of English 168–169, 172; "buy-in" from 45, 50, 52–53; communication styles and classroom dynamics 125–136; completion rates 6; EMI courses 104, 105, 107; evaluation of teachers by 31, 146, 172; false beginners 43–44, 45, 47, 52; habitus 134, 135; international 3–6, 104, 155; motivation and engagement 137–143;

"native speaker learner fallacy" 175; non-native non-Japanese English speaking teachers 176–177; number of 3, 26; purposeful speaking practice 52–53; relationships with 30–31, 140; speaking activities 45–51; textbook choice 52; use of English 51
study groups 203–204
substitutions 48, 119
Sudo, Mikiko 165–173
summarizing 57–58, 81
Super Global University projects 7
supply and demand 25, 26
support 34
Sustained Silent Reading (SSR) 90
syllabi 30, 44, 120, 121

Takaesu, Asako 165–173
talk 125, 128–129, 131, 133
Tamagawa University 174–175
Tamura, Mika 131–132
tatemae 38, 121, 198
taxes 29
teacher training 153
TEAP 104, 154
technical colleges 213
technical support 111–112
technology 109–114; digital components of textbooks 119; online study sites 120; repeated listening 80; smartphones 87, 90, 91, 110
TED Talks 78, 90, 113, 130
TEFL 11, 19
"ten-year rule" 13, 189–190
tenure 15, 17–20, 23, 182; additional duties 148–149; labor contracts 188–189; qualifications required for 21
terms 12
TESOL 8, 11; Japanese teachers of English 165; labels of "native" and "non-native" 178; master's degrees 13; "native speaker fallacy" 174; "native speaker learner fallacy" 175; part-time work 27
textbooks 51–52, 153; CLIL 106, 108; cultural assumptions 108; digital components 119; EMI 106; listening 82
textual borrowing 68
Think-Heads Together learning structure 57
Think-Pair-Share learning structure 57
think time 47

timed readings 56
TOEFL 104, 107; iBT 152, 154, 156n6; listening 75; vocabulary 91
TOEIC 75, 77, 91–92, 107, 115
TOEIC Service List (TSL) 55, 92, 96n14
Tokyo University 9, 10n4
top-down processing 76, 77
Top Global University Project 104, 154
training 153
travel budgets 12, 29
trust 140, 142
TSL *see* TOEIC Service List
two-year junior, vocational, and technical colleges 213

uncertainty avoidance 148
Underwood, Paul R. 54–63, 150–156
unions 187, 193–195, 209–210
university system 32–40; bureaucratic structure 33–34; decision-making 35–36; responsibility 36–37; types of universities 7, 211–215; values 37–39; *see also* institutions
Ur, Penny 49, 53n5, 53n6

values 32, 37–39, 128, 134, 135, 184
videos 110, 112, 113
Virtual Learning Environments (VLEs) 113, 114
visas 28–29
visual images 112
VLEs *see* Virtual Learning Environments
vocabulary 84–96; across courses and curricula 94; advanced learners 93; dialogues 47; discussions 50; English Medium Instruction 93–94, 107, 108; false beginners 45; flipped classrooms 52; general English class 86–87; listening 76, 79, 81, 87–90; mobile devices 113; reading 54, 55–56, 60, 61, 90–91; targets 53n1, 93; TOEFL, IELTS, and overseas study 91; TOEIC and business English 91–92
vocational colleges 213
voice change 101
voice projection 99

Wadden, Paul 3–10, 84–96, 125–126, 165–166, 211–215
wagamama 198
Waring, Rob 54–63

Warschauer, Mark 111
Waseda University 7
White, Merry 130
Wi-Fi 109–110, 112
Wilson, Andrew 95
Wiltshier, John 43–53
women 159–164, 188
Word-Learner 92
word parts 93
word recognition 55–56
work-family balance 162–163
workload 16, 22, 34, 153, 192; full-time work 12; part-time work 29–30; tenure 20
World Englishes 174, 175, 178

writing 64–74, 175; assessment 72–73, 141; controlled language practice 69–70; critical thinking skills 155; genre analysis 66–69; homework 118; impact of Extensive Reading 61; meaning-focused output 94; meaningful tasks 65–66; peer feedback 71–72; presentations 97; speeches 101; teacher-directed feedback 70–71; vocabulary 94

yakudoku 54
Yamada, Haru 130–131
Yoshida, Kensaku 82n2
YouTube 110